IN RETROSPECT
Remembrance of Things Past

F. F. BRUCE

WILLIAM B. EERDMANS PUBLISHING COMPANY
GRAND RAPIDS, MICHIGAN

First published 1980 by Pickering & Inglis Ltd., Scotland
This American edition published 1980 through special arrangement
with Pickering & Inglis by Wm. B. Eerdmans Publishing Co.,
255 Jefferson Ave., S.E., Grand Rapids, MI 49503

Library of Congress Cataloging in Publication Data

Bruce, Frederick Fyvie, 1910-
  In retrospect.

  1. Bruce, Frederick Fyvie, 1910- 2. Biblical
scholars — Great Britain — Biography. I. Title.
BS501.B78A34 1980 220′.092′4 [B] 80-39943
ISBN 0-8028-3537-6

When to the sessions of sweet silent thought
I summon up remembrance of things past —

—SHAKESPEARE, **Sonnet 30**

TO
MY COMPANIONS ON THE WAY

Since all are my brothers and friends,
I say
'PEACE BE WITH YOU!'

Psalm 122:8
(Jerusalem Bible)

CONTENTS

PREFACE

The contents of this book were originally written for publication in *The Witness,* a Christian monthly magazine, and appeared there as a series of articles from 1974 to 1976. They were written by a reader of *The Witness* for other readers of *The Witness,* and many things could be taken for granted as common knowledge which cannot be taken for granted in the same way when they are presented to a wider public. A good deal of revision, expansion and explanation has therefore been necessary.

The Witness circulates mainly, though not exclusively, among the people called Open Brethren. I am myself a lifelong member of this religious community, and have been so much involved with it that a substantial part of my reminiscences must inevitably be devoted to life among the Brethren. For this reason many of the chapters will be of more interest to Brethren than to other readers. They deal with people and affairs very well known among the Brethren but little known outside their ranks. But for the benefit of readers outside their ranks I have tried to be less esoteric in my references than I may have been in the original articles. For the sake of greater clarity I have appended to the work a paper entitled *Who are the Brethren?* which was written for another purpose nearly twenty years ago.

My main activity for most of my life has been carried out in the academic world. This activity has come much more into public view than has my church association; yet even here there is a risk of being too esoteric for non-academic readers.

I hope I have avoided this risk in my 'academic' chapters: at least, I have seen no need to add a second appendix entitled 'What is a University?'

I owe an incalculable debt of gratitude to my relatives and friends, fathers and brethren, colleagues and students, who have helped to make my remembrance of things past so happy. To all of them this work is dedicated; to a few of them I have tried to express a more specific indebtedness, very inadequately, in the following pages. If there is one friend who deserves to be specially named here, it is Cecil Howley, former editor of *The Witness,* but for whose encouragement these chapters might never have been written. He has now been taken from us, but he remains an inspiration to all of us who were his companions on the way.

To all my readers alike I apologize for the prominence of the pronoun 'I' in these pages. It could not well be otherwise, since it is my remembrance and not someone else's that is being recorded; but it is somewhat distasteful to contemplate.

If Shakespeare provides the sub-title for this volume —

> When to the sessions of sweet silent thought
> I summon up remembrance of things past —

a more appropriately Christian sentiment for its presentation to the public is one expressed by my favourite author: 'forgetting what lies behind and straining forward to what lies ahead, I press on . . .'.

F.F.B.

IN RETROSPECT
Remembrance of Things Past

1
My north-east heritage

The north-east corner of Scotland is a region to which no one has ever been ashamed to belong. On all its sons and daughters it has bestowed a distinctive heritage, and part of that heritage is a disinclination to conform to fashions of thought or action current in other parts of Scotland, or of the world, unless those fashions can justify themselves in north-eastern eyes. This has been as true in religious affairs as in other departments of life.

The Romans penetrated the area towards the end of the first century AD, and met with some resistance. They did not think it worthwhile to establish the 'Roman Peace' in those parts. It was, in fact, a native of those parts who is credited with the charge that the Romans 'created a desert and called it peace'.[1] But along the Roman line of penetration a few centuries later the first Christian missionaries entered the area and evangelized it.

In the neighbourhood of Elgin, my native city, the pioneer missionary appears to have been St. Brendan the Navigator. He preached the gospel and planted a church, some time in the sixth century, at Birnie, three miles south of Elgin. The parish church of Birnie, dedicated in his honour, is a Romanesque building which, despite successive restorations, preserves in the main its original structure of

1140. When episcopal administration was introduced to these parts, Birnie was the first see of the Bishop of Moray; the see was later transferred successively to Kineddar, to Spynie, and then to Elgin itself. Elgin Cathedral, founded in 1224, exhibits even in its ruined condition something of the magnificence which won for it the title of 'The Lantern of the North'.

In the seventeenth century the churchmen of the northeast looked with a coolly objective eye on the covenanting enthusiasm which gripped other parts of Scotland and had to be persuaded, by such incidents as the occupation of Aberdeen by a covenanting army in 1639, to conform to the prevalent policy. And to this day there are probably more Scots Episcopalians per head of the population in the northeast than in other parts of Scotland — *native* Scots Episcopalians, that is to say, as distinct from English immigrants.

This independent spirit manifested itself in the adherents of the old religion, as well as among the heirs of the Reformation. Ten or twelve miles east of my native city of Elgin, Morayshire, lies the district called the Enzie (pronounced Ingie) which, at the end of the eighteenth century, had as its priest a remarkable man named Alexander Geddes. Geddes was not only famed as a pioneer in biblical scholarship, but he practised an ecumenicity which would attract attention even in this post-Vatican II age. On one occasion, it is recorded, when his ecclesiastical superiors decided to pay him a surprise visitation, he was not to be found: he had taken a party of guests to Banff, to listen to a Presbyterian preacher.

The school of churchmanship in which I was brought up, however, could boast of no ancient roots in my native region. While it had come to be associated (from the early 1870s) with the Brethren movement, its origins were quite independent of Dublin, Plymouth and Bristol;[2] they are to be found rather in the evangelical revival of 1859-60.

The work of grace during that 'year of the right hand of the Most High' was acknowledged in 1860 by the General

Assemblies of the three main Scottish Churches — Established, Free and United Presbyterian — when they recorded their thanksgiving to God for the outpouring of blessing which had so greatly promoted the spiritual well-being of Scotland. One of the lay leaders of the revival, Brownlow North (1810-75), was an Elgin resident; it was in Elgin that he was converted in 1855.[3] His gifts as a gospel preacher of exceptional seriousness and power led to his being officially recognized as an evangelist (despite his Episcopalian background) by the General Assembly of the Free Church in 1859.

Among various means adopted for the perpetuating and consolidating of the work of the revival was the establishment of the North East Coast Mission — an independent mission with its own board of directors (albeit closely associated with the Free Church), which undertook responsibility for evangelizing the fishing towns and villages from Ferryden (just south of Montrose) to Thurso in Caithness. Soon after the Mission was founded, the need of a superintendent became evident, and to this post one Donald Ross was appointed.

Donald Ross (1824-1903) was born in Alness, Ross-shire, and converted in his teens. At the Disruption of 1843 he naturally joined the Free Church of Scotland. At that time he was a school teacher, but his gifts and vocation were those of an evangelist. About 1850 he moved to Edinburgh, and joined a church at the West Port, where he soon became an elder and was given charge of a mission sponsored by the church. His minister saw that evangelism was to be the young man's life work, and when in 1857 he was asked to find a man to undertake full-time work as a missionary among miners and others around Newmains, Lanarkshire, he recommended Donald Ross. Donald agreed with considerable reluctance, but when once he had set his hand to the plough, he gave himself wholly to the ministry of the gospel for the rest of his life.

His headquarters as superintendent of the North East Coast Mission, from 1860 onwards, were in Aberdeen. This new work was congenial indeed, and he soon associated with himself a number of younger men who were fired with his own evangelistic zeal.

His ten years with the Mission were years of tremendous blessing. The spirit of revival continued with the preachers and great numbers of men and women were converted in those coastal areas. But as time went on, tensions developed. Donald Ross and his colleagues were sturdy individualists of independent spirit, who carried on their work in what they believed to be the best way. But their way was, to an increasing degree, not the way of the Free Church ministers, who (in the best Presbyterian tradition) were anxious to keep the forward movement under ecclesiastical control. Donald Ross himself was a member of the Free North Church in Aberdeen, and his colleagues were all Free Churchmen, but they found to their dismay that their methods were being chiefly criticized, and often positively opposed, by ministers who themselves had been foremost in the activity of the 1859 revival.[4] In 1870, therefore, Donald Ross judged it best to resign his superintendency and withdraw from the North East Coast Mission. Together with two of his fellow-missioners, Donald Munro and John Smith, he formed a new agency, the Northern Evangelistic Society, which was to evangelize the inland towns and villages of the north of Scotland (so as not to trespass on the territory of the Mission they had left). The directors of the new Society were nominated as the Father, the Son and the Holy Ghost, with Donald Ross discharging a subordinate superintendency. The work of the Society was publicized in a new periodical, published in Aberdeen at the beginning of 1871, entitled *The Northern Intelligencer*.[5] The object of this periodical, in Donald Ross's words, was 'to set ungarnished truth before the reader', and its doctrinal basis was stated plainly as follows inside the front cover: 'Eternal salvation is a free, present, attainable, inalienable, imperishable gift — i.e. any man or woman in this world, be he or she the blackest sinner in it, may in one moment be justified for ever from every charge of sin, and may rest as sure of eternal life as he is certain that in himself he never has deserved, and never will deserve, anything but eternal damnation.'

Similar blessing to that experienced along the coast was now experienced inland. But many of the converts were no longer content to remain in their former church fellowship, where their association with the 'new prophets' was frowned upon; worse still, an increasing number of them insisted on being baptized as believers. Donald Ross compared himself to a hen that has hatched out a brood of ducklings, standing and making agitated noises on the bank when they take instinctively to the water. When his thirteenth and last child was born, someone asked him if he was going to have the baby christened, to which he replied emphatically: 'I have had twelve children baptized already, and, if I were to have twelve more, so would they all be.' But his was not a mind to be fettered by tradition, and when he was impelled to think the subject through afresh in the light of the New Testament, he reached a different conclusion and at the age of forty-seven was baptized (in the Dee) by my wife's grandfather (John Davidson of Gowanwell, near New Deer, Aberdeenshire), a considerably younger man than himself. Unlike some of his colleagues and disciples, however, he retained great sympathy for believers who did not see eye to eye with him on this issue: 'Make believers' baptism a matter for forbearance,' he wrote to a friend who was engaged in the formation of a New Testament church. 'Let the basis of fellowship with you be *faith in the Lord Jesus Christ.*'[6]

About this time he resigned his membership in the Free Church of Scotland, but what form of church fellowship he and his converts should enter was not clear to him. He is recorded to have preached on the text 'Come out from among them, and be ye separate' (misinterpreting it, I greatly fear) without being able to tell his hearers where they should go when they did 'come out'. 'We heard of "Brethren" ', he said, 'but only as bad, bad people, and we resolved to have nothing to do with them.' But before long he and his friends made the acquaintance of some of these people, and found them to be not quite so bad as their reputation. In fact, there was a handful of them meeting in Aberdeen, and they joined forces with Donald Ross and other Christians associated with him in the principal mission hall of the Northern Evangelistic Society.

In 1874 Donald Ross left Aberdeen for Edinburgh, and two years later he sailed to North America to undertake pioneer evangelism there. The Northern Evangelistic Society faded away, but its ideals were perpetuated in many Brethren meetings in the north-east of Scotland. Quite a number of these meetings have celebrated their centenary in recent years; some of them have found it necessary to mark their centenary by disbanding. They had served their generation by the will of God.

Other similar meetings in the region came into being quite spontaneously around the same time.[7] Among these was the Brethren meeting in Elgin. The prime mover in the formation of this meeting was John Rae, who had been pastor of the Baptist Church in Elgin. When he resigned his pastorate (about 1872) he was followed by the majority of his flock but, as an old man who recalled the situation once told me, many of them just 'came out to John Rae' and so, in due course, went back to where they had come from. In later years John Rae and his family became well known in North America, but he left the Elgin meeting which he had founded a memento in the shape of a silver communion plate.

John Rae's action is recorded by H. A. Ironside in his *Historical Sketch of the Brethren Movement*: Dr Ironside refers to him as 'my father's uncle by marriage'.[8]

Dr Ironside goes on to tell how some of the leaders of this north-east movement were approached by some Exclusive brethren from Edinburgh, who would have welcomed them into their fellowship — but stipulated that first they should judge the Bethesda question of 1848.[9] They felt unable to engage in such judicial activity on the basis of incomplete and hearsay evidence, and did not see why they should do so in any case. By contrast, they were recognized and welcomed as fellow-ministers of the word by John R. Caldwell[10] and other brethren associated with him, and the meetings with which they were connected came to be recognized as Open Brethren meetings — a recognition which could only be informal and unofficial, but involved a warm practical fellowship.

But we in the north-east did not inherit much that had become accepted tradition in the Brethren movement. We were never terribly impressed when people told us that we should embrace such-and-such an interpretation of Scripture or adopt such-and-such a course of action, because that was what 'the early brethren' taught or did. To use a favourite idiom, it was not to 'the early brethren' that we had 'come out'. We had abandoned one form of religious tradition, and saw no reason why we should take over another; what we did, of course (without realizing it), was to develop our own. Some of our traditions were established by what theologians would call the *via negativa*; their originators took note of what was customarily done in the churches from which they had withdrawn, and thought the safest course was to do something different from that. As late as my own youth it was felt to be rather strange when ministering brethren who visited us from 'the south' (i.e. anywhere south of the Grampians) concluded their services with the apostolic benediction (2 Cor. 13: 14); we all knew that this was how services were concluded in those other places, and (undoubtedly scriptural as the benediction was) felt it a little odd to hear it used at our meetings.

Whereas the Brethren movement started off as an early experiment in ecumenicity, ecumenicity played little part in our north-eastern thinking. Our pioneers had seceded from the main-line churches, and often they expressed their reasons for secession in a way which did not encourage the main-line churches to think of them benevolently as 'brethren dearly beloved and longed for'.[11] Perhaps understandably, the sense of having said 'Good-bye to all that' was more decisively, if more poignantly, felt by those who had previously shared in evangelical fellowship and witness with friends now on the other side of the dividing line than by those who had known only a formal and

7

devitalized church. However that may be, it was useless for visitors from the south to tell us that what we stood for was not what the early brethren had stood for; the early brethren were not our standard of reference.

This was more a general trend than a uniform pattern. For uniformity was never accounted a virtue in the north-east. We were a society of individualists — more so, I suppose, two generations ago than today — and our individualism was as manifest in our church life as in other spheres. There may be something about the Brethren way of worship which attracts individualists; we certainly had no lack of them in our meetings in the north-east, men and women who had no objection to being in a minority of one if that was the right thing to be. I remember a neighbour of ours who was sometimes referred to as 'the church of God in Elgin'; when there was a division in the 'Needed Truth' movement in 1904 he did not follow the Vernal majority but stayed with the Luxmoore minority — indeed, he *was* that minority, so far as our town and district were concerned.[12]

Our individualism showed itself in many ways. We used the *Believers Hymn Book* but did not confine ourselves to the tunes printed in the music edition. Some of our tunes we got from an excellent collection published in Aberdeen under the title *The Northern Psalter*; some we got from more uncanonical sources. For example, we sang 'I heard the voice of Jesus say' to the tune of *The Auld Hoose*, 'Faint not, Christian! though the road . . .' to *Killarney*, 'O Christ, what burdens bowed thy head' to *The Rowan Tree* (to which indeed it was set in a collection called *Songs of Victory*), 'I'm waiting for thee, Lord' to *The Flowers of the Forest* (I recall a funeral service in Tomnahurich Cemetery, Inverness, where this was done very effectively), 'When we reach our peaceful dwelling' to *Just Before the Battle, Mother*, and 'Rise, my soul, behold 'tis Jesus' to a variation on *Ae fond kiss, and then we sever*. Some (not all) of these were highly suitable settings; the tune fitted the words. To this day I associate two or three hymns in the *Believers Hymn Book* with tunes that I have never heard except in the north-east; I have never seen them in print and have no idea of their origin,[13] but in my mind they are wedded to the words. It occasionally falls to my lot to 'lift the tune' in Brinnington Evangelical Church when our regular pianist is away on a Sunday morning; I sometimes have to resist the temptation to start the tune that comes first to my mind.

Again, when I want to give a sample of highly individual biblical exegesis, it is on my store of north-east memories that I draw. The men and women there read the Bible with an independent mind and loved to puzzle out the meaning of obscure passages for themselves. Of course the eccentric excesses into which this addiction to private interpretation could lead may well be imagined, but such excesses were the defects of very positive qualities. Interpretations were not unhesitatingly accepted because some able expositor had voiced them. 'I would be slow to believe that,' said a Peterhead brother[14] to C. F. Hogg at a conversational Bible reading on 1 Samuel 16. What, it was asked, was the significance of the 'horn' of oil from which Samuel anointed David (v. 13)? 'I suppose', said Mr Hogg, 'it would be to hold the oil'; but the questioner was 'slow to believe' that it could have no deeper significance than that. Perhaps he had in mind that David was anointed from a horn, a symbol of strength, whereas Saul had been anointed from a 'vial' (1 Sam. 10: 1), a symbol of wrath, as the King James Version of Revelation 15: 7 indicates. (I have known this distinction between the two containers to be seriously suggested).

C. F. Hogg was, indeed, one of the most esteemed and appreciated of our ministering visitors, but none of us imagined that an interpretation was necessarily right because even he held it. (In more recent years an overseas correspondent found fault with my understanding of 1 Corinthians 13: 10, 'when that which is perfect is come', because it did not tally with W. E. Vine's understanding of it and I ought, surely, to have agreed with *him*.[15] My understanding could well be mistaken, but no north-eastern Scot would change his considered opinion just because a respected authority held a different opinion!)

So much, then, for my regional and ecclesiastical background; the factors which I have mentioned have helped to make me what I am, and I am glad that it has been so. The people I have described are my people, and I think of them with grateful affection.[16] I have been away from that area for so long that nowadays, when I go back on occasion, I find that the leadership has passed to the grandchildren of the leaders I knew. Yet I remain a north-eastern Scot, and have spent a good part of my life applying sandpaper to the more abrasive individualisms that would pass unnoticed in my home territory, in order to make myself reasonably tolerable to the kindly and hospitable southerners among whom I have lived for so long.

Notes to Chapter 1

1. Calgacus, the Caledonian leader, according to Tacitus, *Agricola*, 30.

2. See Appendix *Who are the Brethren?* (pp. 313 ff.).

3. The Brethren meeting in Elgin now has its premises on the site of Brownlow North's residence, on the north bank of the River Lossie.

4. One can understand, of course, that some of Donald Ross's utterances did not endear him to the ministers, as when he published a tract 'suggesting to the ministers to go on strike for a year or more and allow nine pairs of evangelists to be let loose on Scotland, pledging our word that more conversions would be seen through the eighteen than through all the ministers put together in the same time'. Cf. C. W. Ross (ed.) *Donald Ross* (Kilmarnock 1904), p. 45.

5. Its name was changed in 1878 to *The Northern Witness*, and in 1887 to *The Witness*.

6. C. W. Ross (ed.) *Donald Ross*, p. 96.

7. A notable instance was the Peterhead meeting, which came into existence largely through the evangelistic work of a very remarkable man named James Turner, who had been active in the 1859 Revival.

8. *A Historical Sketch of the Brethren Movement* (Grand Rapids 1942), p. 72.

9. The 'Bethesda question' marked the original cleavage between Open and Exclusive Brethren. When J. N. Darby required Brethren generally to follow his lead in excommunicating all who were in fellowship with B. W. Newton (on account of the latter's alleged heresy), the elders of Bethesda Chapel, Bristol, maintained the autonomous rights of their local church and refused to submit to Darby's dictation, preferring to assess each case on its individual merits and not to endorse a blanket verdict of guilt by association. For this policy Bethesda Chapel was in its turn denounced by Darby; to 'judge the Bethesda question' was in effect to concur in his virtual excommunication of Bethesda. See H. H. Rowdon *The Origins of the Brethren* (Pickering & Inglis 1967), pp. 258-266; F. R. Coad *A History of the Brethren Movement* (Exeter ²1976), pp. 157-164, 301-304.

10. John R. Caldwell (1839-1917) was a leader among the Open Brethren in the Glasgow area; he edited *The Witness* from 1876 to 1914.

11. The phrase in which R. C. Chapman of Barnstaple (1803-1902), a leader among the Open Brethren, described the Exclusive Brethren.

12. The 'Needed Truth' movement received its name from the monthly periodical *Needed Truth*, founded in 1888 and still being published. It advocated more strictly demarcated lines of church fellowship than those observed among Open Brethren, which were adopted by those churches of God which seceded from the Open Brethren in 1892. The two parties in the division of 1904 were popularly called after two leaders; the Vernal group was in the majority in Scotland, the Luxmoore group in England and farther afield.

13. It used to be said that when Donald Ross heard a street-singer singing an attractive tune which he thought would fit some hymn, he would follow him or her from street to street until he had mastered it. Occasionally some people have mistakenly thought that a hymn tune, if not the very language of the hymn, was borrowed from popular culture when the borrowing was actually the other way round: I remember a friend telling me how he was mildly scandalized when first he heard a Christian chorus sung to the tune of 'Follow, follow, we will follow Rangers' — but that must have been because his acquaintance with Scottish football antedated his introduction to evangelical Christianity. (On the other hand, people who raise their eyebrows when they hear sacred words sung to the tune *On Ilkla Moor Baht 'At* need to be reminded that that tune was lifted a century ago from the Primitive Methodist Hymnbook.)

14. This brother, a fisherman, once gave a remarkable explanation of the statement that the disciples 'caught nothing' on the occasion mentioned in John 21: 3. 'They should have known better than to expect anything,' he said. 'We are told that they had with them the two sons of Zebedee. These were the men whom Jesus called "the sons of thunder", and it is a fact well known to all fishermen that when there is any thunder in the atmosphere, the fish bury their heads in the sea-bed, and it is impossible to catch any.' This tendency to illustrate Scripture from one's professional experience came to expression in a comment I once heard a speaker in central Scotland make on the groaning creation of Romans 8: 22: he identified this groaning with the creaking noises which he sometimes had heard while working down the pit.

15. W. E. Vine suggested a reference here to the completion of a canon of Scripture, which did away with the need for the gifts of tongues and prophecy (*First Corinthians* [London 1951], p. 184).

16. Some pleasant and informative sketches of life and times in that part of Scotland were given in W. S. Bruce *The Nor' East* (Aberdeen ³1922). The author, no relative of mine (so far as I know), was parish minister of Banff for half a century from 1872 onwards.

2

Home and church

Into this north-east environment, then, I was born in 1910. At the time of my birth my father, Peter Fyvie Bruce,[1] had been actively engaged as an evangelist for over ten years. He himself was a native of Aberdeenshire ('born twice in the parish of Ellon', as I have heard him say), the seventh in a family of twelve children. At the age of sixteen he experienced an evangelical conversion after a period of spiritual concern. Even before that, according to his eldest sister, he showed a reverence for God, always (for example) saying grace before food, even when eating alone.

According to a short autobiographical article which he contributed in June 1949 to the now defunct gospel paper *Good Tidings*, while talking about the way of salvation with a companion who shared his concern on this matter, 'I realized that the work of the Lord Jesus on the Cross was for me, and I said to my friend: "Man, I see it all, I'm saved!" ' When relating this in later years, he would say, 'What did I see? Jesus on the cross for me.' And this was the central note of his gospel witness to the end of his days — 'Jesus on the cross for me'.

At the time of his conversion he worked on a farm, as his father had done before him. He quickly found fellowship with a company of like-minded believers in the village of

Newburgh, at the mouth of the Ythan, and became active in gospel testimony and Sunday School teaching. After a few years he found employment in Aberdeen and joined the St. Paul Street meeting in that city, continuing to give his spare time to gospel witness and Bible study, for which he had an unappeasable appetite. His period of formal education was brief; he left school before his twelfth birthday (although by that time he had begun the study of Latin, which was not an unusual thing in north-east parish schools in those days). But he was a natural scholar and student, who brought to his understanding of Scripture a finely balanced judgment, and I have never had to unlearn anything I learned from him.

When he was twenty-four years old, he was invited by an evangelist in the area (Francis Logg) to join him in a tent mission for some weeks in the summer. He asked for a fortnight to think over the proposition. Before the fortnight was completed, he had decided that, since he had saved a few pounds, he would be willing to spend them in the Lord's service in this way. By the end of the season, he found he had more money than when he started, and decided that this too must be used in the Lord's service. So, having obtained help from God, he continued in this work for fifty-six years until, in September 1955, he had a fatal heart attack while conducting a funeral service. Throughout his life he exemplified Charles Wesley's lines:

'Tis all my business here below
To cry 'Behold the Lamb!'

— and at the end the lines immediately following these came true of him also:

Happy, if with my latest breath,
I might but gasp his name;
Preach him to all, and cry in death:
Behold, behold the Lamb!

For a number of years he was associated with older evangelists — with Francis Logg in the north-east, with

Duncan McNab in the south-west of Scotland (where they manned the horse-drawn Caledonian Bible Carriage) and with William Mackenzie of Inverness in the Scottish Highlands. That he visited the south of England once at least during those years is indicated by the inscription in a copy of William Kelly's *Exposition of Isaiah* which lies before me: 'Presented to Peter Bruce, Scotch evangelist, on his first visit to Brighton, January 1908'.

It was when he was conducting a tent mission in Ross-shire with William Mackenzie that he first met my mother. She was nursemaid in a doctor's family in Dingwall, and it was while the family was on holiday at Rosemarkie, in the Black Isle, that they were introduced to each other. She had recently become a foundation member of a new, Brethren-type church in Dingwall. The cultural tradition of the Highlands, in which she was born and brought up, was considerably different from that of the north-east; I am glad to have inherited something of both.

They were married in 1909 and settled in Elgin, where they lived for the rest of their lives, bringing up a family of seven children, of whom I came first. We grew up in an atmosphere of plain living and high thinking. The living was as plain as could well be imagined; the necessities of life were never lacking, but as for the luxuries of life, we never even thought of them. My mother, in her earlier days, had been greatly impressed by George Müller's *Autobiography*, not realizing at the time that in years to come she would herself enjoy the kind of experiences of which that work was full. The scale was smaller, but the principle was the same. It was a good upbringing; it taught us, among other things, to view money and other material things in their proper perspective. The widow of my late friend S. H. Hooke (who was himself brought up that way) told me that he 'preserved that attitude to money all his life . . . he never refused an appeal for help when he had money, and when he hadn't he never worried but always said "The Lord will provide" — and the Lord did, very often in quite unexpected ways!'

But if the living was plain, the thinking was high. The

principal subjects of conversation were the most exalted and mind-stretching that could well be imagined. Our knowledge of distant lands and their spiritual state was increased by visits from missionaries on furlough, who frequently stayed with us when they were addressing meetings in our area. Missionary meetings, complete with maps, were a welcome change from the more pedestrian programmes which were normal at our place of worship. They also involved a substantial postponement of the usual hour of going to bed. On one occasion Handley Bird, of India, stayed with us for several days, addressing meetings practically every evening. I was discouraged from attending his meetings, being assured that they were not missionary meetings and that I would not understand what he was speaking about. This was a wise judgment; he was giving a series of lectures on the cherubim of glory, a favourite theme of his, which he treated in a highly allegorical manner. I gathered that my father could not follow him all the way; his mind, unlike Mr Bird's, did not run on allegorical lines.

Our local church, as I have said, was founded about 1872.[2] The leading brother from its inception until his death, a year or so before I was born (James Grant of Tyockside), had the distinction of never having been baptized (i.e. by immersion, on profession of personal faith). This was an anomaly indeed, as believers' baptism was our regular practice; but anomalies are things to be cherished; without them life might be insufferably monotonous. In my young days the leading brethren were warm-hearted, God-fearing men, quite ungifted, who nevertheless carried on the services to the best of their ability. There was my father, of course, but he was more often than not away from home doing the work of an evangelist. Looking back, I realize that I found his gospel preaching more interesting than that of our local brethren, but at the time did not understand why this was so. It was only later that it occurred to me that there was about his preaching a coherence and a sequence which distinguished it from a mere stringing together of gospel texts.

15

Our local brethren from time to time told the story of their conversion. This at least made interesting hearing; I heard them tell it so often that I could repeat it almost as well as they could, and when my sisters and I meet, years later, it needs only the quotation of one phrase to reconstruct the whole narrative: what one of us forgets another supplies. One of those brethren, John Dunbar, would tell how he was converted when D. L. Moody, passing through Elgin, stopped and preached on Lady Hill in 1874. Another, George Bowie, would tell how he was first convicted of his spiritual need by a preacher who said (as though addressing him personally), 'Young man, you are going to hell religiously!'

I must have been sixteen years old or so when our gospel service one Sunday evening was addressed by a young man from Lancashire, who had come to the neighbouring town of Lossiemouth, five or six miles away, to spend several months doing locum work in a pharmacist's shop. His text was Philippians 1: 21 ('For to me to live is Christ'), which he expounded by first placing it in its context. He had not well begun to speak before I realized that here was a speaker who (unlike most of the speakers to whom I listened on Sunday evenings) was completely on my own wavelength. His name was Kingsley Melling; in later years I came to know him very well, and we are still on the same wavelength. (He has good reason to have pleasant memories of his time in Lossiemouth; it was then that he met his wife Helen.)

Our local brethren were not qualified to give expository ministry, or even to conduct a conversational Bible reading with profit. To one of them, however, George Bowie, who taught me in Sunday School, I owe a debt; over the years he had read and re-read the Acts of the Apostles until he knew the book practically by heart, and as he was specially prone to base his Sunday School lessons on Acts, I became nearly word-perfect in its text myself. I imagine that this may have stood me in good stead in later years when I came to write commentaries on Acts.

When my father was at home for a weekend (as he

occasionally was), we would have a Sunday afternoon meeting for Bible ministry. Some Christians in the town who attended other churches would come along to hear him, as they had no services of their own at that hour. In my earlier years I was not able to follow his expositions of the Pauline epistles (his favourite passages of Scripture) with the appreciation of which I later became capable. But I remember once, with rapt fascination, listening to his exposition of Nebuchadnezzar's dream-image in Daniel 2. I knew the stories of Daniel in the lions' den and of his friends in the fiery furnace, but that was my first introduction to biblical apocalyptic. (Talking of Daniel in the lions' den, I recall how one day I found in a book a picture of Christian martyrs exposed to the lions in the Roman arena, and asked my mother in surprise why God didn't do the same for them as he did for Daniel; I don't think I was satisfied with her answer.)

I was admitted to membership and first communion in our Elgin church in September 1928, after being baptized by the aforesaid George Bowie in James Street Hall, Lossiemouth (we had no baptistery at that time in our rented premises in Elgin).

For some years a 'Glanton' brother,[3] Duncan Chisholm by name, lived in our town and helped us greatly. The nearest meeting of his own connexion was several miles away. His conscience would not allow him to break bread with us, but he would preach the gospel for us and take part acceptably in our prayer meetings, In addition, he conducted conversational Bible readings on a week-night in his home. From these too I learned a great deal; no wonder, for he was a keen and highly intelligent student of J. N. Darby and especially William Kelly. But I realized one night that his reading had been limited to the literature of one school, when I referred to H. P. Liddon's work *The Divinity of our Lord* and found he had never heard of it. 'Well,' I said, with the precocity of adolescence, 'it's one of the series of Bampton Lectures, like Bernard's *Progress of Doctrine.*' But he hadn't heard of that work either. (That is perhaps not

17

surprising; I was once told, whether correctly or not, that even W. W. Fereday,[4] though he had vaguely heard of it, had never read it.) One elderly 'Glanton' brother (James Burgess, of Rothes, a small Speyside town about nine miles away) regularly attended those Bible readings; when any knotty question arose, he would produce from his pocket a copy of the New Testament in the *New Translation* and say, with an air of finality, 'We'll see what Mr Darby says'. (He had the edge on the rest of us; he had *known* J.N.D.)

Another of the Brethren (Open, this time) on whose wavelength I felt myself to be, though he must have been sixty to seventy years older than I was, kept a tiny shop in Rothes. George Younie was his name; he was a man with world-wide interests. His son, a former dux of Elgin Academy, held a responsible position in the Indian Civil Service. George Younie was a member of the Victoria Institute. He subscribed to biblical and theological journals from the United States as well as from Great Britain. I don't suppose he had much more formal education than my father had a generation later, but he was a truly educated and cultured man. He had been for a number of years a member of the local school board. He told me with relish of a meeting of the school board which had been addressed by a visitor from Edinburgh who tried to persuade him and his colleagues that there was no point in teaching Latin in the local school, which catered only for children up to the age of fourteen. What was the use, asked this visitor, of those children's knowing how the ancient Romans used to talk? 'When he had sat down', said Mr Younie, 'I rose and said, "Mr Chairman, does the speaker intend us to suppose that the only value in learning Latin is knowing how the ancient Romans used to talk?" Man, I never saw a man climb down faster. He thought he was talking to a lot of ignorant country yokels!' If he did, he certainly thought wrong, with George Younie in the audience.

George Younie took an active interest in local and national politics. The prevalent doctrine among us was that Christians, being citizens of heaven, did not take part in the politics of earth. Some of our people may have voted in elections without saying too much about it, but George Younie nailed his Liberal colours to the mast and addressed public meetings, indoors and out-of-doors, on behalf of what he believed to be the rightful cause. Such activity was anomalous, but no one questioned his liberty to engage in it.

Notes to Chapter 2

1. 'Fyvie' was his mother's maiden surname; it has come down as a middle name through three generations.

2. When, in 1939, our church moved to the old West End Mission Hall, on the corner of High Street and Murdoch's Wynd (recently demolished), three of the foundation members were still alive. It was through the generosity of one of them, William Grigor, that the church acquired this building; he was able, happily, to be present at the opening celebrations.

3. The 'Glanton' connexion, so called from the town of that name in Northumberland, originated in 1908 in a breakaway from the extreme Exclusive party, the Raven connexion (so called from F. E. Raven, 1837-1905, grandfather of Anthony Crosland, late Foreign Secretary). Since most of the evangelistic and outward-looking members went with the Glanton group, those who remained behind became even more extreme in their exclusiveness.

4. W. W. Fereday, a prominent Brethren teacher (see p. 101), had been in earlier days one of William Kelly's associates.

3
Conferences

Our appetite for biblical ministry was catered for by a number of annual conferences held at various times throughout the year. We called them 'conferences' but we did not come together to 'confer'; they were really conventions or congresses at which we listened to ministry.

First in the year, and in any case first in order of importance and prestige, was the Aberdeen New Year Conference. It was inaugurated on New Year's Day, 1874, so it attained its centenary in January 1973, and if one may judge by the enthusiastic support it received on the latter occasion, its prospects of another prosperous century are bright. My father began to attend it in 1892, and continued to attend it regularly for over sixty years. In 1923, when I was twelve years old, he took me with him. That was the fiftieth anniversary, and we had reminiscences from brethren who had attended it in the very early days, including one — Walter Fraser, of Dufftown — who had been present at its inauguration. I did not foresee then that fifty years farther on I should be present at the centenary celebration and indulge in reminiscences of the jubilee meetings.

I told Stephen Short on one occasion when we were together in 1972, that I hoped to attend the centenary conference at Aberdeen next New Year's Day, and he asked what kind of speakers we used to have in earlier days. I said, 'Well, C. F. Hogg, W. E. Vine, J. B. Watson, J. M. Shaw, George Goodman, Montague Goodman, Rendle Short, J. C. M. Dawson — you name them, we had them.' The conveners of the conference in those days went for the best, and got it. The conference lasted three days. On the afternoon of the second day reports were given by 'home workers' of evangelistic activities carried out during the preceding year. On the afternoon of the third day we had reports from 'foreign' missionaries; the evening of the third day was an occasion when Sunday School teachers received practical guidance for their special ministry.

The day after the Aberdeen conference finished there was an all-day conference in Peterhead. There, some of the Aberdeen speakers, who were able to spend a further day in the north-east, had an opportunity for further ministry — provided they were acceptable in Peterhead (which could not be taken for granted). In addition to them there might be other speakers at Peterhead who would not have been admitted to the Aberdeen platform. I could name names in both 'unacceptable' categories, but it is better to draw a kindly veil over such matters.

At Aberdeen, as far back as I can remember, the platform was 'closed' (i.e. restricted to speakers invited and announced in advance). At Peterhead it was understood that speakers from the Aberdeen conference would have priority; after all, divine guidance would not have brought them so far north if they had not been intended to minister.

There was greater flexibility with regard to the other speakers. (But it was a Border assembly, not a north-east one, which in 1935 announced its annual conference in one of our magazines in these terms: 'Ministry by A.B. and C.D.; after that as the Lord may lead'.

Around Eastertide we had conferences at Dufftown and Buckie (Buckie and Portessie were joint-sponsors of the latter). The great event of the summer was the Craigellachie Conference in mid-July; it lasted two days. The host assembly for this conference was at Aberlour, two miles up the Spey from Craigellachie; it had been founded in 1869 as the sequel to a mission conducted by Donald Ross (it has now been defunct for some years). But Craigellachie was a more convenient centre; it was then a railway junction, but a real beauty spot. It was also the home of two men of substance among us: Robert Dunbar, proprietor of the Popine Mills, and Edward Grant, inventor of the Standfast plough. (My wife and I have in our home a tangible token of the quality of Robert Dunbar's workmanship — a dining-room table which he made for her grand-parents over a hundred years ago.) The attendance at the Craigellachie meetings was increased by holiday-makers from distant parts — not only from the benighted south of Scotland but even from darkest England (as some of us reckoned it to be). A minor diversion for some of the younger people at the conference was to hear our English visitors' attempts to pronounce 'Craigellachie'.

A few days after the Craigellachie meetings there was a conference at Dingwall; some of the Craigellachie speakers were persuaded to continue their visit to Scotland and to speak there, sampling the attractions of the north-west as well as of the north-east. In August there was a conference at Inverurie; later in the year there were Harvest Thanksgiving conferences in New Deer and Moscorral (near Huntly), and on Christmas Day there was a conference in Inverness.

In my young days most of those conferences had an 'open platform' (i.e. it was open, in theory, for any male to come forward from the floor and address the company). When Craigellachie adopted the 'closed platform' system (complete with chairman) in July 1928, I well remember that there was a public protest by a well-known *laudator temporis acti* at this departure from the 'scriptural pattern'. But, although too often the open platform meant that the race was to the swift and the battle to the strong, nevertheless, when brethren of weight and repute were present there was a general agreement to make room for them. It was at such open conferences that I first heard Harold St. John and H. P. Barker. For the sake of hearing them, it was worth while sitting under the ministry of others who taught us, for example, the important difference between 'in my name' and 'into my name' in Matthew 18: 20.

I recall one conference — at Dufftown, in 1935 — when H. P. Barker ministered on that text. He approached it by a devious route, starting with the incident of the man in Numbers 15: 32-36 who was found gathering sticks on the sabbath day. That was a wrong kind of gathering, but the speaker soon came to the right form of gathering (H.P.B. had not 'abandoned exclusivism'[1] for nothing!) and maintained that '*in* my name' was the only intelligible rendering, not '*to*' or '*unto*' or '*into* my name' — adding for good measure the thought that people were 'gathered together' in the sense of Matthew 18: 20 only when they were *gathered together* (a revolutionary thought to some of his hearers).[2] H.P.B. was too acute an observer of the human pageant not to know what he was about. After a brief interval, during which the platform was occupied by a youthful volunteer who spoke on a completely different subject, a seasoned champion of the 'into my name' rendering leaped into the fray and with animation accomplished (to his own satisfaction) a demolition job on the whole of H.P.B.'s discourse. H.P.B., whose deafness stood him in good stead at times, sat through it with a beatific smile on his face — but even if he didn't hear the message, he had a shrewd idea of its 'main thrust'. (For the benefit of uninstructed readers, let me explain the distinction: every church in Christendom, it was affirmed, is gathered *in* the Lord's name, but to be gathered together *into* his name is something which can be predicted only of an *élite* minority of Christian companies, conforming to a particular pattern — no need to inquire into their identity!)

I recall a speaker at one of these conferences who gave us an address on the significance of Christian baptism based on the incident in 2 Kings 13: 21, where a corpse was thrown hastily into Elisha's grave and revived on coming into contact with his bones. Then there was a speaker who could derive church teaching from Ecclesiastes 10, somewhat as follows:

> v. 1. *Dead flies cause the ointment of the apothecary to send forth a stinking savour:* This speaks of moral evil in the assembly.
> v. 2. *A wise man's heart is at his right hand:* This is because the right is the side of consecration (Leviticus 8: 23, 24).
> v. 7. *I have seen servants upon horses:* This refers to men acting as elders who have no right to such a dignity (with a side-glance at the ban on multiplying horses in Deuteronomy 17: 16).

We had another ministering brother to whom the verb 'repair' meant 'mend' and nothing else, so that he could not abide Sir Edward Denny's hymn

> To Calvary, Lord, in spirit now
> Our weary souls repair —

because, as he insisted, the Lord's Table was not a 'repair-shop'. (I wondered at times if he also misunderstood 'souls' as 'soles' — but that was probably unfair.) Yet he thought he could instruct us, at times, in the niceties of Greek usage. He was, I believe, an earnest evangelist; it was a pity that he was ever encouraged to think that he had the gift of a teacher.

One ministering brother to whom I frequently listened with appreciation — though not always with agreement — was John Brown (1846-1938), who spent the last thirty-odd years of his life in Edinburgh, but had lived for forty years before that in Greenock, in the west of Scotland. In his prime he had been one of the leaders of the 'Needed Truth' secession in Scotland (1892) — 'we expected', he once remarked, 'to carry the whole of Scotland' — but later he returned to the fellowship of the churches which he had left. Some other brethren who did the same reacted vigorously against the 'Needed Truth' position and became more 'open' than they had been before (I think, for example, of L. W. G. Alexander), but John Brown retained many 'Needed Truth' principles, restricting the designation 'church of God', for instance, to a local company of Christians canonically 'gathered together into the name of the Lord'.[3] By calling he was a master-baker, but had taught himself a little Greek and rather less Hebrew. He was wholeheartedly devoted to the

24

Revised New Testament of 1881 and its underlying text, declaring that 'where Lachmann, Tregelles, Tischendorf, and Westcott and Hort agree, you have verily what the Spirit saith', and that 'it is impossible to know the mind of God if you depend on the Authorized Version'. 'Will any one tell me', he would challenge us from the platform, 'that the last twelve verses of Mark's Gospel are the Word of God?' No one, naturally, would have dared to tell him any such thing.

He was given to fine distinctions: he would say that he had been seventy years 'in Christ' and sixty-nine years 'in the Lord' (the latter status dated from his baptism and reception into church fellowship),[4] and he would warn his hearers that they were guilty of 'a very serious misdemeanour, to say the least', if they said, or sang, in reference to 1 John 3:1, that the measure of the Father's love to them was their being called the *sons* of God. After such a discourse some brother was sure to rise and give out No. 26 in the *Believers Hymn Book* ('Behold, what love . . .'); the speaker would endure it with resignation. (I think all who were 'in Christ' were *children* of God, but only those 'in the Lord' were his *sons*.)

Some conference *habitués* had the idea that a speaker was not much good if they could understand all he said. They felt they were getting their money's worth if he was some way above their heads. If I learned anything in those days, I learned not to inflict Greek on Greekless audiences!

John Brown, who combined magisterial ferocity on the conference platform with the most exquisite Victorian courtesy in private life, picked up a good deal of information, on his own confession, by cultivating the company of people better educated than himself. He told me once how in his younger days he found himself occupying a hospital bed next to Dr James Morison, a distinguished expositor in his day, and profited by conversation with him on the Scriptures. John Brown in his turn had many ardent disciples, some of whom went so far as to say, like a man in Buckie whom I remember:[5] 'If John Brown says it, it's right.' As he entered his nineties, some of his disciples thought he was being specially preserved as a witness to the truth (the truth about the church, I suppose), and a few spoke as if they held it not unlikely that he might have been chosen to survive until the Lord's coming. He himself, more modestly, said: 'I have no doubt the Lord is keeping me alive for a purpose. My prayer is that I may rise to his purpose.'

But some of his disciples (possibly carrying his teaching to its logical conclusion) went farther than he approved, and in his closing days he deplored their divisive activities. (Brethren with longer memories than mine savoured the irony of this more than I could.) After his death, it was not to one of them but to me that his favourite Bible was (at his instruction) presented by his widow.

His spoken ministry stands out in my memory largely because of his aphoristic way of expressing himself. 'God will accept from those to whom he has *not* revealed his will what he will *not* accept from those to whom he *has* revealed his will.' (This was a lesson drawn from the contrast between David's disastrous transportation of the ark on the 'new cart' in 2 Samuel 6: 1-10 and the Lord's acquiescence in the Philistines' similar method of conveying it on an earlier occasion in 1 Samuel 6: 7-16.) 'Clerisy is the sin of sins Godward, as socialism is the sin of sins manward.' (Let readers make what they will of that one!)

Among all the varieties of ministry to which I was thus exposed I was able to find my way by using the clue which my father recommended to me in my teens: never to accept anything offered in the way of Christian faith or practice unless I saw it clearly for myself in the Scriptures. This advice I have regularly passed on to others, warning them especially not to accept anything just because I have said it. And another blessing of those early days was that I formed, and maintained, friendships with people whose firmly held and expressed views in some doctrinal areas (especially eschatology and ecclesiology) were poles apart from mine. Divergent beliefs might be the subject of mutual criticism but need be no obstacle to good personal relations.

Notes to Chapter 3

1. *Why I Abandoned Exclusivism* was the title of a pamphlet by H. P. Barker (Pickering & Inglis, no date, but apparently about 1930).

2. It was held by some that the perfect participle passive of Matthew 18: 20 denoted a permanent ecclesiastical status. See next note.

3. He made a point of translating the perfect participle passive in Matthew 18: 20 as 'having been and being gathered together'. On one occasion he came upon a place of worship in some town in Scotland, which announced on its notice-board: 'Christians gathered together into the name of the Lord Jesus Christ meet here.' 'I uncovered my head and worshipped,' he said. For these words betokened a company of Christians which knew itself to be permanently 'gathered together', while it 'met' at the times indicated on the notice-board.

4. Contrast C. F. D. Moule's distinction between the two phrases: 'what you are is "in Christ", and what you are to become is "in the Lord"' (*The Origin of Christology* [Cambridge 1977], p. 59).

5. This good man in later years described me as an 'ecclesiastical liberal'; I suspect he meant it as a criticism, but I welcomed it as a compliment.

4
Books

Children brought up in homes without books are deprived children, intellectually deprived, just as children brought up without adequate food, clothes and shelter are physically deprived or children brought up without affection are emotionally deprived. My siblings and I were deprived in none of these ways; as for books, we grew up with them.

Kind friends presented us from time to time with 'improving' books, written by people who wrote down to what they imagined to be children's level, and with volumes of expurgated Bible stories, such as *Line upon Line*. But, as I recall, we preferred our Bible stories neat, straight from the Authorized Version. In this way we learned many details passed over in silence by writers for children, and increased our vocabulary — gradually. I imagined that Potiphar's wife invited Joseph to join her in perpetrating some kind of falsehood (which I knew in any case to be a heinous offence), and, desiring some light on a detail in the story of Rahab, I asked my father what a harlot was. 'A bad woman,' said he. This puzzled me a bit: Rahab received unqualified commendation in Scripture, so I concluded that before she played her part in the history of Israel she must have been converted from a life of wickedness (theft or drunkenness, perhaps).

There were not many works of fiction in the home into which we were born: if there were more in later years, it was because we brought them home. In my earliest years I recall that George Borrow's *Lavengro* and *Romany Rye* were on my father's bookshelves; I think he picked them up somewhere because they were written by the author of *The Bible in Spain* (a fascinating work, but none too easy for a child to read, as I remember). There was also Bulwer Lytton's *The Last Days of Pompeii*, which I devoured. After a lapse of fifty years I picked it up in a place where I was staying, and found it unreadable. Far different was it with *David Copperfield*, which was left in our home by a lady who spent a few weeks with us. I can still read it with pleasure, and with considerably more understanding than I did in my boyhood: I couldn't really appreciate why such a fuss was made about little Emily and Steerforth. Similar lack of comprehension attended my reading of Southey's *Life of Nelson*, which I received as a school prize in 1919: how, for example, did Lady Hamilton come into the picture? And what were those two lines in mysterious script at the end of the book? My father told me the script was Greek; in later years I recognized the lines as a couplet from Hesiod.

Other works with which I became very well acquainted were Bunyan's *Pilgrim's Progress*, Harriet Beecher Stowe's *Uncle Tom's Cabin* ('Don't read the swear-words,' said my mother, who had read it herself in her youth and had some recollection of Simon Legree's language) and Lewis Carroll's *Alice in Wonderland* (a work with a moral for most occasions). The ten volumes of Nelson's *Encyclopaedia* (published about 1906) provided a plentiful store of general knowledge.

Missionary and other biographies lay around in profusion: David Livingstone, Mackay of Uganda, Frederick Stanley Arnot, Dan Crawford and the like were household names. Of non-religious biographies I recall those of the American Presidents Abraham Lincoln and James Garfield, both by one W. M. Thayer (who emphasized the 'log cabin to White House' pattern of both their lives). One Sunday afternoon a lady came to tea and asked me what I was reading: it was one of these two books. '*My* daughter wouldn't be allowed to read that kind of book on Sunday,' said she — obviously in disapproval of my parents' permissiveness.

A book which was generally acknowledged to be suitable for Sunday reading was *The Works of Josephus* in Whiston's translation. This was a new version of the familiar Bible story, with interesting deviations and additions. Sunday was never a dull day, with literature like that to read. Another fascinating work was *The Two Babylons*, by Alexander Hislop, who undertook to demonstrate, with greater erudition than judgment, that the Roman Catholic order of worship was the perpetuation of the alleged Babylonian cult of Nimrod and his wife Semiramis. Hislop's copious references to classical literature and mythology interested me greatly when I began to study classics at school. I suppose I was about fourteen when my father asked me, 'Have you read *all* of that book?' 'Yes,' said I. 'You've read more than is good for you,' he remarked; but in fact I suppose that what was beyond me simply remained beyond me. He himself had been presented with the book, before I was born, by an old lady in Jemimaville, in the Black Isle, in whose house he saw it. When she realized he was interested in it, she gave it to him, as it meant nothing to her (except that it maintained a 'godly attitude towards the Papacy',[1] to quote the elder Gosse in another connexion). My father gave her in exchange a volume by W. T. P. Wolston, which she might find more edifying.

I quickly realized that I was as liable to acquire misinformation as real information from Hislop. His etymologies were ingenious, if nothing else; there were few words in the religious vocabularies of all parts of the world which he could not derive from 'Chaldee' roots (in common with his contemporaries he supposed that the language which they called 'Chaldee', but which we know as Aramaic, was the ancient Babylonian language; this mistake arose from a misunderstanding of Daniel 2: 4). Thus, words like the Gaelic 'Beltane' (the fire festival of May 1), the Anglo-Saxon 'Easter', the Slavonic 'Zernebock' (the 'black god' of pre-Christian Central Europe), the West Indian 'cannibal' (a Spanish corruption of a word akin to 'Caribbean'), and many others, were given a new significance by means of their 'Chaldee' derivation. On a par with this kind of exercise was Hislop's derivation of French *roi* (king) from Hebrew *ro'eh* (shepherd), rather than from its true Latin origin.

But I learned a great deal from Hislop, even if his main conclusion is as untenable as the arguments by which he sought to establish it. In 1941 I tried, rather as a *jeu d'esprit*, to show how a modern writer would set about establishing the same conclusion in the light of more up-to-date knowledge and published my effort in *The Evangelical Quarterly*[2] under the title 'Babylon and Rome'. A certain Protestant trust took it so seriously that it wanted to reissue it as a propaganda tract; mercifully, shortage of paper in wartime helped to prevent that!

An even more esoteric work, which I acquired in 1926, was G. H. Pember's *Earth's Earliest Ages* (1876); I expected that it would deal with Genesis and geology, but it introduced me to the very unfamiliar territory of demonology.

On ecclesiastical history my father's shelves had Merle D'Aubigné's *History of the Reformation* and Andrew Miller's *Short Papers on Church History*. D'Aubigné was heavy going; Andrew Miller was much more readable.

Dorothy Sayers once wrote a short paper entitled 'A Vote of Thanks to Cyrus', in which she said that she owed a certain debt to Cyrus, for it was he who taught her that biblical history was *real* history, when she found that an authentic character whom she had previously known only from a children's primer called *Tales from Herodotus* figured in the Old Testament narrative. The Old Testament narrative in her youthful mind belonged to the context of church, and Old Testament characters were referred to in an 'unreal' tone of voice, but there was nothing unreal about Cyrus. This lesson was reinforced when in some out-of-the-way manual of general knowledge she came upon the information that the biblical Ahasuerus was identical with Xerxes, against whom the Greeks made that heroic stand at Thermopylae. 'I think', she said, 'it was chiefly Cyrus and Ahasuerus who prodded me into the belated conviction that history was all of a piece, and that the Bible was part of it.'[3]

I had something of the same experience, and two theological writers who brought the lesson home to me were Sir Robert Anderson and John Urquhart. My father possessed most of the works of Sir Robert Anderson, and I was attracted by two of them in particular — *The Coming Prince* (1895) and *Daniel in the Critics' Den* (1902). The former work presented an ingenious interpretation of the oracle of the seventy weeks in Daniel 9: 24-27; but since the whole basis of the argument would be undermined if the Maccabaean date for the composition of Daniel were sustained, the latter book was devoted to an examination and refutation of the case for that date, and a vindication of the sixth-century date. (In later days, when I lectured annually on the exegesis of the book of Daniel, I sometimes recalled with a degree of amusement that it was in Sir Robert's works that I was first introduced to its 'critical' interpretation.) Much of the argument of both books, which dealt with the fortunes of the Neo-Babylonian, Persian and Graeco-Macedonian Empires, overlapped my own field of historical interest. In addition, these books made me aware of some of the problems of biblical chronology. I could not see, however, why Sir Robert took it for granted that Artaxerxes' decree for the rebuilding of the walls of Jerusalem was issued on the first day of his twentieth regnal year — an assumption which was basic to his argument that the interval from the issuing of that decree to our Lord's entry into Jerusalem on Palm Sunday amounted to 69 'weeks' of years of 360 days each, calculated exactly to the very day. In fact, Nehemiah's memoirs do not indicate on which day of Artaxerxes' twentieth year the edict was issued; and to this uncertainty about the beginning of the period in question there must be added the high improbability that the year of our Lord's death was (as Sir Robert reckoned) A.D. 32. As with *The Two*

Babylons, however, so with *The Coming Prince* the collapse of the main conclusion of the book did not prevent me from gathering much valuable information by the way. Sir Robert was much better at exposing the fallacies of others than at avoiding fallacies of his own, more particularly in the area of prophetic interpretation.

John Urquhart's contribution to my education was provided in the third part of his *Inspiration and Accuracy of the Holy Scriptures* (1895), in which he discussed the bearing of historical and archaeological knowledge on the books of Esther and Daniel. His correlation of the data of Esther with the account of Herodotus and with the then recent excavations of M. A. Dieulafoy at Susa made a lasting impression on me.

I still have a volume of 1,000 pages, bought for me (at the price of two shillings, I believe) by a friend from a second-hand bookstall in Inverness, entitled *The Ancient History of the Egyptians, Carthaginians, Assyrians, Babylonians, Medes and Persians, Grecians and Macedonians*, translated from the French of Charles Rollin, on the fly-leaf of which is inscribed in my schoolboy hand, the date of acquisition: 29th December, 1923. Since Rollin died in 1741, his work could not be accounted up to date, but it comprised a digest of everything that the historians of Greece and Rome had to say on the period covered. I found it a storehouse of information.

An uncle of mine had been persuaded to buy on the instalment system, in the mid-1920s, a copy of Hastings' one-volume *Dictionary of the Bible* (1909). Unfortunately for him, he found very little use for it after he had got it. But when I visited his home from time to time, I found much of interest in it, especially in its very full entries on archaeological subjects, and when I was seventeen he made me a present of it. I still have it; but I did not foresee then that the day would come when I should be a contributor to a second edition of Hastings (1963).

Domestic literary resources were augmented by those of our local public library. From it I borrowed, among other things, several of the works of Sir William Ramsay and

Adolf Deissmann, which opened up to me the world of New Testament archaeology and philology. It was from it, too, that I borrowed Edmund Gosse's *Father and Son*. (I gathered, from remarks dropped by my father in later years, that he was seriously relieved that our relations did not turn out like those of the Gosse *père et fils*; this I found rather odd.) Yet another book which I procured from our public library (on inter-library loan) was Peake's *Commentary on the Bible* (1919); my curiosity to see it was stimulated by some reviews I had read, including one entitled 'Satan and the Higher Criticism' (by the then editor of the *Bible League Quarterly*). Again, I did not foresee the day when I would contribute to a new edition of Peake's *Commentary* (1962) and occupy Peake's chair.

Hereby hangs another tale. Soon after I was appointed to the Rylands Chair in Manchester, the Fellowship of Independent Evangelical Churches held its annual assembly in that city. I was invited to address a ministers' meeting on current trends in biblical exegesis. There in the front row sat the late E. J. Poole-Connor, the founding father of the F.I.E.C., by that time 88 years old. After expressing my appreciation of the opportunity to address the meeting, I said that I found my presence there somewhat anomalous. 'In 1933', I said, 'Mr Poole-Connor published a book entitled *The Apostasy of English Nonconformity*, in which the first Rylands Professor at Manchester University figured as Exhibit A. Now the present Rylands Professor is invited to address a meeting of the F.I.E.C. in Mr Poole-Connor's presence. Something has changed somewhere.' There was general laughter, in which Mr Poole-Connor joined as heartily as any. But the change to which I referred had not taken place exactly in the way they thought it had.

I shall have more to say about books later on, but this chapter has dealt with some books that I read before I left home for university in 1928. I must now turn to something else.

Notes to Chapter 4
1. E. Gosse *Father and Son* (London [1907] 1928), p. 90.
2. Vol. 13 (1941), pp. 241-261.
3. D. L. Sayers *Unpopular Opinions* (London 1946), p. 24.

5

Most willingly to school

Tuesday, 24th August, 1915, marked an important epoch in my career: on that day I went to school for the first time and in a manner of speaking, I have been there ever since.

For the first six years I received my education at a primary school, Elgin West End School. From there I graduated in 1921 to the ancient grammar school of our city, Elgin Academy (a school which attained high distinction in 1973 in the BBC 'Top of the Form' contest).

Elgin Academy originated early in the thirteenth century as the Cathedral School of the Diocese of Moray, and was moved from Spynie to Elgin about the time of the foundation of Elgin Cathedral (1224). It began to be called the Grammar School in 1489. In its early years it is said to have prepared youths for the University of Paris, before the University of Aberdeen was founded (1494).[1] About 1800 it was merged with the 'Sang Schule' of Elgin, founded by James VI in 1594 with revenues from the former Maisondieu, and has thenceforth been called Elgin Academy. During my time there the Rector (as the headmaster of many secondary schools in Scotland is called) used to tell new boys and girls each year that they come to 'a school with traditions'. This was true, of course, but I suspect that some of the traditions which he wished them to revere were introduced by himself, and they were none the worse for that. If, like Hugh Miller, I were writing a book on *My Schools and Schoolmasters,* I might go into greater detail than is practicable here. I owe so much to so many of my teachers that it might be invidious to single out names, but there are some to whom I must acknowledge a special debt.

The Rector to whom I have referred, Ian G. Andrew, was appointed to that post in 1922 in his twenty-ninth year. When news of the appointment was published, the majority of the teaching staff sent an open letter to a local newspaper, protesting against the decision to give this post to one substantially younger than most of themselves. This was a discouraging start for a new head, but Mr Andrew had faced greater perils than that — he came to us with a distinguished war record — and amply justified his appointment. In later years he became head successively of Robert Gordon's College, Aberdeen, and George Watson's College, Edinburgh. I recall him with gratitude because of the constant encouragement he gave me.

I think also with gratitude and affection of the lady who first taught me Latin, Miss Mary H. Gerrie. She graduated at Aberdeen University in 1904 and stayed on for a time as Assistant to Sir William Ramsay, who was Professor of Humanity (i.e. Latin) there from 1886 to 1911. Then she came to teach classics in Elgin Academy, where she remained until her retirement. She died in her early nineties in 1974.

The reference to Sir William Ramsay reminds me that she once conveyed to me a message from him: 'Tell him not to dissipate his energies; this has been the downfall of many a young Scot.' I have remembered his advice; I am not sure that I have followed it.

The principal teacher of classics in my time was J. N. C. Clark, an Edinburgh graduate, a man with a singular gift for lucid thought and exposition of the complexities of Latin and Greek grammar and construction. He gave us some rules to guide us in the niceties of usage in these languages which were not only helpful at the time but proved helpful in later years when I became a teacher myself and was able to pass them on to others; yet I have never, to my recollection, seen or heard them so simply expressed outside his classroom. Another thing for which I have always felt grateful to him is that he taught us to learn the accents of Greek words as part of their spelling. Thanks to this piece of pedagogical wisdom on his part, I have found Greek accentuation a much less difficult problem than some of my colleagues, by their own confession, do. What we learn when the mind is plastic tends to stick, and I began Greek under his tuition at the age of thirteen.

Youthful students of the classical languages might take encouragement from memorials set up in the school hall to two very distinguished scholars who at one time had been pupils of Elgin Academy. There was a brass tablet in honour of Hugh Andrew Johnstone Munro (1819-85), first Kennedy Professor of Latin in Cambridge and well known for his great edition of the works of Lucretius (1864). (He is commemorated by another tablet in Trinity College, Cambridge.) Then there was a bust of Sir William Duguid Geddes (1828-1900), a Homeric scholar who became Principal of Aberdeen University (the Aberdeen students of his day called him 'Homer').

Another master of whom I have very pleasant memories was A. B. Simpson, who taught English language and literature, History and Scripture. His two great loves among the subjects he taught were Shakespeare and the Authorized Version. He encouraged us to learn by heart some of the great chapters of the Bible — Isaiah 40 and 55, for example, and Ecclesiastes 12. He cherished great expectations of his pupils, for he taught us to write poetry — at least, he hoped it would be poetry, but at least it was verse, and he saw to it that it scanned. As a schoolboy I had some interesting conversations with him about the Bible. He had been brought up among the 'Ravenite' Exclusives in Linlithgow, where his father was one of their leaders. (In the later 1930s, when I lived in Edinburgh and went occasionally to Linlithgow to address a weeknight meeting, I met his father; by that time his brethren had 'withdrawn' from him[2] and he had found fellowship in a Glanton meeting. This meant that he was free, for the first time in his life, to go along occasionally to the Open meeting, where he had a number of friends; it was there that I met him.) When A. B. Simpson went, in his later teens, to Edinburgh University, he found he had to do quite a lot of sorting out in his mind; happily, an understanding Presbyterian minister helped him to distinguish baby from bath-water, so that he could jettison the latter without damage to the former. (But 'never forget', I once read, 'that one man's baby is another man's bath-water.') Mr Simpson found a congenial spiritual home in the United Free Church (merged, from 1929 onwards, with the Church of Scotland) where before long he became an elder and a very acceptable lay preacher. Although his upbringing had been more restricted than mine, he understood some of my own 'sorting out' problems, and helped me more than I realized at the time. Happily, I was able to convey my mature appreciation to him later. In the teaching profession, as in all others, there are square pegs in round holes, but he was a man who had found his true calling in life: he thoroughly enjoyed teaching and his pupils thoroughly enjoyed being taught by him.

We did not specialize at school as much as is done nowadays: while my principal subjects were Latin and Greek, most of my classmates and myself carried English (with History), French and Mathematics up to the sixth form and university entrance.

Education was highly esteemed in all levels of society in the north-east of Scotland, and practically every boy or girl who was likely to profit by a university career was provided — on a very modest scale — with the financial means of attending university. Moreover, parents and elder siblings counted it a privilege to make whatever sacrifices were necessary to allow promising members of their families to receive a university education. In the Spring 1973 issue of the *Aberdeen University Review* mention was made in the obituary columns of a lady whose family had had the unique distinction of producing eight graduates (seven daughters and one son) in the same generation. That was, as the notice said, 'unique'; but there was a farmer near Keith, about seventeen miles from my home, five of whose sons obtained first class honours in classics at Aberdeen University in the last two decades of the nineteenth century. One of them, A. W. Mair, was from 1903 to 1928 Professor of Greek in Edinburgh University. An older brother of his, John Mair, was for many years minister of Spynie, the adjoining parish to Elgin. (I remember an occasion when John Mair, calling on the Rector at the Academy, came into the classroom during a Latin period and wrote on the board the words *ne si quis*, to see if we could translate them. To us they seemed to mean 'Lest if any one' — which was not all that intelligible. Actually they mean 'Spin if you can'.)

Our brethren in the Open meetings in the north-east were second to none in their veneration of learning. When in 1928 I attained an academic distinction much thought of in those parts, the acclaim with which they greeted the news was enough to turn my head; it was all the greater because I was the son of one of their own evangelists.'One of our local weekly newspapers, in reporting it, improved the occasion by listing a number of men who had received this distinction from 1860 onwards; the list was headed by the name of William Robertson Smith (and this, I think, has left a lasting impression on me).

Notes to Chapter 5

1. As early as 1325 Bishop David de Moravia bequeathed money to finance the attendance at the Sorbonne of four poor students from Moray; this was the origin of the Scots College in Paris.

2. Because he could not agree with some aspects of the teaching of James Taylor, Senior, of New York, who now dominated the connexion.

6
Student days in Aberdeen

Among the Renaissance Popes, none has generally enjoyed a
worse press than Alexander VI (1492-1503). Yet he has one
good deed to his credit which, in the eyes of some people,
goes far to outweigh his less creditable actions: it was he
who, in 1494, issued the Papal Bull which authorized the
foundation of the University of Aberdeen. William
Elphinstone, then Bishop of Aberdeen and Chancellor of
Scotland, took the initiative in presenting the merits of the
case to King James IV. King James, in turn communicated
with the Pope; the north-east, he claimed, stood sorely in
need of the civilizing influence of a university. The Bull was
forthcoming, and eleven years later the university was
opened. Its first Principal was a young Professor from the
University of Paris, who some years previously had left his
native Dundee as plain Hector Boys, but returned to
Scotland as Hector Boethius. At one time there were certain
advantages in belonging to a university founded by a Pope.
In particular, doctors of divinity of such universities were
empowered to exercise a universal ministry in the church[1] —
not even a bishop could claim such a privilege, for a bishop's
ministry was restricted to his own see.

The original University of Aberdeen was established at
King's College, in Old Aberdeen. Nearly a century later

(1593) another university (an inferior, post-Reformation thing) was founded in New Aberdeen, at Marischal College; the two foundations remained separate universities until 1860, when they were merged in one single University of Aberdeen. Before 1832 (when Durham University was founded) Aberdonians were accustomed to boast that their city had as many universities as the whole of England. (Strictly, Old Aberdeen and New Aberdeen were separate cities until the 1890s.) The situations were not really comparable; England's two universities, each with its multiplicity of colleges, were considerably more substantial foundations than Aberdeen's two colleges.

To the University of Aberdeen, then, I went as an undergraduate in October 1928.

During my four years there I specialized in Latin and Greek, but the curriculum was sufficiently flexible to permit the taking of a number of other subjects, and I attended classes in English, Logic and Moral Philosophy in my first, second and third years respectively. In those days classes in some of the older subjects (e.g. Latin and·Greek) lasted from October to March; this was an old custom which had allowed students to work on the land in the summer and pursue their studies in the winter. This meant that during the summer term students had considerable liberty in attending classes which attracted them. (Sir William Ramsay was credited with the epigram: 'The winter makes the prizemen, but the summer makes the scholars.') In the summer term of 1929 another student and myself attended a crash course in beginner's Hebrew provided by the Professor of Hebrew and Oriental Languages, James Gilroy. It provided a foundation on which I was able to build later. The other student who attended the class with me was J. M. R. Cormack, later Professor of Greek in Aberdeen and a distinguished archaeologist; his career was cut short by a fatal illness in 1975.

Among my Aberdeen fellow-students with whom I have kept in touch I think of Charles Duthie, now D.D. and until recently Principal of New College, London; Ralph

Turnbull, now D.D. and well known in evangelical circles in North America; and Ian Begg, now also D.D. and Bishop of Aberdeen and Orkney in the Scottish Episcopal Church. Men have sometimes been preferred to the episcopate for curious reasons; no one was ever worthier of such preferment than Ian Begg, for whom it came as the climax of a career of humble and self-giving service to others. Then there is David Murison, Editor of the *Scottish National Dictionary*, who brought that monumental work to a triumphant conclusion with the issue of Volume 10 in 1976. And I must not omit David Steel, Moderator in 1974 of the General Assembly of the Church of Scotland. I am told that in some quarters Dr Steel is best known as the father of a distinguished M.P. of the same name; there are some of us for whom the M.P.'s chief claim to fame is that he is David Steel's son.

There is, indeed, another fellow-student from those days with whom I have maintained closer and more continuous contact than with any other: that is the fellow-student whom in due course I married. Betty Davidson, as she then was, came up to Aberdeen University in 1929. I used to say that I was attracted to her because she knew Greek, but that was only a minor factor in the situation. She was, on the side of both her parents, a third-generation heir of the Brethren tradition. Her paternal grandfather has been mentioned already as the man who baptized Donald Ross. Her father, when he was born in 1882, was given the christian names Anthony Bellett, which bore witness to his parents' appreciation of Brethren history, for they were intended to commemorate *Anthony* Norris Groves and John Gifford *Bellett*. ('Anthony' has persisted in the family, as the second name of our son and then of his son.) Even her Brethren heritage, however, was not the principal factor in the special relationship which speedily developed between us. Since these reminiscences are intended to be reasonably objective, I will not enlarge on a subject on which I am completely biased, save to say that meeting her was the most important thing that happened to me during my undergraduate career in Aberdeen.

To return to relative objectivity: Charles Duthie, David Steel and I were among the Aberdeen representatives in the Scottish Students' Campaign Movement, a movement founded and led by D. P. Thomson[2] as a means of perpetuating the wave of revival experienced by the east coast of Britain in particular in the early 1920s. In this movement we conducted evangelistic campaigns in various towns of Scotland during the Easter and summer vacations. What good we did to the populations of those towns I am not sure; but the experience was a healthy one for ourselves. Among members of other Scottish universities whom I met for the first time on those campaigns were the late Ronald Gregor Smith (before his death Professor of Divinity in Glasgow), Matthew Black (until recently Principal of St. Mary's College, St. Andrews), John Graham (Emeritus Professor of Systematic Theology in Aberdeen and former Lord Provost of that city), Harry Thornton (who became Professor of Philosophy in the University of Otago, New Zealand). D. P. Thomson had a gift of attracting men who were destined to make their mark.

It was during these campaigns that I first occupied pulpits outside our own small circle of churches. In one town where we were holding a campaign a dear lady of our circle told me that, in thinking of me, she couldn't get out of her head the text: 'Stand fast ... in the liberty wherewith Christ hath made us free, and be not entangled again with the yoke of bondage' (Galatians 5: 1). I assured her that I was exercising that very liberty, but she shook her head unbelievingly.

When we conducted campaigns in industrial towns in Central Scotland, we came up against an unforeseen obstacle. The workers were prejudiced against us because we were students. 'Students?' said they. 'We remember what they did to us in the General Strike.' It was only a few years since 1926, and although my own age-group was still at school then, university students had volunteered to take over a number of the duties (driving trams, etc.) normally done by the strikers. This was not quickly forgotten. I imagine that today students would not volunteer in large numbers for similar duties. But alas! for all their radicalism and sympathy with the workers, they are no more popular with them. 'Students?' said a taxi-driver who was taking me from Piccadilly Station in Manchester to the University. 'That's the filthiest word in the vocabulary of the Manchester working man.' One way or the other, they can't win, which is a great shame, because they are really such delightful people.

The Scottish Students' Campaign Movement, as I have indicated, existed to promote evangelism throughout Scotland, not specifically among students. Christian witness within the university was carried on chiefly by what was then called the Christian Students' Fellowship, the group affiliated to the Inter-Varsity Fellowship (IVF).[3] It is now called the Christian Union, but in those days that designation was borne by the group affiliated to the Student Christian Movement (SCM), to which I also belonged. The Christian Students' Fellowship had been founded in 1922, and was still finding its feet in university life. One enterprise which helped to establish it was a mission to the university in the autumn of 1930, where the missioner was the veteran preacher John McNeill, then aged 76. Another visitor who proved a tonic to the Fellowship was the late Dr Howard Guinness, who paid us a visit and addressed several meetings in 1931; he was at that time a sort of roving ambassador throughout the world for the IVF.

The IVF was much criticized for the alleged rigidity of its confessional basis. I have never found it uncomfortably rigid; the sense in which it is to be understood is set forth very reasonably in the pamphlet *Evangelical Belief*, which has run through many editions (I like the first, pre-World War II, edition best). But when one contemplates the drifting career of the SCM over the years, by contrast with the stability of the IVF (UCCF), it must be concluded that there is much to be said for a positive statement of belief.

To be a member of the IVF group and the SCM group simultaneously, as I was, could have meant that one was rather suspect in the eyes of both groups. For one year I held the office of study secretary on the committee of the SCM group — but this did not prevent the other group from electing me as president for the following year. An old diary reveals that the subject of one of the SCM study groups set up during my year as study secretary was 'How to abolish the slums'. Well, there's no harm in being ambitious, especially when one is young! I recall an international conference organized by the SCM in Aberdeen in the spring of 1930; among the speakers whom I met on that occasion were Dr John A. Mackay (himself a northern Scot), later to become President of Princeton Theological Seminary, and Dr W. A. Visser 't Hooft, later to become first General Secretary of the World Council of Churches. As a separate engagement, Dr Visser 't Hooft addressed a meeting of theologians in Christ's College, Aberdeen, on the theology of Karl Barth; it was the first systematic exposition of Barthianism that had been heard in Aberdeen up to that time.

Aberdeen was later to have a much fuller exposition of Barth's theology when the great man in person delivered the Gifford Lectures there for 1937-38. His lectures, which were based on the Scots Confession of 1560, were published as *The Knowledge of God and the Service of God* (1938). The Gifford Lectures have as their subject natural theology; when Barth was invited to deliver them, he replied, 'I am the avowed opponent of all natural theology.' On the renewal of the invitation, however, he consented — on the ground, perhaps, that sometimes a cause can be helped by the statement of a strong case against it. By that time, however, I had left Aberdeen. I heard two Gifford Lecturers in my time: the first was E. W. Barnes, Bishop of Birmingham, whose lectures were published under the title *Scientific Theory and Religion* (1933); the other was Etienne Gilson of the Sorbonne, whose lectures (on Thomas Aquinas) were published in the book *The Spirit of Mediaeval Philosophy* (1936). Bishop Barnes had achieved much notoriety because of his public pronouncements in two fields (religion and biology) in which he was no expert (he was a very distinguished mathematician); his lectures were therefore very well attended and the venue had to be shifted from an ordinary lecture-room to the Mitchell Hall of Marischal College (normally used for graduations and the like). During one of his lectures, while he was expatiating on the theme of 'Nature red in tooth and claw', a man in the audience interpolated: 'In other words, God is a murderer'. The speaker did not respond immediately, but he ended his paragraph with the words of Psalm 104: 21, 'The lions roaring after their prey do seek their meat from God', and added 'There is your answer, sir'. The man was about to interrupt again, when Principal Sir George Adam Smith, who was in the chair and who knew his Aberdonians, rose and quieted him with a soothing gesture: 'Write to the paper about it tomorrow'.[4]

In those days university professors in Scotland were appointed *ad vitam aut culpam* — for life, or until they committed a fault so serious that it merited deposition. What such a fault might be no one was quite sure; possibly high treason would have qualified. Once upon a time heresy was the most likely cause for deposition, and not only in the Faculty of Divinity, but that time had passed. In due course it came to be felt that, in the interests of all concerned, it would be good to impose a retirement age, so the age of seventy was decided upon. But those who had been appointed under the old order were not bound by this new provision. The last professor, I think, to have been appointed under the old order was the late J. H. Baxter of St. Andrews, who retired from the Regius Chair of Ecclesiastical History there in 1970 after a tenure of forty-eight years.

When I went to Aberdeen the Professor of Greek was John Harrower, who had been appointed in 1886 and carried on until 1931. By 1928 he was over seventy and visibly failing, but in his heyday he was a superb teacher. I suppose he had never done an hour's research in his life, and he was none the less a scholar for that. Time would fail me to count the number of former pupils of his who occupied classical and other chairs in universities and colleges all round the world.

Harrower's father-in-law, Sir William Geddes, had held the Greek Chair for thirty years before him; he then became

47

Principal of the University from 1885 to 1900. Geddes and Harrower between them established an academic dynasty which dominated the Greek Department for three-quarters of a century. The dynasty is worthily commemorated in the Geddes-Harrower Chair of Greek Art and Archaeology.

The Professor of Humanity (as Latin is traditionally called in the Scottish universities) was himself a former pupil of Harrower's — Alexander Souter. Unlike Harrower, Souter was a lifelong researcher, especially in the writings of the Latin Fathers. Among biblical students he is known for his Oxford edition of the Greek New Testament (1910, ^{2}1947), his *Pocket Lexicon to the Greek of the New Testament* (1916) and his *Text and Canon of the New Testament* (1913, ^{2}1954). I suppose that, among all my university teachers, he is the one to whom I owe most. He was much criticized for being more interested in later Latin than in classical Latin. He thought it right that his students should have at least an introduction to later Latin, so he regularly gave this to his second year class, working according to a quadrennial cycle, in which the set texts were (1) Apuleius's *Cupid and Psyche*, (2) the first half of Tertullian's *Apology*, (3) the second half of Tertullian's *Apology*, (4) Augustine's *De Catechizandis Rudibus*. One scholar of my acquaintance affirms that he married his wife, who was a student in the year after him, because he had the notes on the first half of Tertullian's *Apology* and she had the notes on the second half, and he wanted to have the complete set. My wife was a student in the year after me, but that was not my reason for marrying her, because I came in the year that did Apuleius, so she had the notes on the first half of Tertullian's *Apology*, but neither of us had those on the second half.[5]

To the end of his days Souter's studies were concentrated on the Latin Fathers — principally 'Ambrosiaster' and Pelagius. Perhaps his greatest achievement was his editing of Pelagius's commentaries on the Pauline epistles. He used to comment with amusement on the fact that he, a staunch Augustinian, had spent so much of his time and energy on

Pelagius. To him Augustine was 'the greatest Christian since New Testament times, and even if he be not the greatest of Latin writers, he is assuredly the greatest man that ever wrote Latin'.[6] As for the letters of Paul, to whom he professed himself 'passionately devoted',[7] he regarded them as 'the most valuable writings in the world'.[8] Plainly he was a man with his heart in the right place. I do not recall that he ever described Paul as 'the greatest man that ever wrote Greek', but he would surely have endorsed this description — and so, of course, would I.

In later years I completed under his direction a research project on *The Latinity of Gaius Marius Victorinus Afer* (a fourth-century rhetorician and theologian); the typescript of this work, dedicated to Professor Souter's memory, is deposited in the Manuscripts and Archives Section of Aberdeen University Library.

The Professor of English Literature, Adolphus Alfred Jack, was to some degree in outward appearance the embodiment of the popular concept of a professor. He was an eloquent lecturer, whose students were given special delight by his rather mannered recitation of English poetry. About the time I went up to Aberdeen he was involved in a lawsuit which attracted much public attention: a former student sued him for (as he claimed) preventing him from taking his degree. I cannot remember the details, but evidently professors must have had more executive responsibility then than they have now. In my own professorial experience, every executive decision (with regard to examination results or anything else) is taken by Faculty or Senate, so that the idea of prosecuting an individual teacher for causing a student's failure could hardly be entertained. As it was, this case was odd enough: the sheriff described the plaintiff as trying to drive a carriage and pair through the university ordinances. The morning after the dismissal of the case was announced, Professor Jack received a hearty ovation from the Ordinary English Class: I can still picture his appreciative smile and response: 'Thank you, ladies and gentlemen.'

Alexander Stewart Ferguson, the Professor of Logic and Metaphysics, whose lectures I also attended, is perhaps best known for his involvement in Walter Scott's edition of the *Corpus Hermeticum*. John Laird, Professor of Moral Philosophy, was a distinguished philosopher and prolific author. He propounded no system of his own; his strength lay rather in the perception and stating of problems than in providing solutions to them.

Another member of the teaching body whom I came to know quite well was G. T. Thomson, Professor of Systematic Theology. Appointments to that professorship were traditionally made on the basis of a competitive examination. (I can think of worse methods of appointment.) He was the last man to be appointed by that method. (The runner-up was given an honorary D.D. as a consolation prize.) During his Aberdeen years Professor Thomson was profoundly — and simultaneously! — influenced by the Oxford Group Movement and by Karl Barth. The mixture was an explosive one. In due course the former influence waned, but the latter increased, and developed into a devotion to classical Calvinism. He moved from Aberdeen to Edinburgh, where he was, until his retirement in 1952, Professor of Christian Dogmatics.[9] I came to know him originally through attending a university series of open lectures on Christian Evidences which he delivered at Aberdeen in 1931. The so-called Christian Evidences turned out to be an introductory course in Barthianism. The year before (1930) he had attended that lecture by Dr Visser't Hooft. In the afterspeaking he stood up and asked what Barth's German was like. 'Very difficult,' said the lecturer; 'I can read only three pages of him at a time.' Professor Thomson was not deterred; he did his homework sufficiently well to deliver that series of lectures a year later and subsequently he translated the first volume of Barth's *Church Dogmatics* into English.

Notes to Chapter 6

1. This information I owe to A. Ehrhardt *The Apostolic Ministry* (Edinburgh 1958), p. 50.

2. Dr D. P. Thomson, for many years Director of Evangelism in the Church of Scotland, died in March 1974 at the age of 77.

3. Now the Universities and Colleges Christian Fellowship (UCCF).

4. One afternoon the late caretaker and doorkeeper of Hebron Hall came along to one of Dr Barnes's lectures. He was a man of limited education, who knew several big words but was not always sure of their meaning. Seeing me there, he took his place beside me. What he made of the lecture is neither here nor there, but after it was over he turned to me and said, 'Would you say he is an *agnostic?*' Then, on reflection, he added, 'But there's no doubt, he's a great scholar.'

5. Actually, all the notes (and more) are accessible in Souter's edition of J. E. B. Mayor's critical text of the *Apology* (Cambridge 1917).

6. *The Earliest Latin Commentaries on the Epistles of St. Paul* (Oxford 1927), p. 139.

7. *op. cit.*, p. 6.

8. *op. cit.*, p. 3.

9. He was succeeded by Tom Torrance; the appointment of James Mackey as *his* successor in 1979 was the occasion of a *furore* in the General Assembly of the Church of Scotland. Scotland is not Northern Ireland, but the idea that a Catholic should occupy the Thomas Chalmers Chair was more than some Presbyterians could stomach. Yet the appointment was perfectly constitutional, and ministers of the Church of Scotland — whether university representatives or church nominees — constituted the majority of the recommending committee.

7
More Aberdeen memories

Church life in Aberdeen was inevitably richer and more variegated than it had been in my home town. In my time at the University (1928-32) there were half-a-dozen companies of Open Brethren in the city, most of them large and active. Some account of the Brethren movement in Aberdeen has been given by the late James Cordiner in his *Fragments from the Past* (Pickering & Inglis 1961) and by others in the informative little book *Aberdeen Christian Conference Centenary*, 1874-1973, published to mark the hundredth anniversary of the Brethren's New Year Conference. Some of the leading Aberdeen brethren in those days were well-known figures in the public life of the city, and important events among our churches were duly chronicled in the Aberdeen daily paper, the *Press and Journal*, which in the days of its independence was a really great newspaper.

The leading brethren of whom I speak were conscious of their responsibility to the spiritual wellbeing of the city, not only in evangelism but in Bible teaching also. In October 1929, I recall, at a time when some national publicity was being given to views in several quarters deemed subversive of the Christian faith, they organized a series of lectures on the basic truths of Christianity in a public hall in Aberdeen, the lecturer being J. C. M. Dawson of Belfast. I believe that Mr

Dawson's forthright expositions of Christian doctrine at that time were of great help to many who heard him, far beyond the frontiers of the Brethren churches.

There were gradations of outlook and practice from one of those churches to another, but many of their leaders were men of liberal spirit in the proper sense of that noble adjective. In some of those churches it was taken for granted, fifty years ago, that when a missionary sister came home on furlough it was not only the ladies who ought to have an opportunity of hearing her account of the Lord's work overseas. I remember one missionary sister from what was then called Belgian Congo (Emma Holmgreen, later Mrs F. Ray Williams), for whom a valedictory service was arranged on the eve of her return there at the end of her furlough. Several brethren gave short and appropriate messages, but the *pièce de résistance* of the occasion was her reply to them, which took the form of a succinctly-worded application of 2 Corinthians 5: 9, which she rendered: 'We make it our ambition, whether at home or abroad, to be well-pleasing to him'.

There were indeed two elder brethren in Aberdeen in those days who were pioneers, not to say campaigners, for the cause of women's liberty of ministry. The subject was one of general interest at that time, for Scotland's first woman minister had lately been ordained to the pastorate of a Congregational church — the Rev. Vera Findlay (later, after her marriage, the Rev. Vera Kenmure), who died in December 1973. She came to address meetings one Sunday in a Congregational church in Aberdeen. Along with some of my fellow-students, I went to hear her in the evening, and sure enough, there in a front seat was one of those two brethren, William Yuill, leaving for the nonce his own company in Assembly Hall in order to support one of the causes he had at heart. (I remember the sermon; it dealt with our Lord's temptations and was illustrated by copious quotations from Middleton Murry's *Life of Jesus!*) The other champion of women's ministry to whom I have referred, also a member of Assembly Hall, was Dr John A.

Anderson, formerly a missionary with the C.I.M., but at that time living in a very active retirement in Aberdeen.[1] He was devoted to two minority causes, which he defended 'in season, out of season': on the one he published a book entitled *Woman's Warfare and Ministry*; on the other (the post-tribulation rapture of the church)[2] he published a number of studies, notably one entitled *The Church, the Chart and the Coming*.

At Hebron Hall (now Hebron Evangelical Church), which I attended during those years, we did not have quite such controversial personalities as these, though we had no lack of the rugged individualists whom we used to know as 'characters'. The temptation to give a few thumbnail sketches must be resisted. But the occasional clash between such rugged individualists provided mild entertainment for spectators, especially at conversational Bible readings. However, there were no hard feelings, because each individualist could give as good as he got. The church at Hebron Hall was wisely guided by a group of responsible elders — although there was a small recognizable 'opposition', and even, I think, a 'leader of the opposition'. Our elders were as conservative politically as they were theologically. For some time after the Labour victory in the 1929 election the closing prayer of our Sunday morning service would include a petition that there might be 'no rash or hasty legislation', accompanied sometimes by a rather plaintive 'We know not, Lord, why it has pleased thee to allow this government to take office'. This note of bewilderment was replaced by a more cheerful one after the return of the National Government in 1931.

There were a number of notable preachers in Aberdeen in those days, some of whom were well known as preachers far beyond Aberdeen. There was Alexander Frazer, minister of John Knox Church, Gerrard Street, a powerful evangelist and convention speaker, then at the height of his career. In earlier years he had exercised a ministry in the small town of Tain, to which in later years he retired; he is therefore widely known as *Frazer of Tain* — the title of his biography written shortly after his death in 1964 by Dr John T. Carson.³ The foreword to that work was supplied by Dr James S. Stewart, who was minister of Beechgrove Church in Aberdeen during my student days. He was then a young man, but was already laying the foundations of his well-merited reputation as Scotland's greatest preacher. He later moved to a charge at Morningside, Edinburgh, and then to the Chair of New Testament in Edinburgh University, and to the Moderatorship of the General Assembly in 1963.

Notes to Chapter 7

1. See *Autobiography of John A. Anderson, M.D.* (Aberdeen ²1950).

2. To expand this piece of eschatological shorthand, he taught (as against the interpretation of J. N. Darby, W. Kelly and the *Scofield Reference Bible*) that the event foretold in 1 Thessalonians 4: 16 f., 1 Corinthians 15: 51 f., etc., would not follow and not precede the 'great tribulation' of Matthew 24: 21, Revelation 7: 14, etc. Both this view and that which it contradicted are varieties of pre-millennial futurism.

3. Allan Frazer, who accompanied Malcolm Muggeridge on the Palestinian journey described in *Jesus Rediscovered* (London 1969), is a son of the Rev. Alexander Frazer.

8
More about books

Books have exercised an important influence on my mind throughout my life, and I can best do justice to that influence by punctuating my reminiscences from time to time with some account of books that have helped to form my thinking.

Before I went up to university in 1928 I had laid the first foundations of my personal library, and I made substantial additions to it during my Aberdeen years. Naturally, since I was a student of classics, many of my books dealt with classical history and literature. A large number of these have already been inherited by the next generation, but not all.

Before World War II a considerable section of the New Market in Aberdeen (on the corner of Union Street and Market Street) was occupied by a second-hand book dealer named Low. Low's bookstall was one of the two best emporia of that kind I have ever known; the other was David's in Cambridge Market. Even before I went up to university I had begun to patronize Low's on occasional visits to Aberdeen, especially at New Year conference time. I rise from my chair to take down from my shelves some books bought there half a century ago. Here, for example, is C. J. Ball's *Light from the East: An Introduction to the Study of Biblical Archaeology* (1899), a beautifully illustrated volume which I acquired on 3rd January, 1925. My father and I were examining Low's books, and I was obviously attracted by this one. 'Would you like it?' he asked. 'Yes,' said I, 'but it costs ten shillings.' 'That's all right,' said he. I thought he must have suddenly come into a fortune — and in truth he was not usually in a position to fork out ten shillings and expend it on a book just like that. Here is W. F. Moulton's translation of Winer's *Grammar of New Testament Greek* (1882), bought in the same place twelve months later; and here is A. H. Sayce's *The Higher Criticism and the Verdict of the Monuments* (1895), bought there in January 1927.

Sayce was a curious character; he wrote books with that kind of title and was regarded as a champion of orthodoxy by people who read only the titles of his books. I recall a remark once made to me by G. T. Manley, that once you get a reputation for 'soundness' you can write and say what you please. In the book just mentioned Sayce argues, for example, that at one point after another 'the account given by the Book of Daniel is at variance with the testimony of the inscriptions' (p. 526), but people who approved of Sayce because he opposed 'monumental facts' to 'higher critical fancies' overlooked such a statement as that.[1] It is said that when E. B. Pusey died in 1882, the names of Sayce and S.R. Driver lay prominently before W. E. Gladstone who, as Prime Minister, had to decide on the filling of the Regius Chair of Hebrew at Oxford. He decided that Driver was the 'safer' man, and Driver was accordingly appointed. Despite much popular but uninformed opinion to the contrary, Gladstone had no reason to regret his decision: Driver was as cautious as Sayce was erratic. In the same field of study, my copy of William Robertson Smith's *The Old Testament in the Jewish Church* ([2] 1895) was bought, I see, from Low a couple of years later.

In Low's bookstall, as I remember it, volumes in the *Expositor's Bible* series sold at two shillings each. Some of the volumes in that series were not up to much, but others were of first-rate quality — such as George Adam Smith's commentaries on Isaiah and the Twelve Prophets and James

Denney on Thessalonians and 2 Corinthians. Another series well represented on Low's shelves was Williams and Norgate's 'Crown Theological Library', consisting mainly of translations from the German. They were small blue octavo books, and I am told that in some quarters they were known as 'the devil's blue books'. I now have about thirty of them, but the first half dozen were bought from Low about 1929, including some of Harnack's New Testament studies. Harnack's theology reflected a phase of thought which received its death-blow in 1914, but he was a great historian, whose contributions to the history and thought of the early church are of lasting value.

My theological tastes were evidently as eclectic in those days as they are today; from that period I retain copies of E. Griffith-Jones, *The Ascent Through Christ: A Study of the Doctrine of Redemption in the Light of the Theory of Evolution* (a book of which I thought better then than I do now); John Laird, *Morals and Western Religion* (a discussion in dialogue form of some issues of the day); E. Gilson, *The Philosophy of St. Thomas Aquinas* (my interest in both Gilson and St. Thomas was whetted by the former's Gifford Lectures on the latter); A. S. Eddington, *The Nature of the Physical World* (a work of more theological relevance than its title might suggest); W. R. Matthews, *God in Christian Thought and Experience* (his most original contribution to theology, I suppose); N. P. Williams, *The Grace of God* (which came near to suggesting that the grace of God is another way of referring to the personal Spirit of God); W. H. Griffith Thomas, *The Principles of Theology* (an introduction to Christian doctrine organized according to the sequence of the Thirty-Nine Articles); John McConnachie, *The Significance of Karl Barth* (a present from my fiancée for Christmas 1931). I have never been in the position of believing what I do simply because I have never been exposed to any other form of belief!

When books still stand on my shelves, I can consult them and refresh my memory about them. But there were other books which I read in those days but did not own. A number of these, no doubt, I have forgotten; but some still stand out in my memory. During the summer of 1928 I spent a week or two with relatives in whose house I came across J. E. McFadyen's *Approach to the Old Testament* (1926). This is not a very distinguished book, but I am glad I read it when I did; it helped me greatly to see the Old Testament in its own light. A fascinating work which I read not long afterwards was J. A. Robertson's *Hidden Romance of the New Testament* (1920), a title in which the word 'romance' requires to be emphasized. Professor Robertson, an imaginative and poetic soul, occupied the New Testament Chair in what was until 1929 the United Free Church College in Aberdeen (now Christ's College); his opposite number in the University Faculty of Divinity, Professor A. C. Baird, used to complain that his students took Professor Robertson's fancies for facts and served them up as such in essays and examination answers! I found more solid fare in two works by A. S. Peake — *Christianity, its Nature and its Truth* (1908) and *The Bible, its Origin, its Significance and its Abiding Worth* (1913). My fellow-student Charles Duthie read these two works about the same time; not long ago, when we were reminiscing together, we recalled the help and insight which we both received from them. Peake illustrates the opposite principle to that which I quoted from G. T. Manley when discussing Sayce. 'Give a dog a bad name and hang him' operates in the world of theological reputation as much as elsewhere, and in many conservative quarters Peake's name was inseparably associated with some 'way-out' positions (as they were then accounted) taken up in the one-volume Bible Commentary which he edited. Peake, in fact, was a convinced Paulinist in his theology.

As I think of the books I have named (owned and read or read but not owned), I recall others which clamour for mention — George Milligan's *The New Testament Documents* (1913), Adolf Deissmann's *Light from the Ancient East* (1927), Alexander Souter's *The Text and Canon of the New Testament* — but one must stop somewhere. Let me turn to periodicals.

Quite a number of periodicals came regularly to our home in Elgin. Those of expository relevance included *The Witness* and the *Believer's Magazine;* no self-respecting Brethren household was without these two. (One of our local elders remarked to me that he could always tell when some of our members' first love was beginning to cool; they discontinued their order for these magazines.) Later *The Harvester* began to come our way. *Echoes of Service* (taken primarily, of course, for its missionary interest) frequently included papers of expository value by W. E. Vine. Two quarterly papers which were sent to my father at the instance of Mr J. W. Gordon Oswald of Aigas were *The Scattered Nation* and the *Bible League Quarterly.* The former was the organ of the Hebrew Christian Testimony to Israel, and its primary interest was missionary, but its editor in those days was David Baron, a fine biblical expositor, and some of his greatest expository work first appeared in serial form in its pages. My father, I remember, set high store by his writings. The *Bible League Quarterly* was then edited by the redoubtable Robert Wright Hay, who secured contributions from biblical scholars of international renown, such as Robert Dick Wilson and John Gresham Machen. Sometimes those contributions were reports of lectures delivered before the Bible League, for Wright Hay was able to attract men of that calibre to meetings in London. My friend Geraint Llewelyn Jones, son of R. B. Jones of Porth, the great Welsh preacher who was a close friend of Wright Hay, has told me how those men and others of the same quality stayed in his home on their visits to this country and how stimulating he, as a schoolboy and young student, found their conversation.

Some of our friends, who had emigrated to North America, saw to it that American periodicals reached our home. Among these I recall *Our Hope* (edited by Arno C. Gaebelein), *Our Record, Words in Season* and — last but not least — Philip Mauro's paper, *The Last Hour. The Last Hour* was read appreciatively, but not uncritically. We had friends in Nairn, 25 miles distant, who were great Philip Mauro fans. I remember asking one of them if he had seen

Mauro's latest work (I had come across an announcement of its publication somewhere), and he said, 'No, but I can tell you in advance that I'll agree with it'. In our home we took more seriously the apostolic injunction to 'prove all things'; but Philip Mauro was always worth reading. When I was in my early teens the work which later appeared in volume form as *The Seventy Weeks and the Great Tribulation* (1923) was being published in serial form in *The Last Hour;* I read each instalment with intense and mounting interest, which I think reached its climax when he identified the wilful king of Daniel 11: 36 ff. with Herod. Later, his exposition of Revelation, *The Patmos Visions* (1925),[2] was serialized in the same way. I thought then, and I still think, *The Seventy Weeks and the Great Tribulation* to be the better work of the two.

In 1929 I began to subscribe to two periodicals which I have taken regularly ever since — *The Expository Times* and *The Evangelical Quarterly.* The former was, and still is, of great value in keeping the reader abreast of what is being published in the field of biblical exegesis, over and above its original contributions in that field. Someone once asked me, in those early days, if it was 'sound'; I replied, 'Well, C. F. Hogg writes in it' — and that seemed to satisfy my questioner. I probably had in mind a note in which Mr Hogg suggested that the centurion of Capernaum, being a God-fearer, might have known the Greek text of Psalm 107:20 ('he sends his word, and heals them') and applied it to his own situation (July 1918), or one in which he saw a distinction between John's uses of the two Greek words for 'love', *agapaō* and *phileō* (May 1927). (My own first contribution to *The Expository Times,* I see, was a note on the ascension in the Fourth Gospel, in July 1939.)

As for *The Evangelical Quarterly,* I first came to know about it from a favourable editorial reference in *The Witness* to its second issue (April 1929), which contained an article by Professor A. Rendle Short on our Lord's virgin birth. I was encouraged to secure that issue and its predecessor, and have taken every issue since then. My first contribution to it was an article on 'The Earliest Latin Commentary on the Apocalypse' (that of Victorinus of Pettau) in October 1938. Naturally, I did not then foresee my own thirty-one years' occupation of the editorial chair of the *E.Q.*

Notes to Chapter 8

1. *Monumental Facts and Higher Critical Fancies* was the title of one of Sayce's more popular works (London 1904). An example of the regard in which he was held by conservative Christians is provided in the preface to the original *Scofield Reference Bible*, where he is listed among five named 'learned and spiritual brethren' to whom the editor was 'indebted for suggestions of inestimable value'.

2. A later edition of this work appeared under the more cumbersome title: *Of Things Which Must Soon Come to Pass* (Grand Rapids 1933).

9
South of the Border

On 7th December, 1931, I crossed the border into England for the first time; until then, I had never been farther south than Edinburgh and Glasgow. I was now in my final year at Aberdeen, and my advisers encouraged me to think of proceeding from there in October 1932 to the classical school in Cambridge. But this could not be done without fresh financial resources, so I travelled to Cambridge in December 1931 to sit the entrance scholarship examination set by a group of colleges of which the college of my choice, Gonville and Caius, was one. To the question 'Why Cambridge and not Oxford?' the answer must be that my principal advisers themselves were Cambridge men. And to the question 'Why Gonville and Caius College in particular?' the answer must be partly that Professor Alexander Souter, whom in those days I regarded as an oracle (and wisely so), was himself a Caius man, and partly that the director of classical studies in Caius (H. T. Deas)[1] had himself graduated at a Scottish university before going to Cambridge and would therefore understand the position of a student who, having obtained one degree, found himself reverting to undergraduate status all over again. Whatever the reasons were, I am glad that I went to Cambridge rather than the other place, and I am glad that, of all the Cambridge colleges, the one to which I went was Caius.

To Cambridge, then, I went in October 1932. One advantage of having graduated at another university was that I was able to complete the bachelor's course at Cambridge in two years instead of three. Gonville and Caius College bears the names of two founders: first, Edmund Gonville, who established the original foundation (Gonville Hall) in 1348, and then, John Caius, who procured its elevation to the status of a college in 1557. John Caius was a doctor of medicine and physician successively to Edward VI, Mary Tudor and Elizabeth; partly, no doubt, because of the precedent set by him Gonville and Caius College has fostered distinguished medical men, the most noteworthy being William Harvey (1578-1657), discoverer of the circulation of the blood.

As I think back to my Cambridge teachers, I suppose the one who influenced me most was Peter Giles, Master of Emmanuel College and University Reader in Comparative Philology. He too had been an Aberdeen graduate before he came to Cambridge, fifty years before I did. As I specialized in Group E (Language) for Part II of the Classical Tripos, I attended his lectures, which were designed (in theory, at least) to prepare candidates for the special papers in that group. Actually, he tended to ignore his lecture notes and discourse on a great variety of interesting subjects; he was a master of general knowledge as well as of comparative philology. One could get up the examination data from books; what he gave us was much more interesting.

Another discursive lecturer was T. R. Glover (Public Orator of the University), who talked as much about modern America as he did about ancient Rome (the subject on which he was supposed to be lecturing). He warned us at the beginning of his lecture course that he regularly said 'Wordsworth' when he meant 'Virgil', and *vice versa*; the warning was quite necessary. He could never understand, he said, why so many people went into raptures over the line of Propertius: *sunt apud infernos tot milia formosarum*. For, said he, its plain meaning is 'There are so many thousands of beautiful girls in hell' — and why should anyone want to go into raptures about that?[2]

As a Christian and a classical historian, Glover had a natural interest in the historical setting of early Christianity. His best known work in this field was *The Jesus of History* (1917), which for a generation enjoyed very great popularity. For myself, I found more help in my younger days in his *Jesus in the Experience of Men* (1921). His *Paul of Tarsus* (1925) can still be read with profit; it certainly exhibits his admiration for the apostle. *Christ in the Ancient World* (1929) and *The World of the New Testament* (1931) were further contributions; the latter is a specially attractive work.

Glover was a stormy petrel in Nonconformist life, not least around the time of his presidency of the Baptist Union in 1924. But his basic allegiance was never in doubt, and he felt himself specially at home in evangelical company, as when he spoke at the banquet in Caius hall to mark the jubilee of CICCU in 1927. Ten years later, to mark the centenary of D. L. Moody's birth, he contributed an article to *The Times* which showed a lively and sympathetic appreciation of 'Moody: The Man and his Message'.

C. F. Angus, of Trinity Hall, lectured to us on Ancient Philosophy. In his first lecture of the 1932-33 session he told us that Cambridge differed from Oxford in its curious regard for *facts*. What he had in mind was the uncritical readiness — as he saw it — with which some Oxford scholars (including two, John Burnet and A. E. Taylor, who went to chairs in Scottish universities) ascribed to Socrates elements in the doctrine of ideas which Plato put into his mouth.

I went to A. S. F. Gow, of Trinity College, for lectures on the poet Theocritus (3rd century B.C.) — and excellent lectures they were, which I found very helpful when, some years later, I had to lecture on Theocritus myself. In 1950, Mr Gow incorporated their substance in a valuable annotated edition of Theocritus. I presented our daughter Sheila with a copy of this when she was studying Theocritus at St. Andrews; she left it behind her, with many other

65

things, when she and her family made a hasty departure from Uganda for Australia in 1974. Perhaps it will yet turn up safe and sound; it is unlikely that Idi Amin would have made much of it.

F. E. Adcock (later Sir Frank Adcock), Professor of Ancient History, was a scholar whose lectures scintillated with epigrams. Talking of the readiness of Cyrus and Darius to extend their patronage to the religious cults of their subject nations (like the Jews), he remarked: 'The Great King was always willing to bow down in the house of Rimmon if there was anything to be picked up on the floor.'

I attended a course of lectures by Professor E. J. Rapson, of the Chair of Sanskrit, as part of the Group E requirements for Part II of the Tripos. I am glad to have had the opportunity of reading some of the Vedas in the original. Since 1935 I have not done much with Sanskrit, but Monier-Williams' *Sanskrit-English Dictionary*, a prize from those days, still stands on my shelves and is consulted from time to time.

Of all the scholars whose lectures I attended, however, none could compare in academic excellence with A. E, Housman, then Kennedy Professor of Latin. During my first year in Cambridge I attended a course of lectures which he delivered on Lucretius; and it still gives me pleasure to recall that I once sat at Housman's feet. The same lecture course was attended by a very distinguished undergraduate of Trinity College, J. Enoch Powell. Mr Powell was believed to lead a hermit's life in Trinity; no one, we were given to understand, had succeeded in getting to know him socially. He seemed all set for an academic career of exceptional eminence; he became a Fellow of Trinity at the age of 22, Professor of Greek in Sydney at the age of 25, and was elected Professor of Greek at Durham two years later, but he did not take up that appointment, because on the outbreak of World War II he joined the army, in which he rose from private's rank to that of brigadier. His political progress since the end of the war is a matter of public knowledge.

Housman I remember as a patient and considerate

lecturer, who would write an unfamiliar German name or word on the blackboard for the benefit of students who might not otherwise get it right. Occasionally his capacity for mordant sarcasm appeared, as in his reference to a French commentator on Lucretius who, in the 1920s, had written in derogatory terms of an earlier German commentator, a far greater scholar than himself. 'There had been a war, I understand, between their two countries,' said Housman, 'and the Frenchman thought it his patriotic duty to disparage the other scholar because he was a German.' Housman himself was notoriously severe on many German scholars, but not because they were Germans.

Housman was greatly venerated by an aged Fellow of Caius, W. T. Vesey, to whom I used to go for tuition in Greek and Latin verse composition.[3] Mr Vesey (whose surname in earlier days had been Lendrum) was delighted to learn that I was attending Housman's lectures. 'He's the greatest scholar we have had since Bentley,' he said, 'and *I* think he's greater than Bentley.[4] And yet,' he went on, 'when he was elected to the Chair here, what do you think was the majority in his favour?' Of course I had no idea. Mr Vesey held up one finger. It would have been a breach of confidentiality, I suppose, had he *said* what the voting was! Older scholars said that Vesey was an indefatigable lobbyer on Housman's behalf back in 1911, when the Kennedy Chair fell vacant through the death the previous year of J. E. B. Mayor[5] (at the age of 85). Perhaps, if he had not lobbied quite so hard, the majority might have been higher; one can never be sure about that sort of thing.

Without drawing up an order of merit, one may safely place Housman (1859-1936) among the three greatest classical scholars that Cambridge has ever known. Bentley came first in point of time; next was Richard Porson (1759-1808), Fellow of Trinity and Professor of Greek, who edited several plays of Euripides and established the laws of tragic metre. Bentley, Porson and Housman combined in a rare degree the qualities of industry and perseverance with those of genius and imagination; without such a combination no scholar can approach their achievements in the field of textual criticism.

Mr Vesey once told me that the best student he ever taught was an Aberdeen graduate, A. W. Mair.[6] Mair had an exceptional feeling for Greek style, and his quality as a composer of Greek verse amounted, as some rightly judged, to 'Attic genius'. 'And didn't you also teach Mair's contemporary, Souter?' I asked. 'Souter?' replied Vesey. 'A learned creature!' (Greek verse composition, evidently, had not been Souter's strong point.)

Of my fellow-students whom I came to know personally, many were members of the Cambridge Inter-Collegiate Christian Union (CICCU). Some of us who were contemporaries still keep in touch by means of an occasional prayer-letter. The editor of this prayer-letter is Jack Earl, lately Principal Inspector in charge of Religious Education with the Department of Education and Science. As I look down the alphabetical list of over sixty participants, I note the names of David Adeney, formerly Principal of Disciples' Training Centre, Singapore; Howard Belben, formerly Principal of Cliff College; H. Martyn Cundy, formerly Professor of Mathematics in Chancellor College, University of Malawi; Sir Maurice Dorman, formerly Governor-General of Malta; Ivan Neill, formerly Provost of Sheffield Cathedral; John Wenham, until recently Warden of Latimer House, Oxford, and others whom I remember very well, though they are not so much in the public eye, perhaps, as those mentioned. A little senior to me was Robert E. D. Clark, who took his Ph.D. during my undergraduate period in Cambridge. In those days he attended Panton Hall fairly regularly on a Sunday morning; I recall a brief meditation he gave there one morning on our Lord's words in John 18: 8: 'If therefore ye seek me, let these go their way'. Over the years Dr Clark has become very well known as a writer on the borderlands between scientific research and Christianity, but I have always found specially helpful an earlier work entitled *Conscious and Unconscious Sin* (1934), in which he makes a penetrating contribution to practical Christianity.

Three members of my own college whom I came to know fairly well were J. B. Skemp, subsequently Professor of Greek in Durham (a position from which he retired in 1973), R. J. Hopper, for twelve years my colleague as Professor of Ancient History in Sheffield, and H. Islwyn Davies, lately Professor of Religious Studies in the University of Ife (Nigeria). Another contemporary was J. N. Sanders, who later became Dean of Peterhouse (his own college) and a distinguished New Testament scholar until his premature death in 1961 (his best known work is probably the volume on the Gospel of John in Black's New Testament Commentaries).

One name which must not go unmentioned in any Cambridge retrospect is that of Basil Atkinson, father-in-God to successive generations of CICCU men for half-a-century until his death in 1971. Basil (as he was always affectionately called) was a classical scholar with a special interest in philology, and held a senior appointment in Cambridge University Library. He was a regular, and sometimes explosive,[7] participant in the CICCU Daily Prayer Meeting, held each midday in the Henry Martyn Hall, and was much in demand as a leader of Bible readings. In 1933 he published a little book called *Is the Bible True?* It was not the best of his books; in fact, it would convince only those who were antecedently disposed to accept his answer, which was Yes. A ditty set to a well-known tune circulated in the CICCU at that time, as follows:

> Basil, Basil,
> Give me your answer, do;
> Tell me, tell me,
> Is the Bible true?
> Crusaders continue to spout it,
> Though Buchman is guided to doubt it;
> But now one can get
> For half-a-crown net
> A glorious answer from you!

The 'Buchman' in the ditty was Frank Buchman, founder of the Oxford Group Movement. I don't think, in fact, that he was 'guided' to doubt the *truth* of the Bible, but at times his followers, if not he himself, doubted its *relevance*.[8]

The ranks of Tuscany made merry over one section of Basil's book where he argued that since, according to 1 Timothy 3: 2, 'a bishop must be . . . the husband of one wife', it followed that ordinary Christians might, in principle, have more than one. So far as he himself was concerned, the question was purely theoretical; he was a lifelong bachelor. But he attached more than theoretical importance to his conviction that the dead, even the dead in Christ, have no existence whatsoever between death and resurrection. He did not publicize this conviction, because he knew that it would give offence to many fellow-evangelicals, but his friends knew that he held it, and towards the end of his life he expounded it in his last book, *Life and Immortality* (1969). Some of his friends might be tempted to say (more or less as Henry Pickering once said about Caleb J. Baker), 'Dear Basil knows better now that he is with the Lord'. But all his friends (and they were many) would agree with an obituary tribute by David Jackman, which said: 'He was clearly God's man for the hour. He quickly became known for his uncompromising stand for Biblical Christianity, and was fearless in his defence of the truth. Indeed, he stood by the CICCU in a day when scarcely any other senior members of the university did, and became a trusted adviser to CICCU presidents and committees right up to the present day.'

The CICCU struck me in those days as being much less interested in the intellectual side of Christianity than its counterpart in Aberdeen had been. One reason for this was that, while entry into the Scottish Universities was almost entirely conditional on academic attainment, it was not necessarily so with Oxford and Cambridge in those days. The 'tough' was an unacademic type who might distinguish himself in the athletic field but, in the words of an IVF publication of 1933, 'will not have the inclination, or perhaps even the intelligence, to listen to argument'. Nowadays one would ask what on earth such a person was doing at university, or how on earth he managed to get in, but things were different then. CICCU men were encouraged to cultivate the company and acquaintance of such people, with a view to winning them for Christ, but to keep at arm's length 'the religious man who is in error'.[9]

The implication was that the 'tough', being more developed in brawn than in brain, would not be able to shake a CICCU man's faith, whereas the religious man in error, especially if he were a student of theology, might do this very thing. And this may have been a wise policy; not many CICCU men in those days would have been equipped to defend their faith in intellectual debate. Only a few of them, even prospective ordinands, read for the Theological Tripos. No more did I, but at least my studies enabled me to put the New Testament writings into their historical and philosophical context. When, thirty years later, I was invited by the CICCU to go to Cambridge for a weekend to lead the Saturday evening Bible study in the Union Debating Hall and preach the Sunday evening CICCU sermon in Holy Trinity, I was greatly impressed by the change for the better which I immediately recognized in this as in other regards.

Mention of the Sunday evening CICCU sermon reminds me that during my undergraduate years I had the opportunity of hearing some of the leading evangelical preachers of the day who came to Cambridge week by week during term in this connexion. Among them were G. R. Harding Wood, A. E. Richardson, H. Earnshaw Smith, J. Stuart Holden and T. C. Hammond. I recall one occasion when Montague Goodman, a well-known Christian lawyer, was the preacher. An after-meeting was held in a CICCU member's room in a neighbouring college to continue a discussion of the subject of his address, and two or three men were converted there and then. It was the kind of setting in which he could be a superb advocate for the gospel. I thought at the time that he acquitted himself more effectively than many professional preachers who came to deliver the CICCU sermon, and I still think so.

In the summer term the CICCU held a Sunday evening open-air meeting in the market square. It was at one of those meetings that I first met Donald Coggan (later Archbishop successively of York and Canterbury and now Lord Coggan of Canterbury and Sissinghurst). He went down from Cambridge shortly before I came up, to enter upon his Lectureship in Hebrew in Manchester University, but he must have been on a visit to Cambridge that particular weekend. He was editor of the IVF Magazine, and also editor of the history of the IVF, *Christ and the Colleges,* which appeared in 1934. Lady Coggan, then Miss Jean Strain, was in those days IVF Travelling Representative for Women Students.

The CICCU ran a mission to the university every third year; as I was in residence for two years only, I did not experience a CICCU mission. Towards the end of my residence preparations were afoot for a mission in the following academic year, led by Archbishop Howard Mowll of Sydney.

A mission which I do remember was organized by other Christian groups than the CICCU; it was held early in 1933. One of the missioners was W. R. Inge, Dean of St. Paul's. I went to hear him evening by evening for the week of the mission in the University Church, Great St. Mary's. Half way through the week he caught influenza, and his last addresses had to be read for him; no matter, the book containing them, *Things New and Old,* was published the following Monday, and first Dean Inge himself and then his substitute read from an advance copy. The book still stands on my shelves; it is one of his better works. Years later, when I read his *Diary of a Dean* (1949), I found this remark on it: 'No doubt this little book has shared the fate of my other literary efforts. I am rather sorry, for I put into it all that I most wanted to say as an old man talking to the young' (p. 169). I wrote to tell him that one of his student hearers at least remembered his words with appreciation. I hope my letter gave him some momentary happiness; I fear his old age was unhappy, after the death of Mrs Inge, his 'dearest Kitty', in 1949.

Notes to Chapter 9

1. In due course he was my son's tutor too, when he in his turn went up to Caius in 1955.

2. He was then preparing his chapter on 'The Literature of the Augustan Age' for Volume 10 of the *Cambridge Ancient History* (1934), on p. 519 of which he quotes this as 'a beautiful line with a double spondee to restrain excessive sorrow'.

3. By all accounts, verse composition in Greek and Latin is not much cultivated nowadays. That is a pity. But it is a much greater pity that less and less importance is attached even to *prose* composition in these languages. It is impossible to attain real mastery in the handling of any language whether ancient or modern, without practising composition in it.

4. Richard Bentley (1662-1742), Master of Trinity and Regius Professor of Divinity, was unsurpassed as a classical philologist and textual critic. His *Proposals for Printing a New Edition of the Greek Testament* (1717) aimed at establishing the text of the Nicene or ante-Nicene age, and anticipated the principles of Lachmann and his successors.

5. J. E. B. Mayor had taught my own teacher Alexander Souter, who greatly revered his memory. Passing a portrait of Mayor in St. John's College, Souter remarked to a common friend, 'I always feel like genuflecting when I pass that portrait.' T. R. Glover, in his Loeb edition of Tertullian's *Apology* (1931), tells how he and Souter attended Mayor's lectures on that work — 'the strangest of all lectures' (p. xxv). Elsewhere Glover spoke of himself and Souter as the idle and the industrious apprentice. Glover was not at all idle, but Souter was much more on Mayor's wavelength (see p. 51, n. 5).

6. See p. 40.

7. On one occasion when an undergraduate in prayer made a not unfriendly reference to the Pope, the place was shaken by a loud 'No!' from Basil.

8. Another opportunity for CICCU versification was provided by a pep-talk from Sir Montagu Beauchamp, Bart. (a veteran survivor of the Cambridge Seven who set out for China as missionaries in 1885), based on the uncanonical text: 'Water boils from the bottom.' This provoked the limerick:

> The Reverend Sir Montagu Beauchamp
> Said, 'These fellows know nothing; I'll teauchamp.
>   "Water boils from the bottom":
>   If that hasn't got 'em,
> There's nothing can possibly reauchamp.'

9. B. F. C. Atkinson, in *Effective Witness*, ed. F. Houghton (London 1933), p. 53.

10

Cambridge and London

Mention of Dean Inge's addresses reminds me of another series of addresses — not a university mission this time but a straightforward lecture course on Catholic doctrine — given in the Cambridge Guildhall by two Dominican scholars, the veteran Father Hugh Pope and a younger colleague, Father Aelfric Manson. This course lasted for a week; I attended the last lecture, which dealt with the life to come. It was on a Saturday evening, I remember, and in another room in the Guildhall a group of people had met for community singing. At times there seemed to be an undesigned coincidence between the two rooms: for instance, when Father Hugh was talking about the relation of the immortality of the soul to the resurrection of the body, one could hear in the distance the strains of a familiar song about an American folk-hero whose 'body lies a-mouldering in the grave, But his soul goes marching on'. The exposition followed the lines of traditional orthodoxy, although Basil Atkinson would not have agreed with it. After the lecture, those of us who were interested were invited to further informal discussion in Fisher House, the Catholic chaplaincy. I remember it as the first time I was involved in serious theological conversation with Roman Catholic scholars.

I have already referred to the University Church in Cambridge, Great St. Mary's. On Sunday afternoons during term the university sermon was preached there. Occasionally I attended it and heard a variety of eminent theologians and churchmen. Among them I recall N. P. Williams, O. C. Quick, W. H. Frere (Bishop of Truro), Norman Sykes, W. R. Matthews (then Dean of Exeter). I remember the subject of Dr Matthews' sermon, because it was a summary of his thesis in *God in Christian Thought and Experience* (1930), a work of his which I had read a couple of years before. From time to time a more general address to students would be arranged in Great St. Mary's; it was on such an occasion that I first heard William Temple, and on another such occasion that for the one and only time I heard A. F. Winnington-Ingram (then Bishop of London), whose intellectual stature fell somewhat short of Temple's.

But Caius College Chapel played a greater part in my life at Cambridge than Great St. Mary's did. In my time there Matins and Evensong were said regularly on Sundays and Evensong on other days; there was also a communion service before breakfast every morning during term. I did not attend with perfect regularity, but often enough to be counted a member of the chapel community. From time to time I would read one of the lessons, and during one Long Vacation term I served as chapel clerk. I am glad that I had this opportunity of becoming thoroughly conversant with the Anglican service of morning and evening prayer (according to the pattern of 1662). Occasionally I communicated there; the first occasion on which I did so was my birthday on Wednesday, 12th October, 1932. (It is my diary, not my memory, that helps me to be so precise!) The service in Caius Chapel was exceedingly simple; how elaborate an Anglican communion service could be I discovered a week or two later when I attended a choral eucharist in King's College Chapel before a missionary breakfast in aid of the Universities Mission to Central Africa. The celebrant was the then Bishop of Zanzibar.

The services in Caius Chapel were the responsibility of the

Dean of the College, H. C. L. Heywood (who later became Provost of Southwell Minster). One of his virtues was a readiness to acknowledge his own shortcomings. Once he decided to intone certain parts of the evening service. The responses of the college choir were tuneful enough, but his own attempts at intoning the preceding versicles were not successful. He could scarcely sustain a monotone, but when it came to the change of note in the last two or three syllables of the versicle there was ignominious collapse. At least it was not all that ignominious, because, after an embarrassed silence, the Dean said (with his slight and rather engaging stutter), 'I'm sorry. That's what comes of trying to do something you know perfectly well you can't do.'

More embarrassing was the phase during which the Dean came under the influence of the Oxford Group Movement, and in the course of his short chapel sermons would confess his latest sins, as he took them to be (like giving sixpence to a student who was collecting money for a raffle). He was a kind and honest Christian, if somewhat lacking in worldly wisdom. On one occasion he had me to breakfast with him to tell him who the people called Brethren were and what they stood for. Occasionally he held in his room a gathering of ordinands and others who shared their interests, to engage in improving discussion or to listen to a visiting speaker. One visiting speaker whom I heard was Rabbi Israel Mattuck, a leading liberal Jew, who presented a Jewish view of the crucifixion of Jesus. Another visiting speaker was a young Fellow of Caius, already making a name for himself in biochemistry and other fields — Dr Joseph Needham, later to become Master of the College, a great man and an unconventional believer. One of his epigrams sticks in my memory: 'People who take holy communion ought to be holy communists' — all right, if one spells the last word with a small 'c'!

My real spiritual home during those years in Cambridge, however, was Panton Hall. After Matins on Sunday in Caius Chapel there was just comfortable time to remove my surplice (we wore surplices in chapel on Sundays, ordinary college gowns on other days) and walk or cycle to Panton Hall to participate in the communion service there. There, on the first Sunday morning of my first term, I received a warm welcome, together with a few other students up for the first time, including R. J. Hopper of Swansea (whom I have mentioned already) and Clifford Sims of Rotherham, whose death towards the end of 1972 brought sadness to so many of his friends. The front rows of seats on Sunday morning during term were usually occupied by university people — CICCU men and their friends. Some of them who had never experienced a Brethren-type communion service before were so favourably impressed that when they returned home they sought out a similar company of people — sometimes to get a rude shock.

The majority of the church-members at Panton Hall were, I think, people with local roots, but they were strengthened by others who had come to Cambridge from other parts. I think in particular of the late Theodore Rendle, manager of Chivers' establishment at Histon, and of Archie Hanton, who had recently established his medical practice in Cambridge. These two men freely placed their very considerable gifts at the disposal of the church in Panton Hall: Mr Rendle had great administrative ability and Dr Hanton's qualities as a minister of the word were already widely acceptable and most helpful. Archie and Mary Hanton kept open house for undergraduates on Sunday afternoons — a service which they continued so long as they lived in Cambridge. For my part, I found with them a home from home, and thus was laid the foundation of a lifelong friendship. Another lifelong friendship was established with Dr Hanton's assistant in the practice, William Thomson Walker (now of Tunbridge Wells). He later rendered me a unique service when, on 19th August, 1936, he stood by me in a momentous hour: he was best man at my wedding.

The visiting ministry at Panton Hall was of a high order. The Brethren there were able to call on the help of some of our ablest expository teachers in the south-east of England. Some of them I had heard before; others I heard for the first time. I had heard both George and Montague Goodman in Scotland; in Cambridge I heard them more frequently and had the opportunity of meeting them socially. On my first Sunday at Panton Hall the visiting preacher was the late Scott Mitchell. It was there, too, that I first heard and met E. W. Rogers. I have a lively memory of the first occasion when I heard F. A. Tatford at Panton Hall and got to know him personally through being invited to have lunch with him in the home of Mr and Mrs Rendle; that was about the time when he began his long career as Editor of *The Harvester*. It was in Panton Hall, too, that I first met Cecil Howley, later to become Editor of *The Witness*. He was regarded as a promising young man. Some promising young men remain promising (and nothing more) for the rest of their lives; with him the promise of youth has been more than amply fulfilled, for I do not think that in those days one could have foreseen the rich literary ministry which he was destined to discharge, over and above his oral ministry.

I recall my first visit to London: it was on a Saturday in November 1932, when Dr and Mrs Hanton took me with them from Cambridge to one of the Bloomsbury Bible readings.[1] The two speakers on that occasion were George Goodman and J. B. Watson; they dealt (as far as I recall) with chapters 12 and 14 of 1 Corinthians and applied them to present-day church life.

During my Cambridge years I found it convenient to spend some time in London in the vacations, especially in the summer vacation, making use of the facilities of the British Museum Reading Room. During these London visits I was made welcome in the homes of two former Editors of *The Witness* — Henry Pickering and J. B. Watson, both of whom were elders in Grove Green Hall, Leytonstone. One evening when I called at the Pickering home I met a recently married young couple who were also visiting there — Howard and Eleanor Mudditt. Although I was immediately attracted to them both, I could not then have predicted my close association with the future proprietor of the Paternoster Press: Howard was then employed in the Bank of

England, and already gaining a well deserved reputation for Bible ministry.

Among the Brethren's meeting-places in London which I visited in that period of my life I remember the old Welbeck Hall (attended in earlier days by the second Lord Congleton), to which I went one Sunday morning. This (I think) was the last occasion that the church met there before merging with the church at Rossmore Road and moving to the latter place (but retaining the name Welbeck Hall). I also recall visiting Malden Hall (Kentish Town), Loughborough Hall (Camberwell) and Glenfarg Hall (Catford), when I paid a visit to friends who worshipped in these places, and Denmark Hall (South Norwood), to which Scott Mitchell sent me one Sunday evening to speak in his place.

Among London preachers whom I went to hear in those days were J. Stuart Holden and Albert D. Belden (once each). On a Sunday night when I went to hear Dr Belden in Whitefield's Tabernacle he preached against the Incitement to Disaffection Bill then going through the Commons. The scripture text was Galatians 5:1. I found it difficult to see any relation between the freedom of that text and freedom to incite H.M. Forces to 'disaffection' (which was threatened by the bill).[2]   On two occasions — in 1933 and 1934 — I went to the Bible Day rally then organized each summer by the Bible Testimony Fellowship. One of these two meetings was held in the Alexandra Palace and the other in the Crystal Palace. The main sessions seemed to be designed largely for whipping up a spirit of fervent 'rallying to the Bible'; but some of the 'sideshows' had more positive content. At the latter I remember hearing Sir Charles Marston speak on recent discoveries in biblical archaeology and Sir Frederic Kenyon speak on the Codex Sinaiticus, recently acquired by the British Museum — a notable contrast between the enthusiasm of the amateur and the precision of the scholar.

Reference to the Codex Sinaiticus reminds me of the ballyhoo which in some quarters greeted its purchase by the British Government and people from the Soviet authorities for £100,000 on Christmas Day, 1933. The Leader of the Opposition in the Commons said that what was wanted was more of the Sermon on the Mount on the statute book and less of it in the British Museum. Another kind of opposition to the deal was launched by the *Daily Express,* which tried to revive the fable that the Codex had been forged nearly a century before by Constantine Simonides and then, when this balloon was swiftly pricked, argued that the deal was illegal or immoral because the Codex had been stolen by Tischendorf from its true owners, St. Catherine's Monastery on Mount Sinai.

When I say that the Codex was purchased by the British Government and people, I mean that half the cost was defrayed by the Treasury and the other half by voluntary subscription. There lies before me a receipt from the British Museum, dated 27th January, 1934, acknowledging a contribution of £1 from one member of the British people. I have sometimes shown it to my students to impress them with the fact that, at a time when undergraduates were much more impecunious than they are today, one of them had a sound sense of financial priorities.

As for the main purpose of my going up to Cambridge, suffice it to say that in 1933 and 1934 respectively I sat Parts I and II of the Classical Tripos, satisfied my examiners, and found myself at the end of the course with sufficient money to finance a period of post-graduate research.

Notes to Chapter 10
1. For many years a committee of brethren in the London area has organized series of Bible addresses in Bloomsbury Central Church on the Saturday evenings of each February and November.
2. This I regard as a more serious misuse of the text than that mentioned on p. 44.

11
Tales from Vienna

Having graduated at Cambridge, I betook myself for post-graduate study to the University of Vienna, in Austria (founded in 1365). The attraction of Vienna as a place to study lay chiefly in the prestige of Paul Kretschmer, for many years Professor of Indo-European Philology there and author of authoritative works on the history of the Greek language and the formation of Koine Greek. Kretschmer was a Berliner by origin and retained his native accent. 'You must not think', said an Austrian student to me, 'that we understand him any better than you do.' Kretschmer was in his late sixties when I went to Vienna. On his sixtieth birthday in 1926 he had been presented with a complimentary volume of essays (a *Festschrift*); on his seventieth birthday he was presented with another, to which I, as a former student of his, was invited to contribute; he lived on to have his eightieth and ninetieth birthdays similarly honoured. Vienna provided an opportunity to sit at the feet of several other scholars of worldwide renown. There was Karl Mras, best known for his editing of Eusebius, whose Viennese vernacular was at times as difficult (for me) to follow as Kretschmer's Berlin accent. One course which I attended was devoted to the Hittite language and literature; in it I was initiated into the reading of the cuneiform script.

It was conducted by Robert Bleichsteiner, adherent of a school which found in one or another of the many languages of the Caucasus area an explanation for all linguistic phenomena in the Indo-European field which could not be accounted for in Indo-European terms.

When I went to Vienna in the late summer of 1934 it was not the peaceful city that it now is. It was still recovering from the attempted Nazi coup of July in that year, in which Chancellor Dollfuss was assassinated. His successor, Chancellor Schuschnigg, occupied his uneasy seat until Hitler's annexation of Austria in 1938. Political *graffiti* included such sentiments as 'Next widow, Mrs Schuschnigg' and 'Give for the Schuschnigg Memorial Fund'. This last was a parody of an official exhortation, 'Give for the Dollfuss Memorial Fund' (the implication was: there isn't a Schuschnigg Memorial Fund yet, but there will soon be one; you might as well make a donation to it too while you're at it).

When I matriculated at the university, one of the documents which I was required to sign was a declaration that I did not belong to (i) the Nazi party, (ii) the Communist party, (iii) the Styrian Home Guard. The Nazi and Communist parties I knew; the Styrian Home Guard I had not heard of, and I never met any one who belonged to it. However, I knew I didn't belong to it, so I signed the declaration with a good conscience. Of my Austrian fellow-students (all of whom were required to sign the declaration) the majority must have signed it with a mental reservation because, apart from Jewish students, they seemed to be Nazis to a man (or woman). My first experience of a student demonstration was one afternoon when a scholar, expelled from Hitler's Germany, was billed to give an open lecture in the university. The cause of free speech was preserved by the strong-arm tactics of the police against the demonstrators. 'You'd better clear off,' said a lecturer to a Greek student and myself; 'it may come to shooting.' So far as I know, it didn't come to shooting on that occasion, but one never could tell. The university buildings were permanently guarded by armed police, to whom we had to show a pass as we went in. When I saw our amateur student militants in England in the later 1960s, I used to reflect on the real militants whom I had known in Central Europe thirty-five years before: ours (happily) had not begun to learn what militancy means.

Those most to be pitied were the Jewish students, who could read all too plainly the writing on the wall (both in the biblical sense and in the literal sense). Vienna had a large Jewish population. The city was divided, for postal and other administrative purposes, into several numbered districts; the second district was almost entirely Jewish. One entered the second district from the first by a bridge over the Danube Canal. 'What is that bridge called?' ran a popular jest. If an unwary stranger answered with its official name (the Joseph Bridge), he would be told, 'No, it's the "translation into Hebrew".' (The German word for 'translation' — *Uebersetzung* — also means 'crossing over' in the literal sense.) It is not surprising that in those years the suicide rate among Viennese Jews, especially of the professional class, was inordinately high. I have often wondered what happened to some of my Jewish friends in Vienna, but never discovered.

I found congenial lodging in a Protestant *pension* not far from the university. The manageress was a pious and business-like German lady, a lover of Jesus and a devotee of Hitler — no unusual combination in those days! The *pension* had some permanent residents but also accommodated visitors or travellers on their way through Vienna. One such overnight visitor was J. Edwin Orr, then doing his 10,000 miles of miracle to Palestine.[1] Our first meeting was brief, but it was evident then that here was no ordinary man.

As for church fellowship. I found that with a small company of believers meeting in a ground-floor room in the Zentagasse. The best-known couple in this fellowship were Benno and Maria Brandt, two of the finest Christians whom it has ever been my good fortune to know. I was given the freedom of the flat where they lived with their five children, and was treated as a member of the family. Benno Brandt had been a major in the old Austrian Imperial Army and had seen service during World War I on the Russian and Italian fronts. He combined the natural dignity and code of honour proper to his military calling with a transparent Christian humility and charity, 'an Israelite indeed, in whom was no guile'. He augmented his very modest officer's pension with what he earned as a glass-blower in a small family business. His wife, who was considerably younger, was (and still is) a cheerful, outgoing personality, who could make a stranger feel immediately at home. She played the harmonium at meetings in the Zentagasse and co-operated with her husband in doing a great deal of good by stealth. From their own slender resources they did what they could to help others worse off than themselves. Several members of the fellowship were unemployed, and the state unemployment benefit hardly sufficed to keep them up to subsistence level, especially when they had families to support. In the post-war years Major and Mrs Brandt, and since her husband's death Mrs Brandt, have been actively engaged in Christian relief work beyond the Iron Curtain.

Among others in the same company I remember Richard Meitner, a colporteur with the British and Foreign Bible Society, who had quite a gift for expository ministry. Like many other residents in Vienna, he was a Czech by birth. He spoke a very classical German himself, and took pains to correct mine when it was less than classical. He specially deprecated my use of certain Viennese colloquialisms which I picked up in conversation with some of the other believers. 'Ah!' he exclaimed, when I once dropped such an expression in his hearing; 'where did you hear that? Only unintelligent people use that expression.' He had a good idea where I had picked it up, and he was right — but it was by no means from an 'unintelligent' source.

Another member of the group, a policeman, was a cousin of the Great Dictator, who was himself, of course, Austrian by birth and upbringing. This man's mother was a Hitler. But he did not advertise his distinguished relationship. But once we had a visit from a German brother, a member of the Weidenest community, who was on his way home from the Balkans and addressed a week-night meeting in the Zentagasse. After the meeting he was introduced to our policeman brother, mention being made of the special relationship, and he almost genuflected — in spirit at least, but physically he raised his arm in the appropriate salute. Technically, I suppose, the policeman would have been within his rights in arresting him on the spot, for the Nazi salute and greeting were illegal in Austria at that time. Not that it made any practical difference; there was some truth in the current saying: 'In most countries everything is allowed which is not expressly forbidden; in Germany everything is forbidden which is not expressly allowed; in Austria everything is allowed which is expressly forbidden.' The easy-going Austrian temperament was manifest at all levels: even an authoritarian government was easy-going in its authoritarianism.

As part of an economic warfare against Austria, the German government had imposed a heavy tax on German citizens visiting Austria. This cut down the number of German holiday-makers in Austria (which was the intention); it also meant that visits from German ministering brethren to Vienna were much less frequent than they normally were; we had to depend on the chance of their stopping off in transit. We also had visits from brethren in other neighbouring countries.

I remember one such visitor from Romania, a member of the German-speaking community in Transylvania. He spent a weekend in Vienna and ministered on the Sunday morning from Psalm 110, saying that the enemies who were made the Lord's footstool were people like ourselves — formerly enemies but now willing subjects. This was a new thought for his hearers, and certainly a different interpretation from Paul's in 1 Corinthians 15: 24-27. But my chief memory of his visit is of the Sunday evening, after the day's services were over, in the home of Major and Mrs Brandt. The visiting brother was a little, rather self-assertive man, with a large, patient-looking wife. The conversation got around somehow to the role of women in church and home and he said, 'I always stand on the standpoint: "The husband is the head of the wife".' I thought the time had come for something to be said on the other side, so I asked if the name of an English preacher called Spurgeon was known in their part of the world. Yes, his name was known, so I told how Spurgeon, addressing a bridal couple once, said, 'We frequently hear it emphasized that the husband is the head of the wife, but the wisest man who ever lived said that "a virtuous woman is a crown to her husband" — and everyone knows that a crown is worn on top of the head.' 'That', said he, 'is not in the Bible.' Nowadays I should (I hope) have been wise enough to leave him with that last preposterous word, but then, in my mid-twenties, I was tactless enough to direct his attention to Proverbs 12:4. That is not really the way to win friends and influence people.

My association with these believers did me good in a number of ways — first and foremost, because of the spiritual support which their warm fellowship provided. It also did my German much good, for they insisted that I should minister frequently, and as no one was in a position to interpret for me, I had to get used as quickly as possible to speaking publicly in German. It would have been ungracious of me to misuse their language more than I could help, so I prepared my addresses carefully, with German grammar and dictionary as well as Bible. The German Bible we used was the Elberfeld Bible, a version begun in 1855 by J. N. Darby's associates, Carl Brockhaus and J. A. von Poseck, with his encouragement, to be a counterpart to his own French and English versions.

I saw quite a lot of the Society of Friends in Vienna. In the grim years immediately after World War I the Friends undertook a great deal of relief work in Central Europe, and they continued to maintain an international centre in Vienna. Among other things, this centre provided facilities for Austrian and foreign students to meet together and to hear visiting lecturers. One lecturer whom I remember hearing was Dr Rufus Jones, a well-known American Quaker.

The Friends' centre was quite near St. Stephen's Cathedral, in the city centre. With some friends I attended midnight mass there on Christmas Eve, 1934. The main impression it left with me was the look of sadness on the faces of so many of those present — mainly, I think, older people.

On another occasion, towards the end of that same year, as some of us left the Friends' centre late one night, we saw what appeared to be a small but well-guarded funeral procession: the body of Chancellor Dollfuss was being conveyed from its temporary resting-place to a more permanent tomb.

In those days there was a sizeable Russian colony in Vienna — refugees from the Revolution of 1917. Most of them were aristocrats by birth. Some of them had resources outside Russia and were able to live in reasonable comfort; others had no resources and had to make do as best they could, earning a meagre livelihood in ways to which they had not been brought up.

Vienna itself was suffering from having become the capital of a small, impoverished republic, after being designed as the capital of a great empire covering most of east-central Europe. Ramshackle as the dual monarchy of the Austrian Empire and Apostolic Kingdom of Hungary was, life within its frontiers before 1918 was more comfortable for most of its subjects than life has been for many of them or for their descendants since then. The balkanization of all that area has been disastrous; but the example of that disaster has not prevented the putting into effect of the same process in other parts of the world in more recent times. It is easy in retrospect to blame the peacemakers of 1919 for not insisting that, whatever political changes might be necessary, large economic units should not be broken up into small, mutually exclusive units. What I saw in the 1930s was sufficient to make me a Common Marketeer for the rest of my life, although that phrase, in its modern sense, was not then current.

Note to Chapter 11
    1. See J. E. Orr *The Promise is to You!* (London 1935), pp. 27-29.

12

Czechoslovakia and Hungary

When I was about to set out for Central Europe in the summer of 1934, I was given a letter of introduction signed by the then Editor of *The Witness*, Mr Henry Pickering. (I still have it, though I no longer use it.) It was written in holograph on *Witness* notepaper and addressed 'To all the Lord's people everywhere'. But the reactions to it when I produced it varied. In Czechoslovakia, F. J. Křesina took it gladly and said, 'Ah, a letter! I always like brethren who bring letters.' But in Hungary, Aladár Ungár dismissed it indignantly and said, 'Why do you show me this?' — meaning that he was prepared to accept a fellow-believer at face value, without requiring third-party certification.

I

Czechoslovakia and Hungary were two countries which I visited more than once during my time in Austria. The 'conference' habit, so well established among Brethren in this country, had taken root in Czechoslovakia; I attended conferences in Prague, Brno and Bratislava. Bratislava, the capital of Slovakia, was only a tram-ride away from Vienna. There an evangelical work had flourished for many years through the ministry of Frederick Butcher.[1] When he and Mrs Butcher first settled there in 1900, Slovakia was part of Hungary, as was also an area of modern Yugoslavia with Slovak settlers among whom a similar work was carried on. During my period of study in Central Europe Mrs Butcher's increasing feebleness made it necessary for them both to return to England, but Mr Butcher paid several visits to Czechoslovakia between then and the outbreak of World War II, and it was moving to see the affection with which he was welcomed by his friends and converts on such occasions. The Brethren groups in Czechoslovakia were rather closely modelled on the life-style of their Anglo-Saxon counterparts, but the kiss with which brethren greeted each other was an indigenous Slavonic gesture. In this and many other respects Mr Butcher was a completely naturalized Slovak.

Bratislava stood at the junction of three linguistic areas — Slovak, German and Hungarian. It had, in fact, three names: in addition to its Slovak name Bratislava (brotherly glory) it was called Pressburg by the German-speaking people and Pozsóny by the Hungarians (to whom, as I have indicated, Slovakia belonged up to the end of World War I). Czech and Slovak are closely related languages — as close, I suppose, as English and Scots. In the Brethren's meetings in Bratislava, and especially at conferences, one could hear all these languages. Conference addresses were regularly interpreted into another language than that used by the speaker.

When I mentioned the Anglo-Saxon influence on the life-style of the Czechoslovak brethren, this was due not only to Mr Butcher's long ministry but also to the fact that some of the leading Czechoslovak brethren themselves had spent some formative years in English-speaking countries. Mr Křesina, for example, was trained in one of the homes for missionary candidates established by Huntingdon Stone (of whom he always spoke in terms of warm gratitude). His brother-in-law Jan Siracky had spent some years in the Ford works at Detroit, Michigan, and learned his church principles at the feet of T. D. W. Muir. In 1927 he came back from America with his wife (Mr Křesina's sister) and settled in Slovakia, where he maintained his evangelistic and teaching ministry until his death in 1974.

In Ruthenia (ethnically and linguistically part of Ukraine), which in those days was the eastern-most province of Czechoslovakia, missionary work was carried on by S. K. Hine (in Mukačevo), D. T. Griffiths (in Užhorod) and A. C. McGregor (in Chust). The frequent conferences provided opportunities for meeting these and other brethren.

I remember one occasion on which Richard Meitner and I travelled back by train from a conference in Brno with some members of a peasant community who left before we reached the Austrian frontier. Some women among them were talking in rather agitated terms of a situation which was causing them disquiet, and I was called in to express an opinion. The situation was this: a girl from their group had gone to take up employment in one of the cities and came back with her hair cut. 'We wept much,' said one elder sister, 'because we were afraid that she might enter into the resurrection life with her hair cut and so wear this badge of shame throughout eternity.' What did I think? 'In the resurrection', said I as authoritatively as I could, 'everything will be perfect' — and this utter platitude actually seemed to give them considerable comfort!

Between the wars, Czechoslovakia was the one really liberal democracy in Central Europe. I recall one symptom of the public freedom which it enjoyed: while walking along a street in Brno once I heard familiar strains and, moving in their direction, entered into a square where a uniformed Salvation Army band was playing. There was a Salvation Army presence in Austria and Hungary, but I never saw or heard a uniformed open air meeting in progress in either of these countries. Czechoslovak freedom was an offence to neighbouring regimes and was not allowed to endure. But friends of Czechoslovakia still repeat the words of a great Czech, Jan Amos Comenius, spoken on an earlier occasion

(360 years ago) when his country lost her freedom: 'I believe before God, that after the storms of wrath have passed, rule over what is thine will once more return to thee, O Czech people!'

II

The ethos of Hungary and of Hungarian evangelicalism was quite different from what one found in Czechoslovakia, but equally exhilarating. My first visit to Hungary began on New Year's Eve, 1934. I travelled by bus from Vienna to Budapest. This visit was paid at the invitation of Aladár Ungár, a man of about my own age, whom I had met in Vienna some weeks previously. At that time he himself did not live in Budapest (although he moved there later); he lived in Miskolc, about 90 miles farther east, where he maintained a Christian bookshop as one of several forms of his ministry. He arranged for me to spend a few days in Budapest on my way to Miskolc.

In Budapest there was a large and comprehensive evangelical free church, embracing in its fellowship, one might almost say, dukes and dustmen — at any rate aristocrats and dustmen. It included a large number of professional people, the most outstanding of whom was Ferenc Kiss, Professor of Anatomy in the University of Budapest. Professor Kiss acted as spokesman for evangelical Christians with pre-war, war-time and post-war governments alike. He bearded both nationalist and communist bureaucrats in their dens, shook his finger in their faces and said 'You know ... !' — and such was his international distinction that he got away with things which an ordinary churchman would not have dared to attempt. On that New Year's Eve in Budapest he interpreted for me as I delivered a message appropriate to the time of year. He was a seasoned interpreter, and had the reputation of making good in interpretation the deficiencies of those for whom he was interpreting. One young evangelist from the United Kingdom paid a visit to Hungary and sent back glowing reports of the blessing that followed his preaching. But he had Professor Kiss as his interpreter, and those who knew said that the blessing was due much more to the interpreter's renderings into idiomatic Magyar than to the original speaker. Kiss was a tower of strength to every good cause in Hungary.

That New Year's Eve meeting was preceded by a prayer meeting, at which I reckoned that about two-thirds of the vocal prayers were offered by sisters. One of the sisters, Mrs von Nadossy, with whom I stayed on my visits to Budapest, was the widow of a former Chief Constable of Budapest. She provided hospitality for a number of visiting preachers from overseas, including the late Theodore Roberts of London, of whom she spoke with veneration — 'a very blessed man,' she said. Germany, Austria and Hungary had no objection to the ministry of English brethren who were regarded as odd-men-out in their homeland, like Theodore Roberts and G. H. Lang.[2] In Czechoslovakia, on the other hand, they were not encouraged: first put matters right with your brethren at home, said the Czech brethren (who, as I have mentioned, appreciated letters of commendation).

There was a strong Christian Union in the University of Budapest, its patron (needless to say) being Professor Kiss. It went by the designation *Pro Christo*. I remember addressing them on at least one occasion.

Miskolc was the centre of a really remarkable spiritual work, carried on mainly by Jewish Christians, who seemed to have managed to preserve friendly relations with other Jews. Aladár Ungár was himself a converted Jew; his first experience of Christian service had been with the Salvation Army, in Britain and in pre-Hitler Germany. His wife, Emmchen, was a sweet German lady (Gentile, not Jewish). Aladár always spoke of her mother as one from whom he had derived great spiritual help as a young Christian. He carried out an extensive preaching and teaching ministry in Hungary and in the neighbouring German-speaking lands; after the war he settled in Germany, and died there.

But the most outstanding Christian in Miskolc was a lady,

Annie Roth by name, a Jewess by birth, She owned a photographic business in one of the main squares of the city, then called Nicholas Horthy Square, after the Regent of Hungary. Her renown as a photographer was such that members of high society, for all their disinclination to patronize someone of Jewish birth, went to her to be photographed. Her studio served as a Christian meeting place, to which Jewish and Gentile neighbours came for Bible study and discussion. I recall one such Jew who was introduced to me as being a great *Talmudkenner*. Among Gentile members of the fellowship was a teacher in a local high school who, on hearing on one occasion that my next port of call was Bratislava in Slovakia, said, 'It seems odd to us that Slovaks can also be believers. We have always thought of them as our enemies.'

There was constant agitation in Hungary between the wars for the regaining of those areas of the former Kingdom of Hungary which had been sliced off by the Treaty of Trianon and apportioned to Austria, Czechoslovakia, Romania and Yugoslavia. Stickers with the words *Nem, nem, soha* (no, no, never) were ubiquitous (meaning 'We will never agree to the dismemberment of Hungary'), and in public places and public vehicles a four-clause national creed was displayed: 'I believe in one God. I believe in one fatherland. I believe in the justice of God. I believe in the restoration of Hungary.'

This agitation had its repercussion in the neighbouring lands where there were Hungarian minorities, even in such a democratic state as Czechoslovakia. On one occasion when I was crossing from Hungary into Czechoslovakia, Aladár Ungár asked me to take a few Hungarian hymnbooks which had been ordered by Hungarian Christians in Bratislava. This was perfectly legal; my taking them simply saved the postage. But before he gave them to me, he ripped out a page in each — the page containing the Hungarian national anthem. I don't know if the Hungarian anthem was actually banned in Czechoslovakia, but he was taking no chances.

As for the work in Miskolc, this received a heavy blow

CZECHOSLOVAKIA AND HUNGARY

during the war with the intensification of anti-Jewish action in 1944. Between March and June of that year Adolf Eichmann was put in charge of the deportation of Hungarian Jews to extermination camps, and 381,600 Jews were deported in those three months. Annie Roth was one of the victims. If she was spared for any length of time in the extermination camp to which she was taken, I can well believe that a work of grace was started there; but I know no further details.

Another place which I visited in Hungary was Dombovár, some 90 miles south-west of Budapest. This was the home of János Laub, a Hungarian evangelist, with his wife and family. In addition to his evangelistic work, he advertised his services as a private teacher of English, but he did not seem to have much of a clientèle. He and his family lived more or less at subsistence level; I recall with gratitude how they showed me the kindness of God. They also suffered through the war; at the end of it (as I learned from Aladár Ungár) their two sons were taken prisoner by the invading Russians and never heard of again.

Mr Laub took me once to a village some miles from his home where there was a German-speaking settlement of Swabians. I gave them a Bible talk and then there was some discussion which before long they turned to international politics. It was on the eve of the Italo-Abyssinian War, when relations between Britain and Italy were strained. 'Mark my words,' said one wiseacre, 'if it comes to war between England and Italy, England has never lost a war yet.' It was remarkable what a hold this conviction, that England had never lost a war (and therefore would never lose one), had on the minds of ordinary people in Central Europe. I thought of Bannockburn, but held my peace.

Notes

Notes to Chapter 12
1. See W. T. Stunt, etc. (ed.) *Turning the World Upside Down* (Bath 1972), pp. 350 f., 359 f.
2. See p. 114.

13

Edinburgh days

My original intention when I left Cambridge was to spend two years at the University of Vienna, and possibly to present myself as a Ph.D. candidate at the end of the second year. I came home for the summer of 1935, and towards the end of September travelled south to London to get the boat train for the continent. On my way south I broke my journey for a weekend in Yorkshire, where my fiancée was teaching, and on the Saturday morning received a letter, forwarded from Elgin, from the Professor of Greek in Aberdeen (Archibald Cameron) drawing my attention to a vacancy in the Greek Department at Edinburgh University and suggesting that if I was interested in it, I should write direct to the Edinburgh Professor of Greek (W. M. Calder). After discussing the matter with my fiancée, I decided to do so, and wrote to Professor Calder, asking him to send his reply to me at 14 Paternoster Row, London (which some older readers will recognize as the pre-war address of Pickering & Inglis). Instead of going on immediately to Vienna I waited in London until I heard from him. At last I received a letter, dated 6th October, offering me nomination as Assistant in Greek and inviting me to present myself at the beginning of the new session on 15th October. I wrote back accepting his offer and then went off to Vienna to collect some things which I had left there over the vacation, to make my apologies to Professor Kretschmer for discontinuing my course of study with him and to take leave of my friends. Then, on 15th October, I arrived in Edinburgh to start my new work.

Had I been an American, the non-completion of a Ph.D. course might have been a serious handicap in my future academic career. (Here I must resist the temptation to write the article which I may write one day, on the menace of the Ph.D. cult!) As it was, it made not the slightest difference. The thesis which I had started to write, on Roman slave-names, was not entirely lost: sections of it were published in a couple of journals.[1]

The opportunity of a foothold on the academic teaching ladder was attractive although, had I not seized that opportunity, another would have come my way before long. An even weightier consideration was marriage. It was not unusual for the likes of me in those days to serve, Jacob-like, seven years for Rachel; but seven years is long enough. In those days we had the idea that a man ought to be able to support his wife before getting married; and most education authorities then required women teachers to resign when they got married, so my wife could not have continued to practise her profession even if she had wanted to. Next year, then, we were married in King's College Chapel, Aberdeen. After spending our honeymoon in Austria, Hungary and Czechoslovakia, we set up house in Learmonth Avenue, Edinburgh. In Edinburgh, the following summer, our firstborn, Iain, arrived — which meant a third person to be maintained on our annual salary of £250.

A university assistantship in Scotland was the lowest form of academic life, lower than an assistant lectureship in England. It was renewable year by year, without increment, for three years: then it terminated. But when one is young three years seems a long time, and at the end of the three years, we reckoned, something else would come along — and it did. But at the time a university assistantship was at least the lowest rung of a very desirable ladder, and we were as happy then at the bottom of the ladder as we were later at the top.

The vacancy occurred because of the resignation of Kenneth W. Luckhurst to take up a post on the secretariat of the Royal Society of Arts. One of my colleagues commented on the fact that one member of the Brethren should be succeeded by another: 'if I were superstitious', he said, 'I should begin to think there was something in it.' The head of the Greek Department, Professor Calder (later Sir William Calder), was like myself a native of Morayshire and a graduate of Aberdeen University, although from Aberdeen he went to Oxford, not Cambridge. He followed in the steps of Sir William Ramsay and was, like him, a leading authority on the archaeology and geography of Asia Minor. In later years he was kind enough to read my commentary on the Greek text of Acts and to send me detailed comments which meant that the second and third editions were considerably more accurate than the first on such matters as the frontier between the provinces of Asia and Galatia. A man who had plotted the Roman milestones along that frontier, as he had, enjoyed a decided advantage in this field over other students of Acts!

Among other members of the departmental teaching staff, I made a lifelong friend in a man well remembered by all his pupils but (because he published very little) not widely known in the world of scholarship — P. B. R. Forbes, who died in 1978 in Sunderland, his home town, after living there in retirement for twenty-five years. Rarely if ever have I known a man with such an infallible sense of good Greek usage. During my three years in Edinburgh I spent a good deal of time in his company, for he and I shared a kind of office in the Old Gibson Library in the north-east corner of Old College, to which students came to us for tutorials; and I picked up more knowledge of Greek idiom from him than he probably realized.

Edinburgh University boasted many eminent men on its senate and teaching staff in the 1930s. I recall A. E. Taylor, Professor of Moral Philosophy and a distinguished

Platonist; V. Gordon Childe, Professor of Prehistoric Archaeology, who had the engaging habit of revising his opinions frequently and referring in public to 'that very bad book I wrote last year'. This at least is better than the attitude which refuses to reconsider any position once public commitment has been made to it in print. G. T. Thomson, whom I had known in Aberdeen as Professor of Systematic Theology, was now Professor of Christian Dogmatics in Edinburgh. Another acquaintance of Aberdeen days who had come to Edinburgh was Donald Campbell, Lecturer in Humanity (Latin); he was killed by an I.R.A. bomb in the left luggage department of King's Cross Station on his way home from honeymoon in 1938.

My first pupils were only a few years younger than myself. Some of them have risen to exalted heights, but I cannot claim much credit for that. I think of John Brough, now Professor of Sanskrit in Cambridge, James Whyte, now Principal of St. Mary's College, St. Andrews, and Robin Wilson, now Professor of Biblical Criticism in St. Andrews and the leading British authority on Gnosticism. There was also Roy Stewart, well known today as a contributor to evangelical journals and the author of an important work on *Rabbinic Theology* (1961). Another Edinburgh student at that time, but not a pupil of mine, was William Duff McHardy, who had been a fellow-student (one year junior to me) in Aberdeen, where he had graduated in Arts and Divinity. He then came to Edinburgh to take an honours course in Semitic languages (which was not available at Aberdeen). From there he went on to higher things: he was Samuel Davidson Professor of Old Testament Studies in the University of London from 1948 to 1960 and Regius Professor of Hebrew at Oxford from 1960 until his retirement in 1978. He is probably best known as Director of the New English Bible (in succession to C. H. Dodd and G. R. Driver).

In Edinburgh we found a congenial spiritual home in Bellevue Chapel. Bellevue Chapel had been a German church before World War I, and in 1919 it was acquired by one of the companies of Open Brethren in Edinburgh, with whom it remains to this day. It was a special pleasure for me to go back there in September 1969, to take part, along with Stephen Short, in their jubilee conference. The brethren in Bellevue Chapel were guided in the 1930s by an exceptionally wise and able body of elders, including Peter Manson, Frank Balfour, Rice Alexander, Andrew Brown and Addison Graham. The first two of these were partners in the well-known legal firm of Balfour and Manson. In view of the tribute I have just paid to the wisdom of those elders, it would ill become me to question the wisdom of an extraordinary course they took in 1936, when they invited two young men of twenty-five years old to join their number — Archie Wyse (now in Largs) and myself. No doubt the stability of our seniors was more than sufficient to compensate for the immaturity of our youth. They entrusted me with some secretarial responsibility, in addition to which I had a share in the young people's work of the church.

My wife and I find it pleasant at times to review the back pages of our guest-book — a wedding gift from Benno and Maria Brandt — and call to mind some visitors who stayed in our home in our early married years, including visiting preachers. One such visitor whom we entertained was F. J. Křesina of Czechoslovakia, in whose home I had stayed in Prague. But no visiting preacher was more welcome than John P. Lewis of Bangor, Co. Down. He had been an occasional guest in my parents' home (my father and he saw eye to eye on prophetic interpretation) and he stayed with my wife and me on a few occasions, both in Edinburgh and later in Leeds. He was excellent company, but one had to be mentally alert when he was around, because of his habit of suddenly asking catch questions. 'Tell me, Mrs ———,' he said to one of our Bellevue ladies, 'can a man marry his widow's sister?' To which she, very seriously, replied, 'Well, it *would* be legal, I suppose, but it wouldn't be scriptural, would it?' I felt that his nerves must have been badly affected during the Irish troubles of 1916-22, for when he walked along an Edinburgh street he would jump and throw his hands up when a car backfired. He had a detailed knowledge of the Bible, and a fresh and unconventional approach to its interpretation, and this made him a stimulating person to listen and talk to. When he died in 1940 his widow sent me a pocket edition of Nestle's Greek New Testament which he had used. I continued to use it — literally as a pocket edition — until it fell to pieces after several years.

I came to know quite a number of the Brethren groups in the vicinity of Edinburgh through taking Sunday services for them — from Dunfermline to Dalkeith, Galashiels and Hawick, from Falkirk to Tranent and Cockenzie. I remember a weekend in Hawick which I spent with the parents of William Landles, and first made the acquaintance of him and the lady who shortly afterwards became his wife. The mention of William Landles reminds me of the part played by some of our brethren in modern Scottish poetry. In addition to him one thinks specially of the late Robert Rendall of Orkney, an exceptionally gifted and attractive man, and the list could be further extended.

From time to time Edinburgh was visited by chief men among the Brethren, who came to give series of addresses in one or another of our meeting-places. It was in Edinburgh, for example, that I first heard W. W. Fereday, who on two occasions during my time there gave Bible lectures in the Tollcross meeting (now Bruntsfield Evangelical Church) — one series on Pentateuchal typology and the other on the messages to the seven churches of Revelation.[2] One quality of his ministry stands out particularly: his memorable way of expressing himself. I have a clear recollection of every address I ever heard him give. For all his gift of lucid and incisive exposition, he was not an original thinker; he rarely ventured beyond the bounds mapped out by his one-time mentor William Kelly.

There come to mind some special occasions in the wider religious life of Edinburgh during our time there. In October 1936 we attended a special meeting in the Church of Scotland Assembly Hall to mark the quatercentenary of William Tyndale's martyrdom. The principal speaker was Professor

101

Daniel Lamont, that year's Moderator of the General Assembly of the Church of Scotland. The chairman was Dr Alexander Stewart, a leading minister in the Free Church of Scotland, and the lesson was read by a Congregationalist, so by the standards of 1936 it was a fairly 'ecumenical' occasion.

The Assembly Hall was also the principal venue for a series of meetings held in Edinburgh in 1937 to commemorate the centenary of D. L. Moody's birth. There were quite a number of people who remembered one or other of Moody's visits to Edinburgh in 1870, 1873-74 and 1891. There were some reminiscences from speakers who knew Moody or had heard him preach: one thing above all that was emphasized in those reminiscences was that Moody was so devoid of any special attractiveness in appearance or speech that the results which attended his ministry could not be put down to personal magnetism or mass hypnotism but must be ascribed to the power of God working through him. But the meetings were predominantly evangelistic in character: the same gospel as Moody had preached was preached afresh. Some American speakers were over for the occasion; outstanding among them was Dr Harry Ironside, then minister of Moody Memorial Church, Chicago, who was equally welcomed in Bellevue Chapel and in the High Kirk of Edinburgh (commonly called St. Giles' Cathedral), where he preached from John Knox's pulpit.

Of another important Edinburgh gathering — the international Calvinistic Congress held in July 1938 — I cannot speak at first hand, because we were away on holiday when it met. But I knew many of the participants, from the Honorary President (Professor Daniel Lamont) down to some student-members; it really was an ecumenical occasion, for the membership embraced Anglicans, Presbyterians (of all sorts), Baptists (Strict and General) and others not so readily identifiable in denominational terms.

By the summer of 1938, however, the pillar of cloud was lifting from Edinburgh and an onward move was indicated.

Notes to Chapter 13

1. In *Glotta* 25 (1936), pp. 42-50, and *Proceedings of the Leeds Philosophical Society: Literary and Historical Section* 5 (1938), pp. 44-60.

2. He expounded the historicist interpretation of the messages to the churches, according to which Ephesus represents the church of apostolic days and Laodicea the apostate church of the period immediately preceding the parousia. 'Some of you may wonder', he said, 'whether the believers who first received these letters knew that they had this further application. No, they did not, and it was not intended that **they should.**'

14
Yorkshire life begins

As the three years of my Edinburgh appointment were coming to an end, it was necessary to think of something to replace it, so I applied for two or three posts. One of these was a teaching post in a South African university. It would, I fear, have been an academic dead-end: however, I was interviewed for it along with two other candidates in South Africa House, Trafalgar Square, during the Easter vacation of 1938. (Lancelot Hogben, author of *Mathematics for the Million* and similar works, was a member of the interviewing committee.) One of the other candidates was K. D. White, lecturer in Greek in Leeds University. After the interview I took the night sleeper from London to Aberdeen (we spent our vacations in the north-east) and at York there arrived, to claim the berth above mine, an old friend, P. S. Noble, then Professor of Latin in Leeds, who was due to go to Aberdeen in October to succeed Alexander Souter in the Chair of Humanity. (He is now Sir Peter Noble, Principal Emeritus of King's College, London.) I told him the object of my London visit and he said, 'If you get the South African job, well and good. But if they give it to White, you should certainly apply for his post in Leeds. Let me know what happens and, if necessary, I'll speak to Edwards (Professor of Greek in Leeds) about you.' In a few days, news came that

K. D. White had got the South African post, his position in Leeds University was advertised, I applied for it and was appointed. It was, as I have seen more and more clearly ever since, the best thing that could have happened for me just then.

To Leeds, then, we went, bidding a reluctant farewell to Edinburgh. My nonagenarian friend John Brown sent me a letter: 'Edinburgh if not Scotland will miss you,' it said. 'But O! England. England needs you for the Truth and Testimony's sake.' Just how much of what *he* would have regarded as the 'Truth and Testimony' England has received from me is anybody's guess. However, in England I have lived and taught ever since.

During the summer of 1938 we paid a short visit to Leeds to do a little house-hunting. At Leeds City Station we were approached by a lady who was looking out for a young couple with a year-old boy — for us, in fact. This was Mrs Daisley, mother of Donald and Ruth Daisley of Eastbourne and the late Norman Daisley of Sanderstead. As it happened, the house in which we were specially interested was in the next street to hers, and there we spent the next nine years, receiving no little kindness from her and her husband and family. We moved to Leeds at the end of September, at the height of the Munich crisis. The first important event to take place after our move was the birth of our daughter Sheila at the end of November (but she regards herself as a Scot, not a Yorkshirewoman).

The whole atmosphere of Leeds, both city and university, was quite different from that of Edinburgh. Our moving there was the start of a twenty-one years' residence in Yorkshire (nine years, as I have said, in Leeds, and then twelve in Sheffield) and, although we were as far from being Yorkshire folk at the end of that time as at the beginning, we were made to feel at home. It was pleasantly strange at first to be addressed as 'love' by shop assistants and tram conductors, but even when the strangeness wore off, the pleasantness remained. Not all visitors to the county felt like this, however. During World War II many civil servants and others were evacuated from the south to Yorkshire, and some of them, or at least their families, found their exile irksome. One day on a bus in Leeds I overheard two ladies from the south sharing their grievances over the shortcomings of the northerners. 'And all this calling you "love",' said one. 'It's civility we want, not love.' I should have regarded the civility as part of the love; I'd sooner be called 'love' than 'sir' any day.

Leeds University was not marked by such relics of social stratification as could still be found at that time in Edinburgh University. It belonged to the 'Redbrick' category of universities — those founded between the mid-nineteenth century and the outbreak of World War I. The ethos of 'Redbrick' is different from that of the more ancient foundations which I had previously known, and different also from that of the 'Plateglass' or 'Greenfield' institutions which mushroomed in the twenty-five years or so after World War II. All my teaching life since 1938 has been spent in 'Redbrick' universities, and I have found life in them highly congenial.

My new chief, Professor W. M. Edwards of the Chair of Greek in Leeds, was an unusual man. He had been born into a military family and himself embarked on a military career, being an officer in the Royal Garrison Artillery until his later thirties. He then went to Oxford as an undergraduate, taking his B.A. at the age of forty and becoming a Fellow of Merton College the same year. Three years later he was appointed Professor of Greek in Leeds. He was an accomplished linguist, speaking Welsh, Gaelic, Russian and Hebrew as well as the commoner European languages. I was told that he had spent one summer in Kintail in order to perfect his knowledge of spoken Gaelic. I remember how he proposed a vote of thanks to a guest lecturer at a meeting of the Yorkshire Society for Celtic Studies and recited in faultless Gaelic a stanza from *M'Crimmon's Farewell*. On another occasion he came into my room to see me about something or other, and found me reading the Hebrew text of Judges. Immediately he threw back his head and recited, in Hebrew, Samson's song of victory, 'With the jawbone of an ass . . .' He was a bachelor until the age of sixty-two, when he saw the light and married a lady lecturer in the Department of Zoology.

In addition to my Greek lecturing, I gave one lecture a week to the Honours School of Latin, on the history of the Latin Language. The Professor of Latin, E. J. Wood, who succeeded Peter Noble in October 1938, was (like his predecessor and myself) a graduate of Aberdeen and Cambridge. So was the Head of the Department of Mathematics, Professor W. P. Milne, who had many interests beyond mathematics. He was the leading spirit in the Yorkshire Society for Celtic Studies, and in his retirement he wrote a novel, *Eppie Elrick* (1955), in which he endeavoured to preserve as much as he could of the old dialect of Buchan, the north-eastern corner of Aberdeenshire, in which he was born.

Another Professor of Mathematics was Selig Brodetzky, at that time also President of the Board of Deputies of British Jews. He was a man of international repute and no mean political penetration. I recall an article of his, written a few months before the outbreak of World War II, in which he argued that when the fortunes of the Jewish people were lowest the fortunes of mankind as a whole were lowest. He reckoned that the fortunes of both would deteriorate farther before there was any improvement — and how right he was! His appreciation of global strategy at that time was illustrated by his assurance that in a world conflict all would be well so long as Gibraltar, Suez, Singapore and Panama remained in the right hands. (It would be good to think that our rulers still bear in mind such elementary considerations of global strategy.) After the war he went to Israel and became President of the Hebrew University of Jerusalem.

I found myself involved on a basis of personal friendship with several members of the large Jewish community in Leeds, especially after the University appointed Dr Simon Rawidowicz as Lecturer in Mediaeval and Modern Hebrew. There was already a lecturer in Old Testament Hebrew — J.

N. Schofield — but he was attached to the Department of Theology, the head of which was E. O. James, Professor of the Philosophy and History of Religion. When, however, the lectureship in Mediaeval and Modern Hebrew was established about 1941 by the munificence of Sir Montague Burton, a new Department of Hebrew was formed, with Mr Schofield as head and Dr Rawidowicz as his colleague. Dr Rawidowicz was a Russian Jew by origin — he used to recall how pleasant life in Tsarist Russia was in the old days, apart from the occasional pogrom — but received his higher education in Berlin, where he continued to live and work until the advent of Hitler made it expedient for him to leave Germany. He and his wife and boy became firm family friends of ours. Once or twice I went to synagogue with him, and have had the experience of hearing my name announced in synagogue as a visitor more or less as a visitor's name might be announced at the outset of one of our Brethren services. At the end of the war he went to Brandeis University, Waltham, Massachusetts, as Professor of Mediaeval Jewish Philosophy.

Talking of Jews reminds me of the new director of a Christian mission to Jews in Leeds, who thought of experimenting with new techniques in the Christian approach to Jews. One weekend he organized a special series of meetings on 'neutral ground' and roped me in to participate in two of them. One was to be a lecture by me on 'Jews and Christians in the closing decades of the Second Temple' — innocuous enough and well enough received. But it was followed by an epilogue in which an earnest Hebrew Christian told the story of his conversion and appealed to his hearers to follow his example, whereat there was considerable spitting on the floor and muttering of 'Apostate'! I was a little embarrassed, as I felt my lecture was the bait for my successor's hook. It is not that I think the plain presentation of the gospel is ever out of place — *tout au contraire* — but those members of the audience who felt that they had been attracted to the meeting under false pretences had some ground for their complaint. The epilogue had not been advertised, and even when it was introduced by the chairman, the terms of the introduction were: 'Mr X will say a few words about his religious experiences.' Had the advertisement of the meeting included the statement that 'Mr X will tell how he came to believe in Jesus' or 'Mr X will commend his Saviour', the situation would have been more honest, though the audience might have been smaller. No one expects a preacher of the gospel to be neutral, and it is folly to pretend otherwise.

Next evening there was a brains trust, with Jews and Christians on the panel, and the aforesaid director (himself a Hebrew Christian) acting as question-master. I fear it was not a success. Several questions were asked by Hebrew and Gentile Christians in the audience about the meaning of various Old Testament passages which were given a messianic interpretation in tradition (not in the New Testament). These were submitted to a young rabbi who was an able expositor and to myself, and all too often exegetical honesty compelled me to agree with the rabbi, to the dismay of the questioners, who felt that I was letting the side down.

During my years in Leeds several factors combined to move my centre of academic interest more and more towards Biblical studies. Not long after we went to Leeds, the need to lay hands honestly on a little extra money impelled me to become a candidate for the Crombie Scholarship in Biblical Criticism. This scholarship consisted of a sum of money awarded by examination; it was open to honours graduates in classics of any of the Scottish Universities. In June 1939 I went to St. Andrews (where the examination was held) and was duly awarded the scholarship (I was the only candidate that year). The subjects on which I was examined included the critical study of Pentateuchal introduction, of Judges (in Hebrew) and of John and Ephesians (in Greek). I had not previously had to study any part of the Bible (especially of the Old Testament) at the same academic depth.

While the University of Leeds made provision internally for the study of the Old Testament in Hebrew, it did not in those days make similar provision for the study of the New

Testament in Greek. Candidates for theological degrees went for their New Testament lectures to Wesley College, Headingley, where they had the great good fortune to sit at the feet of Vincent Taylor, Principal of the College. But soon after the outbreak of World War II, Wesley College was closed 'for the duration' and its staff directed by Conference to circuit work. (The building became the local headquarters for the W.R.N.S.; some wag put up a notice at the entrance to the drive: 'Quiet, please; wrens nesting'.) There were still a few candidates for theological degrees at the University, and I was asked to give them some lectures in Greek New Testament. There was no reason why I should not (the New Testament is part of the corpus of Greek literature) and in fact I did so very readily. About the same time a theological library belonging to the Diocese of Ripon — the Holden Library — was transferred from its former premises to a room in the Brotherton Library of Leeds University. This was a great boon, and it was far more adequately stocked at that time than the theological section of the University Library.

Even with the addition of Greek New Testament teaching, I was not overburdened with academic duties during the war years, and as Leeds was spared aerial bombardment on the scale that many other English cities had to endure, my civil defence duties as air raid warden and fire-watcher did not exact a heavy toll of time or energy. I therefore had leisure for further study and employed some of it in reading for the Leeds University Diploma in Hebrew, which was instituted when Dr Rawidowicz came to join Mr Schofield, and which I was awarded (with others) in 1943.

Then, the formation in 1938 of the Inter-Varsity Fellowship Biblical Research Committee, to promote advanced Bible study, was a major force in propelling me in this direction. One of the ways in which the Committee endeavoured to promote its aims was the organization of summer schools, and for some years I taught at these summer schools as the Committee's New Testament specialist, while Dr W. J. Martin of Liverpool University served as Old

Testament specialist.[1] It is a commentary on the situation of biblical scholarship in the IVF thirty years ago that a predominantly Anglican committee should have had to enlist the services in this way of two of the people called Brethren, who moreover were not professional theologians but teachers in the Arts Faculties of two secular universities.

I may have more to say of the Biblical Research Committee later. At the moment this only need be added: another of the Committee's projects was the launching of a series of technical commentaries on the Greek text of the New Testament. Only two of such commentaries were destined to be completed: E. K. Simpson's on the Pastoral Epistles (1954) and mine on Acts (1951). The volume on Acts was the product of ten years' work. Some by-products of this work which appeared *en route* were a Tyndale New Testament Lecture, *The Speeches in the Acts of the Apostles* (1942), and a more popular work, *Are the New Testament Documents Reliable?* (1943) — later renamed *The New Testament Documents: Are They Reliable?* (from 1960 onwards).

Note to Chapter 14
1. It was a sad loss to the cause of biblical scholarship when Dr Martin died in February 1980.

15

Brethren in Leeds and elsewhere

During our nine years in Leeds (1938-47) we found congenial church fellowship with the Christians who met in Fenton Street Gospel Hall. When we first settled in Leeds, there were four companies of Open Brethren in the city, the other three meeting respectively in Joseph Street, Ladbroke Place and Moor Road (the last of these was a breakaway from Fenton Street). Of these four only the Joseph Street company remains; it meets in the same building but its postal address has been changed. Not long after we came to Leeds, a new company was formed in the Harehills area. In addition, shortly before we came to Leeds, the Fenton Street church began an outreach work on the Scott Hall housing estate, in a temporary structure which was well named Hope Hall. I say 'well named' because the hope was well founded; the work there flourished and in due course it became an independent church, which replaced the temporary structure by a more stable one but kept the original name. The daughter church continues to flourish while the mother church has disappeared.

Before World War II, plans were approved for the

reconstruction of Leeds city centre which involved the demolition of the Fenton Street building to make way for a new road. The church did not own the building; it rented an upper room above a garage. To make provision for the eventual move, a modest building fund was started, but with the outbreak of war the plans for reconstruction were put into cold storage and the older brethren tended to remain content with this situation and say 'It will last our time'. It did — only just. One night in 1940 a number of bombs fell on the city, and on setting out from home next morning I met one of our older brethren who had got up bright and early to go down town and see how the hall had fared. 'I've been to see the hall,' he said. 'It's all right.' Some of the younger members could almost have wished that one of these nocturnal bombs had landed on the empty building and forced some action on our elders! When at last the building was demolished according to plan, the church moved to temporary premises in the city centre, and when these ceased to be available it was now too weak to acquire new premises in which to continue its existence as a viable community. A pity, for it had been a live and strong church in its day. The moral of this cautionary tale will no doubt be apparent.

Among the elders in Fenton Street (whom, after fitting probation, I was invited to join) were T. H. Daisley (husband of the lady who met us at Leeds City Station), A. W. Davies, F. E. May and J. T. Fewings. All of these, with their wives and families, were delightful people to know, and the same could be said of the members of the church as a whole. Mr Davies was a gifted and sensitive man, of artistic and studious tastes, who was perhaps not as much appreciated as he might have been. As I got to know him better, I discovered that we had much in common. He was more interested in philosophical theology than I was. When the two volumes of Reinhold Niebuhr's Gifford Lectures on *The Nature and Destiny of Man* were published in 1941-43, I recommended them to him; he bought them and read them with appreciation. Niebuhr would not have been approved literary fare for most of our church elders thirty years ago.

As for Mr May, it was through him that I first became personally acquainted with G. H. Lang. I had corresponded with Mr Lang occasionally before coming to Leeds, but had not met him. He came to Leeds from time to time and stayed with the May family, whom he had known for many years (in fact, Mr May was converted during the Torrey-Alexander mission in Bristol in 1904, during Mr Lang's pastorate of Unity Chapel in that city). Mr Lang's visits to Leeds and to Fenton Street caused some fluttering in the dovecotes, not so much because of any controversial element in his spoken ministry as because of the judicious distribution of his latest booklet, whatever it might be — *The Rights of the Holy Spirit in the House of God* (1938), perhaps, or *Firstfruits and Harvest* (1940). One Thursday evening in the earlier part of the war he gave a talk at Fenton Street on Matthew 24, which was more graphically illustrated than could have been arranged, for there was considerable activity as a number of German bombers flew over Leeds bound for a raid on Sheffield. He started reading the chapter (from the RV, of course)[1] and had got to the first clause of verse 6, 'And ye shall hear of wars and rumours of wars . . .', when the local anti-aircraft artillery began to open up. He waited for the first burst of gunfire to die down, and continued unperturbed: '. . . see that ye be not troubled.' It was an enriching experience to get to know Mr Lang, although it required at times considerable resolution to resist the strength with which he would press his convictions on one (in the most gracious possible manner, indeed).[2]

Another visiting speaker whom I heard once at Fenton Street and who left a lasting impression on many members of his audience was Dr V. P. Martzinkovski of Haifa. He was a man of exceptional personality; I once heard Professor Rendle Short describe him and his wife as 'salt of the earth', and Rendle Short did not throw such compliments around carelessly. Dr Martzinkovski was Russian by birth and his wife was German, but I think they had both acquired Polish nationality. In pre-revolutionary days he had been a professor of philosophy in Moscow and secretary of the SCM in Moscow University. He was keenly interested in the work of the Russian philosopher and mystic V. S. Solovyov, on whom I believe he was once invited to give a lecture in the Hebrew University of Jerusalem. He told us of a conversation he once had with Chief Rabbi Kook in Jerusalem, in which they talked of the Messiah; he tried in vain to persuade Dr Kook to agree that the latter's portrayal of the character of the expected Messiah was remarkably similar to the recorded character of the historical Jesus of Nazareth.

During the war the circle of our friends was increased by military personnel who were stationed in Leeds (where the Royal Army Medical Corps and the Royal Army Pay Corps both had headquarters) and by members of certain branches of the Civil Service which were transferred there from London in accordance with the policy of dispersal. One member of the RAPC stayed under our roof for a considerable time: Gordon Stephens, now of Bristol. It was during his period of military service in Yorkshire that he met his wife Winifred, a Harrogate girl. Among the civil servants whom we came to know was G. Ritchie Rice (now of Bexhill-on-Sea), in charge of a department of the Ministry of Supply. Charles Fraser-Smith, formerly of Morocco and now of Bratton Fleming, Devon, was nominally attached to Mr Ritchie Rice's department; actually he was engaged on specially secret and exciting work of 'national importance'.

As regards the oral ministry of the word, the great annual occasion in Yorkshire in those days was the Whitsuntide conference in Bradford. People with long memories said that in the 1940s it was not a shadow of its former self; but after all, wartime conditions made a difference, and it was still able to attract some of the ablest expository teachers of our circle. There I renewed acquaintance with Cecil Howley, whom I had not met since Cambridge days; there too I first met and heard H. L. Ellison, who had lately returned to England from Romania and whose ministry was then blowing like a fresh and invigorating wind among the Brethren in this country, dispelling cobwebs and recalling

115

us to first principles. My own generation found him exhilarating, but our seniors found him somewhat disconcerting. Today Mr Ellison is venerated as a wise elder statesman, but those who did not know him between thirty and forty years ago, when he was busy dislodging us from our ruts, have missed something that to people like myself is a treasured memory.

Then there was the Yorkshire Missionary Conference, held each autumn in Leeds, which provided some opportunity for expository ministry as well as for missionary reports. And it seemed to a newcomer that every little assembly in the county held its own annual conference on one Saturday or another in the summer. I soon found myself involved in these conferences: the first was at one of the meetings in the Bradford area, soon after the outbreak of war in 1939; I remember it especially because I found myself yoked with the late Edwin Lewis, whom I had not met before — a kindred spirit indeed, as I quickly discovered.

As the years went on, opportunities for wider ministry came my way: in 1943 I presented my first paper to the Victoria Institute[3] (which at that time was passing through a phase when it was run by retired Lieutenant-Colonels, whose reaction to my paper on 'The Sources of the Gospels' was sceptical); at Eastertide of that year I was included for the first time on the panel of speakers at the Glasgow Half-Yearly Meetings,[4] while in November 1945 I made my debut as a Bloomsbury speaker.[5] A first invitation to the Glasgow or Bloomsbury platform might be regarded as a probationary experiment; but in the eyes of some of my friends the receipt of a second invitation meant that one had joined the establishment. I am not so sure: I don't think I am really establishment-minded.

This reminds me of a later occasion — in October 1953 — when I was invited to give the ministry one evening at the Westminster Missionary Meetings. That was the first occasion when I met George Patterson, then recently home from Tibet. A few weeks previously he had married Meg Ingram, of Aberdeen and Kalimpong, whom I had known

116

since her babyhood. He gave a brief report at the same session. George is not only not establishment-minded: he is — or at least in those days he was — positively anti-establishment-minded. He told me afterwards that before he gave his report he was taken aside by one of the conveners and told that he must make no reference to this, that and the next thing. (No doubt the convener knew what he was about.) 'But it doesn't matter,' said George to me; 'you said all the things I was told not to say, and at the end the chairman expressed the hope that your message would be published!' (It was; it appeared in *The Witness* for December, 1953 under the title 'The Apostolic Witness'.) Which may go to show that what matters is not so much what is said, but the way it is said. (In this connexion C. F. Hogg once said that some people were down on him like a ton of bricks if he so much as looked over the wall, whereas they would let Harold St. John come into the orchard and pick the apples!)

But of all the conferences in which I became involved at that period of my life none meant so much to me as the North Midlands Young People's Holiday Conference. This was a residential weekend conference, of generally MSC character[6] (although its purpose was primarily expository and only secondarily missionary). It was held in its earlier years at Kingsmoor School, Glossop (formerly the seat of Lord Howard of Glossop but subsequently demolished to make room for a housing estate); then at Lyme Hall, near Stockport; and after that at Scarisbrick Hall, near Southport. It was launched in the unpromising circumstances of 1940 and was the only conference of its kind in England to be held that year or for some years thereafter.

In June 1943 I went from Leeds to address a Saturday evening meeting in Worksop, Notts. One of the people present was K. G. Hyland, who then lived and worked in the neighbouring town of Retford. After the meeting he spoke to me and said, 'Have you had a letter from a man called Pickering?' The answer was 'No'; in my ignorance, at that time I knew only one 'Brethren' family named Pickering, but my ignorance was soon to be corrected. Not long afterwards, I received a letter from Arnold Pickering of Stockport, secretary of the holiday conference referred to, asking me if I would come as one of the speakers for Easter weekend, 1944. I went as a speaker and came away as a member of the committee, and remained on the committee for almost thirty years. Nowhere in all my life have I found more congenial or spiritually helpful fellowship than with the other members of that committee — men of the calibre of Arnold Pickering and the late K. G. Hyland, J. B. Inglis and George Price (father of Mary Batchelor of Stockton-on-Tees and Margaret Young of Banbury), one of the noblest souls I have ever known. (If I mention no other committee-members' names, it is because those named may be taken as samples of the lot.) In the earlier years of the conference we could enlist the co-operation of such speakers as Montague Goodman, Harold St. John, Rendle Short and Latimer Short; in later years we invited speakers considerably younger than ourselves, but the standard of ministry was well maintained. If one were tempted to draw a comparison between the young members of the conference party in the 1940s and their successors in the 1970s, it would be best to resist the temptation. I will say just this: thirty years ago they had greater capacity for expository digestion than the new generation has; perhaps the conditions of wartime had something to do with that. The new generation has problems of its own to cope with, and I find much cause for encouragement as I see how it does cope with them.

Notes to Chapter 15

1. The Revised Version of 1881-85 was, in Mr Lang's judgment, 'the most trustworthy of English translations for general and public use' (see his autobiography, *An Ordered Life* [London 1959], pp. 49, 90).

2. Two minority convictions which he was prone to press were (*a*) a variety of premillennialism technically called 'selective resurrection and rapture' and (*b*) an insistence on the autonomy of the local church and indeed of the individual servant of God so thorough-going that he deprecated all central or inter-church direction or even co-ordinating of missionary work.

3. The Victoria Institute, or Philosophical Society of Great Britain, was founded in 1965 to investigate the areas where religion, philosophy and science overlap. Its proceedings are published in the journal *Faith and Thought*. See p. 182.

4. These Half-Yearly Meetings for biblical ministry, arranged by a committee of brethren in Glasgow, have been held in the spring and autumn of each year ever since 1865.

5. See p. 80, n. 1.

6. The MSC (Missionary Study Class) movement was launched in 1912 by Professor and Mrs A. Rendle Short of Bristol; individual classes were formed in local Open Brethren churches, and periodic conferences brought members together.

16

Biblical research

During my years in Leeds, as I have mentioned, several factors combined to move the centre of my academic interest into the biblical area. Let me mention one or two more.

On 2nd June, 1939, I received a letter from the late W. E. Vine asking if I would be able and willing to help him in reading the proofs of his *Expository Dictionary of New Testament Words*. A Cambridge clergyman, who had helped in this way with Volume I (which had just appeared) found himself unable to do the same for the succeeding volumes. I reckoned that my acceptance of Mr Vine's invitation would be a help to me as well as to him; so I agreed, and I am glad to this day that I did so. In the event I read the typescript before it went to the printer as well as the proofs as sets of them came every three weeks or so, and the accurate attention to the New Testament text which this work involved greatly increased my detailed acquaintance with it. Mr Vine was a good classical scholar and his *Expository Dictionary* (1939-41) embodied the fruit of nearly a lifetime's study of the Greek New Testament. Nothing on this level of scholarship had appeared in Brethren circles since William Kelly's death; Roy Coad rightly says that it was 'as useful a work as any produced by Brethren since G. V. Wigram had sponsored the *Englishman's Concordances* to the Greek and Hebrew texts of the Bible a century before'.[1] I wrote an appreciation of

Volume I which, at the publishers' request, was (in a slightly expanded form) printed as a foreword to Volume II, and I was asked to write forewords to Volumes III and IV also.

Since then I have written forewords for many other books, but mostly for younger writers less well known than myself. Another senior author for whom I was asked to do the same service as for Mr Vine was G. H. Lang. By the end of 1939 Mr Lang had completed his *Histories and Prophecies of Daniel* and had it accepted by a publisher. It had just been set up in type when the publisher went bankrupt. Oliphants (publishers of Mr Vine's *Expository Dictionary*) showed an interest in it and asked me for an opinion. When I sent it in, they asked that it should be adapted as a foreword, and as such it appeared when the book was published by them in 1940. Five years later I similarly provided a foreword for his commentary on Revelation — to find, when it was published, that he had added a clause to it. (Practitioners of the higher criticism who have access to the work are invited to identify the added clause!)

Now here is a curious thing. I found a greater tendency among my brethren to suspect me of sympathy with Mr Lang's eschatology because I wrote forewords to these two volumes of his than to suspect me of sympathy with Mr Vine's eschatology because I wrote forewords to three of *his* volumes. I wonder why? (In fact, my eschatological understanding differs from both of theirs.)

Another work on which I assisted a senior author was the second edition of Alexander Souter's *Novum Testamentum Graece*. The first edition was published in 1910. The Greek text was that presumed to underlie the Revisers' New Testament of 1881; Souter's contribution was the compiling of a critical apparatus which was printed at the foot of the page. The access of knowledge over the thirty-five years which had elapsed since the first edition appeared made it necessary for the critical apparatus to be brought up to date. Reading the proofs of the revised apparatus meant a further deepening of my New Testament education. The proof reader must share the responsibility for failure to correct obvious slips: one such slip is the statement (in Latin) on p. ix that 86 folios of Papyrus 46 (the Chester Beatty Pauline papyrus) are missing out of a total of 104; in fact, 86 folios *survive* out of the original 104. To have let this pass rather detracts from the *summa doctrina diligentiaque* with which the learned editor credited his former pupil in his Latin preface to the second edition.

But the main stimulus to my New Testament study in those years was provided, as I have indicated already, by the Biblical Research Committee set up by the IVF in 1938. The primary purpose of the formation of this Committee was to do something to roll away the reproach of anti-intellectualism, if not outright obscurantism, which had for too long been attached to English evangelicalism. Few of us on the Committee could claim much in the way of theological expertise, but we saw what had to be done. We formed a wider group of interested men and women which was called the Tyndale Fellowship for Biblical Research; we organized annual Tyndale Lectures in Old and New Testament and convened conferences, summer schools and study groups.

In July 1941, a week or two after Hitler's invasion of Russia, a conference was held at Kingham Hill School, Oxfordshire, to plan strategy. The leader of the conference was the Rev. G. T. Manley, a former mathematical don and a veteran missionary statesman; other senior friends present included Dr D. Martyn Lloyd-Jones and Professor Donald Maclean of the Free Church College, Edinburgh. But most of the participants were more or less of my own age-group: I recall W. J. Martin (whom I have mentioned already), John Wenham, Stafford Wright, Geoffrey Bromiley, Stuart Barton Babbage, David Broughton Knox (now Principal of Moore Theological College, Sydney) and the late Alan Stibbs (Vice-Principal of Oak Hill Theological College, London). It was at this conference that I was invited to join the Biblical Research Committee: my name, as I learned later, had been mentioned at one of the Committee's early meetings in 1938; it was wisely decided, however, 'that this gentleman's name should be kept on the list of those in whom the Committee is definitely interested, but that for the present no action should be taken on the suggestion to invite him . . .'! At the Kingham Hill conference the Committee had an opportunity to see and hear me, and decided that I was reasonably harmless. In any case, I had already begun my commentary on Acts at the Committee's instigation and brought a sample of my work to the conference.

One by-product of the conference was that the IVF was presented with *The Evangelical Quarterly* by Professor Maclean, its editor and joint-founder. In consequence my association with it began, at first on a very modest scale — but *The Evangelical Quarterly* must in due course receive fuller mention. In addition to resolutions to hold an annual summer school and make provision for two annual lectures (the Tyndale Lectures in the Old and New Testaments), the conference decided to take preliminary steps to produce a one-volume Bible dictionary and — a specially momentous decision — to secure a residential centre and library for Biblical research. The dictionary did not appear until 1962; the residential centre — Tyndale House, Cambridge — was secured in September 1944 and dedicated in January 1945. Before the acquisition of Tyndale House we held our summer schools and other meetings in Oxford or Cambridge colleges. Early in January 1944, we held a winter meeting in Trinity College, Cambridge, and a distinguished German guest, Dr Franz Hildebrandt, looked in on us at one of our sessions. His reactions have been placed on permanent record.

In 1943 Charles Raven, Master of Christ's College, Cambridge, published a study of Romans 1-8 entitled *Good News from God*. Dr Hildebrandt, Lutheran pastor and refugee from Germany, and a warm friend of Professor Raven, was so shocked by what he considered to be a travesty of the good news set forth in Romans that he composed a reply, based on 1 John, entitled *This is the Message* (1944). The successive chapters of this work took the form of dated letters addressed to 'My dear Charles'. Chapter 4, dated 6th

123

January, 1944, begins with a description of the session of our meeting which he had attended, at which the speaker, 'one of the chief apostles of continental theology in this country', answered questions 'with a dose of cynicism hardly less infuriating than the sweet soft patronizing voice near the chair which never failed to come to his support' — which led Dr Hildebrandt to leave with the reflection that it is written 'ye are the salt of the earth' and neither 'the pepper' nor 'the sugar' and with the conviction that he 'would rather err with Charles Raven than be saved with X, Y, Z' (p. 42). It can now be revealed (as they say) that 'the pepper' was G. T. Thomson from Edinburgh and 'the sugar' J. A. G. Ainley. We imported Professor Thomson to teach some Reformed theology to our English constituency, but his warmest admirers (of whom I was one) would readily admit that certain of his ways took some getting used to! But cynicism was a wrong diagnosis.

In the earlier days of the Tyndale Fellowship we were glad of the help of established senior scholars who held public appointments, as Professor Thomson did. But we were able also to enlist the interest and collaboration of one or two others from private life. I think in particular of two elderly Greek scholars of 'independent means' — among the last survivors, surely, of that once estimable class of gentlemen. These were E. K. Simpson, an Independent layman, and H. P. V. Nunn, an Anglican clergyman (both bachelors).

Mr Simpson, an Oxford graduate, was a keen student of the vocabulary of the Greek New Testament, and made several contributions of great value in this field of study, including an article on 'Vettius Valens and the New Testament' in *The Evangelical Quarterly* for 1930 and his Tyndale New Testament Lecture for 1944, *Words Worth Weighing in the Greek New Testament*. One reviewer of the latter work remarked that it sent the reader to his English dictionary as often as to his Greek one — a reference to Mr Simpson's distinctive and elegant English style, which drew freely on words and phrases borrowed from his well-loved Puritan classics. His retiring temperament kept him from receiving the public recognition which might otherwise have been his. For two years he occupied the post of Lecturer in New Testament Greek in the Free Church College, Edinburgh, during the last illness of Professor J. R. Mackay (co-founder of *The Evangelical Quarterly*). Lectures on Ephesians which he gave during that period later formed the basis of his exposition of that epistle in the *New International Commentary on the New Testament* (1957). His most substantial literary work was his commentary on the Greek text of *The Pastoral Epistles*, published by the Tyndale Press in 1954. The scholarship of this commentary won ready admiration and respect from critical scholars whose position on the authorship of these three epistles Mr Simpson undertook to overthrow on lexical grounds. Dr Vincent Taylor, for example, found its 'learned and careful study of words . . . very valuable, especially his references to classical equivalents. Modern students will often disagree . . . but his opinions are always worthy of study, particularly his treatment of the "ransom-passage" in 1 Timothy 2: 4 and his "Note on the meaning of *huper* in certain contexts" . . . The commentary is one that no close student of the Pastoral Epistles can afford to miss'.[2] The style of Mr Simpson's more polemical passages moved Dr Taylor to describe the work as 'this swashbuckling and entertaining commentary' — a description well justified by the published work, but oddly inconsonant with the author's self-deprecating and almost timid personality and his high-pitched, quavering voice. For the closing years preceding his death in March 1961 Mr Simpson's eyesight became so enfeebled that further literary activity became impossible for him.

Mr Nunn, a Cambridge graduate, was best known to successive generations of theological students for his *Elements of New Testament Greek* (Cambridge University Press). I think it was John Wenham who first put him in touch with the Tyndale Fellowship; John had some correspondence with him regarding his *Elements* (and in fact that manual has now been superseded by John Wenham's own work with the same title).

In earlier days Mr Nunn had lectured in St. Aidan's College, Birkenhead, but gave that work up because of indifferent health and led a retired life in Stockport. Despite his indifferent health he lived to a good old age. He did much good in a quiet way by giving free tuition to promising boys whose financial circumstances would otherwise have hindered them from going on to higher education. Some of these fully justified the time and care he devoted to them. He was specially interested in the authorship of the Fourth Gospel; in 1927 he wrote a scholarly little book entitled *The Son of Zebedee,* to which William Temple contributed a foreword. His *What is Modernism?* (1932) took issue with what he saw as the influence in England of the French School of Alfred Loisy and others. (The fact that the article on 'John, Gospel of' in the eleventh edition of the *Encyclopedia Britannica* [1911] was written by Baron Friedrich von Hügel may suggest that he had a point there.) His association with the Tyndale Fellowship gave him an opportunity for the fruitful use of his gifts. He wrote several articles for *The Evangelical Quarterly,* and in 1946 the Tyndale Press published a monograph of his on *The Fourth Gospel: An Outline of the Problems and Evidence.* His last work, *The Authorship of the Fourth Gospel* (1952) — for which I wrote a short foreword (as also for E. K. Simpson on *The Pastoral Epistles*) — dealt mainly with the external and partly with the internal evidence. Unfortunately (perhaps in part because of his health problems) he could not resist treating writers of different views from his own with a peevish sarcasm which, together with a certain stylistic heaviness, tended to put readers off. He died at the beginning of 1962.

Tyndale House — which, as I have said, was dedicated as a residential library for Biblical research at the beginning of 1945 — was a most exciting enterprise. It is a large house standing in spacious grounds in Selwyn Gardens, Cambridge. The grounds were commodious enough to make room, after some years, for a separate library building and a separate residence for the warden: but at first the warden and his family lived in the house itself and the library was accommodated in what is now the dining room (with overflows in adjacent rooms). The acquisition of the house and foundation of the library were made possible by the farsighted generosity of the late Sir John Laing. His name, at his own desire, was not divulged at the time — but any visitor to Tyndale House who cared to inspect the Latin inscription on the foundation stone of the library building might note the identity of the person who laid that stone in place and draw such conclusions as he pleased.[3] The library has justly attained international renown; it can boast the possession of some rare publications which are absent even from the holdings of its gigantic neighbour — Cambridge University Library. Tyndale House has been for over thirty years now the visible headquarters on earth of the Tyndale Fellowship.

Those who remember the Tyndale Fellowship in its first beginnings have ample cause for wondering gratitude to God as they see how the aspirations of the original Biblical Research Committee have been fulfilled. Today, in the British universities alone, there are between twenty-five and thirty teachers of biblical and related studies who are associated with the Tyndale Fellowship. They owe their university positions, of course, not to their evangelical faith but to their ability to compete with others in the open academic market. This is something which our friends in some other countries, notably in the United States, find it difficult to understand. Some of those friends have the idea that a known attachment to the evangelical faith tends to be a handicap to appointment or advancement in the field of secular education. Perhaps it is a consolation to some of them to think so, but wherever academic freedom is a reality and not a matter of lip-service, a man or woman's personal faith or church connexion should be neither a handicap nor an asset, any more than one's political affiliation.

In addition to those in university teaching posts, one might think of many more similarly placed in theological colleges and colleges of education throughout Great Britain and Ireland, not to speak of others in universities, colleges and seminaries in other lands. If ever there was any substance in the idea that evangelical Christians were afraid of Biblical and theological scholarship, it has long since been given its deathblow. When, back in 1943, I edited for publication by the Inter-Varsity Press *Some Notes on the Gospels* by D. M. McIntyre (late Principal of the Glasgow Bible Training Institute), the review in *Theology* (July 1944) by R. H. Fuller described Dr McIntyre's conclusions as 'generally similar to those of Conservative critics before 1914' but welcomed, with what I interpreted as pleasant surprise, 'this readiness of the IVF to discuss critical problems'. The *Expository Times* (April 1944) was more forthcoming: it devoted over two appreciative editorial columns to the little book, discerning in it 'both a grasp of the essential problems of New Testament study and also an independence of judgment that throw a clear light on the whole situation out of which the Gospels arose'. Today it would not be necessary to republish the writings of a deceased scholar in order to fill a gap in the theological student's equipment, but that was the situation then. (For myself, the experience of editing the writings of a deceased scholar, both on that occasion and once or twice subsequently, has given me, I like to think, some insight into the practical solution of certain problems of Biblical criticism.)

A comparison of the IVF *New Bible Commentary* of 1953 (edited by Francis Davidson, Principal of the Glasgow Bible Training Institute, who died on the eve of publication) with *The New Bible Commentary Revised* which was published in 1970 provides a good idea of the new resources in evangelical manpower which the intervening years produced. Although the first edition did not appear until 1953, work on it began about 1945, and contributors had to be raked together from all available quarters. Some were specialists in the areas they dealt with (e.g. E. J. Young on Daniel) but many were not. Even so, promise of what was to come was evident in the inclusion among the contributors of such younger scholars as Donald Robinson (now Bishop in Parramatta, N.S.W.) and Andrew Walls (now Professor of Religious Studies in the University of Aberdeen).[4] In my copy of the first edition I find one or two cuttings of reviews. One is by T. W. Manson in the *Manchester Guardian* (23rd November, 1953): 'On critical questions the positions taken by the contributors are extremely conservative; and curiously enough, I have the impression that they are more unyielding in the Old Testament than the New.' I thought this last judgment was right, and I wrote to tell him why, in my opinion, this was so. (He found the reason I suggested to be 'a very convincing one'.) Geoffrey Lampe, in the *Church of England Newspaper* (12th February 1954), said: 'As we should expect, the Commentary is conservative in its handling of critical questions, but to those who know the IVF only through the rigidly fundamentalist opinions of some of its affiliated bodies, the liberalism (in the best sense of the word) of this book will come as a surprise.' He meant a pleasant suprise; an *unpleasant* surprise was reflected in a review in *Watching and Waiting* (1954, pp. 36 ff.), the writer of which felt 'under a disagreeable and painful necessity to refer to several features which to him are most disquieting', though he conceded that the work might be 'of real value to the discerning user'. The inference to be drawn from these varying assessments is that the Commentary was a reasonably sound piece of work.

Notes to Chapter 16
1. F. R. Coad *A History of the Brethren Movement* (Exeter|2|1976), p. 221. (See p. 295 with n. 2.)
2. *The Expository Times* 66 (1954-55), p. 76.
3. There is a photograph of this stone in Roy Coad *Laing: The Biography of Sir John W. Laing, C.B.E.* (London 1979), opposite p. 161. The inscription records the laying of the stone on 21st April 1956.
4. Some senior and highly respected scholars also figured among the contributors, such as Professor Daniel Lamont of Edinburgh. It is interesting to speculate why his introductory essay on 'Revelation and Inspiration' was displaced by one from a younger writer in the second printing of the first edition.

17

Some more books

While I was engaged in the activities mentioned in recent chapters, it was necessary not only to make use of whatever library facilities were available but also to build up a working collection of books for ready reference. Before my entry on wedded life I could buy books with a relatively carefree mind — not only in the biblical field, such as the first edition of the *Chester Beatty Biblical Papyri* in several volumes (1933 and following years), but more widely, such as the first public edition of T. E. Lawrence's *Seven Pillars of Wisdom* (1935). But the responsibilities of bringing up a family on a modest salary compelled more careful budgeting. Second-hand bookstores and publishers' remainder lists were valuable sources of inexpensive acquisitions, and the occasional review copy was most welcome. Not far from where we lived in Leeds there was a little man, Mr Loftus, who had a small second-hand bookstore on the ground floor of his house, but the books spread out from there and invaded most of the house, leaving precious little *Lebensraum* for himself and his wife. He seemed to sell books according to their size: a small book was threepence, a middle-sized one sixpence, a large one a shilling, while a folio might be priced at as much as half a crown. From him I bought (for threepence, I think). T. E.

Page's edition of the Greek text of Acts (1895): I acquired it, I see, on 19th December, 1939, and found its innate value to be out of all proportion to its size and price.

Downtown in Leeds there was another bookstore, Austick's, where I bought, during the war, the index volume of Schürer's *History of the Jewish People in the Time of Christ* (English translation, 1885-91). What had happened to its companion volumes no one knew. But when, some years after the war, T. & T. Clark reissued the work, they did not reissue the index volume, so I was glad indeed to have it when at last I procured a set of the reprinted volumes for myself. (Now a completely revised and up-to-date English edition of this work is being produced[1] — a great boon to the student of Judaism and Christianity in the three centuries from the Maccabees to Bar-kokhba.)

When I went to St. Andrews in 1939 to sit the examination for the Crombie Scholarship, one paper in which was devoted to Pentateuchal criticism, I picked up from a second-hand bookstall two volumes which gave a different point of view on that subject from that presented in the standard textbooks: W. L. Baxter's *Sanctuary and Sacrifice: A Reply to Wellhausen* (1895) and James Orr's *The Problem of the Old Testament* (1908).

Visits to Cambridge, Oxford and Edinburgh afforded welcome opportunities of augmenting my collection. I was able to complete my holdings of the works of Ramsay, Harnack and Deissmann. My holdings of Deissmann were completed in 1947 when Cecil Howley transferred to me a duplicate copy of *Light from the Ancient East* (together with one of Brown, Driver and Briggs' *Oxford Hebrew Lexicon*). I picked up everything I could find by James Rendel Harris, realizing as I did so that he became increasingly eccentric towards the end of his long life. Dalman's *Words of Jesus* (1902) and *Jesus-Jeshua* (1929) were added as they became accessible — the former second-hand, the latter remaindered. I found them intensely interesting because of the light they shed on the Aramaic background of the Gospels. I was able also to pick up remaindered copies of C. C. Torrey's *The*

Four Gospels (1933) and *Our Translated Gospels* (1936), which propounded the inadmissible theory that our Gospels as they stand are translations of Aramaic originals. Another work in this field is C. F. Burney's *The Aramaic Origin of the Fourth Gospel* (1922): my copy of this, bought in 1942, had belonged to an Oxford scholar, some of whose notes on separate sheets of paper were left inside the volume, together with the offprint of a review of the work by G. R. Driver, inscribed by him to the owner. V. H. Stanton's *The Gospels as Historical Documents* (three volumes, 1903-20) were acquired in those years; Bishop Stephen Neill speaks of this work as 'a monument of patient and careful industry, which in my opinion has been undeservedly forgotten'.[2]

Another three-volume work is Eduard Meyer's *Ursprung und Anfänge des Christentums* ('Origin and Beginnings of Christianity', 1921-23). It is surprising that this important work has never been translated into English, when so many less deserving works have been translated. Meyer was Professor of Ancient History in the University of Berlin, who had made contributions of outstanding authority to the history of the ancient Near East and classical antiquity. When, against this background, he turned to consider the history of Christian beginnings, the result was, in the words of W. K. Lowther Clarke, 'a theological event of the first magnitude'.[3] Aware of his limitations in biblical and theological study, Meyer informs his readers that he equipped himself by reading the relevant German works of the ten preceding years, confident that whatever was of real importance for his subject must have found its way into them. (I remember how I once mentioned to Wilfred Knox, when my commentary on the Greek text of Acts was approaching completion, that it probably suffered because of my lack of acquaintance with recent theological — as compared with classical — publications. He smiled, and said that he considered that to be no great handicap!).

But as I was equipping myself for producing something on Acts in particular, and on the New Testament in general, there was no author whom I found more helpful than J. B.

Lightfoot. His Pauline commentaries, his volumes on the *Apostolic Fathers*, his *Biblical Essays*, found their way to my shelves. 'If I had my way', says Stephen Neill, 'at least five hundred pages of Lightfoot's *Apostolic Fathers* would be required reading for every theological student in his first year. I cannot imagine any better introduction to critical method, or a better preparation for facing some of the difficult problems of New Testament interpretation that yet remain unsolved.'[4] I applaud his sentiments, but in my experience first-year theological students would need to know more Greek than most of them do in order to read Lightfoot's *Apostolic Fathers* with understanding. Did Bishop Neill, I wonder, adopt this policy himself during his period of office as first Professor of Religious Studies in the University of Nairobi?

But there is one of Lightfoot's volumes to which I owe a special debt: his *Essays on the Work entitled 'Supernatural Religion'* (first published in the *Contemporary Review* between 1874 and 1877, and then in book form in 1889). The genesis of this work was an anonymous volume published in 1874 under the title *Supernatural Religion*. The author (W. R. Cassels) believed that religion would benefit if it were relieved of its supernatural, as opposed to its ethical, content, and tried to support this case by popularizing a German school of thought which represented the canonical Gospels as being late second-century productions and therefore devoid of historical trustworthiness. The circulation of this anonymous work was greatly promoted by a quite unfounded rumour that its author was a well-known bishop, whom natural caution allegedly prevented from revealing his identity. The real author was plainly not a master of the field of study in which he operated, and a scholar like Lightfoot might not have thought it worthwhile to turn aside to demolish him, but for the fact that he went out of his way to cast doubts on the good faith of Lightfoot's friend and colleague, B. F. Westcott. That was enough to stimulate Lightfoot to action, and a very conclusive demolition job he accomplished. *Supernatural Religion* was killed stone dead, but the *Essays* which achieved this end retain great positive value to the present day. They review the second-century evidence for the antiquity and circulation of the Gospels (evidence which could now be strengthened at various points in the light of later discoveries) and do so in such a way that the reader can still enjoy what Professor Kingsley Barrett calls 'the most amusing book of New Testament criticism I know'.[5] I myself found the book of great help when writing my own paperback on *The New Testament Documents*.

The German views which Cassels endeavoured, albeit ineptly, to popularize, were those put forth by F. C. Baur and his colleagues at the University of Tübingen. I made it my business to get hold of such of Baur's works as were accessible, notably the English translations of his *Paul, the Apostle of Jesus Christ* (1873-75) and *The Church History of the First Three Centuries* (1878). Baur was right in seeing how crucial for New Testament study were questions raised by historical criticism, and the questions he asked were the right questions. But it was Lightfoot who pointed the way to the right answers. The questions remain, but thanks to Lightfoot's once-for-all achievement they are seen to be first-century, not second-century, questions. The study of Gospel origins and relations, the inquiry into the interaction between Paul's Gentile mission and Jewish Christianity — these and other quests must be pursued within the context of the first century.

Another nineteenth-century continental writer whose works on early Christianity I read with interest was Ernest Renan. The most popular of these works — his *Life of Jesus* (1863) — was the least important of the series, but I found much of value in his *St. Paul* (1869) and *The Apostles* (1866), even if he is not in the same street as Baur. With even greater interest I studied two twentieth-century works: Joseph Klausner's *Jesus of Nazareth* (1929) and *From Jesus to Paul* (1944). Although Klausner was Professor of Modern Hebrew Literature in the Hebrew University of Jerusalem, he was also an authority on the history of Israel's messianic hope, and he more than any other writer introduced me to the

Jewish background of the New Testament writings. It was illuminating, too, to see our Lord and the apostles (especially Paul) through the eyes of a modern Zionist.

The study of J. W. Jack's *The Historic Christ* (1933), a remaindered copy of which I picked up during a holiday visit to Aberdeen, compelled me to get a hold of Robert Eisler's *The Messiah Jesus and John the Baptist* (1931), to which Jack's book was a reply — a monument of misplaced ingenuity, and yet a repository of miscellaneous learning for the reader who can distinguish fact from theory. I see that I made some reference to it in *The New Testament Documents* — probably because I had met some people who were unduly impressed by it. A remaindered copy of Eisler's *Enigma of the Fourth Gospel* (1938) was added to my shelves about the same time. I still find it more fascinating than most works of detective fiction — perhaps because of its affinities to that literary *genre*.

Other books on Jesus and the Gospels which I acquired during those years were Rudolf Otto's *The Kingdom of God and the Son of Man* (1943) and C. J. Cadoux's *Historic Mission of Jesus* (1941), both review copies; and R. H. Lightfoot's *History and Interpretation in the Gospels* (the Bampton Lectures for 1934) and *Locality and Doctrine in the Gospels* (1938), the last of these being remaindered. The two books by R. H. Lightfoot indicated lines along which Gospel studies were being pursued at that time in Germany. My introduction to Gospel criticism was effected by W. W. Holdsworth's *Gospel Origins* (1913), followed by B. H. Streeter's *The Four Gospels* (1924). E. B. Redlich's *Introduction to the Fourth Gospel* (1939), a very helpful book, introduced me to Johannine criticism, and his *Form Criticism* (1939) was my first textbook on the discipline denoted by its title. B. S. Easton's *Christ in the Gospels* (1930) was another short work which I read with profit. More substantial, and specially helpful, was William Manson's *Jesus the Messiah* (1943).

On Paul I borrowed from the library of the Hostel of the Resurrection in Leeds two volumes by Wilfred Knox: *St.*

Paul and the Church of Jerusalem (1925) and *St. Paul and the Church of the Gentiles* (1939). Somehow or other I have never acquired a copy of either of these works for my own library. I did acquire Kirsopp Lake's *The Earlier Epistles of St. Paul* (1911) and G. S. Duncan's *St. Paul's Ephesian Ministry* (1929), also the first two volumes of Lake and Foakes-Jackson's *The Beginnings of Christianity* (1921-33), a five-volume work on Acts which had been familiar to me from my Cambridge days. In recent years I was able to acquire the fourth and fifth volumes, which were reprinted by the Baker Book House of Grand Rapids in 1965. More recently they have reprinted the third volume, J. H. Ropes's unsurpassed study of *The Text of Acts* (1926). C. J. Cadoux's *Ancient Smyrna* (1938) stood for long on the remainder shelves of a Leeds bookshop; its price was gradually reduced from 25 shillings to 5 shillings, and then I bought it. When the library of the defunct Leeds Clergy School was handed over to the University Library, duplicate copies were offered gratis to any member of the staff who was willing to take them away; one which I secured at that time was B. F. Westcott's commentary on Hebrews (1889).

Two four-volume reference works which I bought second-hand at a ridiculously low price in those days were Smith's *Dictionary of Christian Biography* (covering the first eight centuries AD) and Cheyne and Black's *Encyclopaedia Biblica*. The value of the latter work, published towards the end of the nineteenth century, was greatly impaired because T. K. Cheyne, the principal editor, became increasingly unbalanced during the period of its production — a fact which not only affected his own articles in the last two volumes but those of other contributors, for he persisted in editing and amplifying them in the interests of his 'Jerahmeelite' theory.[6] In later years I have had to warn students against accepting his articles uncritically; I first realized the necessity of this when a girl in Sheffield submitted to me an essay on King Saul which was an attempt to summarize Cheyne's article under that heading.

Nor must I omit books given to me by friends: Mrs A. S. Lewis's edition of the *Old Syriac Gospels* (1910), for example, which I received from W. E. Vine, and a volume presented in 1863 to Thomas Newberry by some of his admirers in London, containing a transcription of the Greek New Testament text of *Codex Sinaiticus,* and annotated in Newberry's hand. This volume I received from G. H. Lang, who sent me quite a number of books when he left his large house at Walsham-le-Willows in 1945 for a smaller one at Wimborne. On the fly-leaf of this particulur volume he wrote an inscription to me followed by the admonition (in Greek): 'O Timothy, guard the deposit' (1 Tim. 6: 20). I suspect I have *not* guarded the specific deposit that he had in mind; but then, I never undertook to guard it.

Among other volumes once owned by very important people which have come into my possession is a copy of *The Hebrew Language,* by Henry Craik, inscribed 'Henry Groves with much love from his affectionate mother, Harriet Groves'[7] — a birthday present dated 27th November, 1860 (the year in which the book was published).

Notes to Chapter 17

1. This new edition is revised and edited by Geza Vermes and Fergus Millar, under the organizing editorship of Matthew Black; the first two of the three projected volumes were published in 1973 and 1979 (by T. & T. Clark, Edinburgh, publishers of the first English version).

2. *The Interpretation of the New Testament, 1861-1961* (Oxford 1964), p. 120.

3. *New Testament Problems* (London 1929), p. 118.

4. *The Interpretation of the New Testament,* p. 57.

5. 'Joseph Barber Lightfoot' *The Durham University Journal* 64 (1971-72), p. 195. On p. 197 Professor Barrett suggests that this work, rather than *The Apostolic Fathers,* might well be recommended reading for first-year theological students.

6. The theory that the Old Testament is mostly concerned with the fortunes not of the nation of Israel but of the Jerahmeelites, a desert tribe of the southern Negev mentioned in 1 Samuel 27: 10; 30: 29. In the interests of this theory the Hebrew text had to be emended out of recognition. It is sad that, when a scholar suffers such intellectual deterioration, publishers can be found to collaborate with him in destroying his reputation. Cheyne's commentary on *The Book of Psalms,* published in 1888, is a fine work of linguistic and exegetical learning and Christian sensitivity; the revision of it which appeared in 1904 was a disaster, and it is a shame that it was ever published.

7. Actually, his step-mother.

18

Biblical teaching in the University of Sheffield

As my time in Leeds went on, the fact that I was devoting more and more of my extramural study to biblical matters meant that my prospects of advancement in the classical field were diminishing. After the end of the war several vacancies occurred in senior Greek and Latin posts in a number of universities (the previous incumbents having had their period of office extended 'for the duration'), but these went, as was just, to men and women whose studies were concentrated along the main roads of classical research. On the other hand, university posts in the biblical field were fewer, and were likely to be filled by candidates who had completed the regular biblical and theological curriculum.

One day in the spring of 1947 I was on my way to deliver a morning lecture when I met a colleague who asked me if I had seen an advertisement in *The Times Literary Supplement,* announcing that the University of Sheffield was instituting a new Department of Biblical History and Literature in the Faculty of Arts and was inviting candidates to apply for the post of Senior Lecturer in charge of this department. I had not seen the advertisement, but looked at it in the Senior Common Room and decided to apply for the post. After a few weeks I was invited to attend for interview,

138

and found that two other men (both, as it happened, Presbyterian ministers) had been similarly invited. When the three of us had been interviewed separately, I was called back to meet the interviewing committee and was told by the Vice-Chancellor, who was in the chair, that they had decided to offer me the post. I accepted it with gratitude and alacrity.

I had the idea then, and nothing that I learned subsequently made me change my mind, that one reason why I was preferred over my two fellow-candidates was that I was a layman. At that time there was a strong anti-clerical sentiment in influential quarters in the University of Sheffield. Some members of the university, I gathered, were not too happy about the institution of the new department, but once that had been decided upon, they made up their minds that it should not provide a bridgehead for any ecclesiastical authority. I wondered idly if this had anything to do with the fact that no Anglican was short-listed for the post; but I have no idea if any Anglicans actually applied for it (although statistical probability would suggest that some did). The healthy policy of confidentiality in such matters means that even successful candidates cannot know why they were chosen; still less can unsuccessful candidates know why they were passed over. This is worth saying, for I have sometimes known unsuccessful candidates explaining confidently why, despite their undoubted merits, they were not appointed; and, where I have had inside information, they have always been wrong. Let me add that the anti-clerical bias of which I have spoken is happily a thing of the past in the University of Sheffield: my successor there from 1967 to his retirement in 1979, Professor James Atkinson, is a well-known churchman and canon-theologian; and the present occupant of the chair, Dr John Rogerson, is also an Anglican clergyman (and, what is more important in my eyes, a former pupil of mine, from my earlier Manchester days).

While this was taking place, the University of Leeds was taking steps to expand its theological department and instituted two new lectureships — one in New Testament

Studies and one in Church History and Doctrine. I sat on the committee which dealt with both these appointments. The man appointed to the New Testament post was Dr Matthew Black (subsequently Principal of St. Mary's College, St. Andrews). Leeds was fortunate to secure him, but it could not hold him for long, because higher things were in store for him north of the border. However, the appointment of a full-time New Testament expert would have meant that the marginal teaching in this subject which I had been giving was no longer required. My successor in Leeds was a former student, Miss Olwen Parry, who had taken classical honours with us and then gone on to Cambridge to distinguish herself in the Classical Tripos there. When I tendered my resignation she had just completed her Cambridge post and was ready to fill the vacant place, which she has adorned ever since.

As for us, we moved to Sheffield, and stayed there for twelve years. We were able to find a house which suited us in every way, and was conveniently accessible both to the university and to the schools in which our son and daughter were enrolled.

The advertisement announcing the Sheffield vacancy described the teaching to be given in the new department as 'non-doctrinal'. I tried, for my private amusement, to turn the concept of 'non-doctrinal teaching' into Latin, with absurd results. What was meant, of course, was that the teaching should be marked by scholarly objectivity, as befitted teaching in a university department, and that it should be free from theological or sectarian bias. It would not have occurred to me that Biblical History and Literature could be taught otherwise in an academic context; I took it for granted that my methods should be those which I had followed thus far in teaching the history and literature of ancient Greece and Rome. But the way this self-evident requirement was expressed moved my former Edinburgh colleague, P. B. R. Forbes (who had a nice gift for satirical composition), to send me the following lines, specially written for the new post:

HYMN
FOR A SCHOOL OF BIBLICAL STUDIES IN A SECULAR UNIVERSITY
(2 Timothy 4: 3)

Come, all ye sons of Science,
That magic name of awe,
And Medicine, and Music,
And Arts (poor thing), and Law;

Here shall we speak of gospels
That to your peace belong,
And faith that hath moved mountains
And filled men's mouths with song.

Fear not ye be converted:
The University
For truth has strictly ordered
No bias here shall be;

Here shall we hold the balance
That weighs the creeds divine
In scales that may not falter
Nor thus, nor thus, incline:

That so, with faith unfaithful,
We tread the narrow way —
Of truth (but not too much truth) —
That lies 'twixt Yea and Nay.

This composition I framed and hung in my room so long as I taught in the University of Sheffield. (On moving to Manchester I kept it in a drawer: Manchester is as secular a university as Sheffield, but Manchester's tradition in biblical teaching had been established for more than half a century when I went there.)

When I started work at Sheffield in October 1947 I was warmly welcomed and made to feel at home at once. Some of my new colleagues were already known to me, such as the Professors of Latin (J. D. Craig) and Greek (Jonathan Tate). They were both committed Christian men: the former a Scottish Presbyterian, the latter an Irish Protestant by birth who from intellectual conviction had, together with his

141

wife, become a Roman Catholic. But it was not only from Christian colleagues that I received help and encouragement. The Dean of the Faculty of Arts at that time was the Professor of French, G. T. Clapton, who professed an atheistic brand of existential philosophy, but he gave me all the advice and assistance which the Dean of a Faculty could give. He and others likeminded might have had initial misgivings about the institution of a biblical department, but when once it was instituted and filled, they, with their colleagues, determined that it should be as academically strong a department as was possible.

At the end of my first year, I was joined by a second member of the departmental teaching staff. This was Dr Aileen Guilding, an outstanding Oxford graduate in theology, whose special field of study was the Jewish synagogue lectionary in use at the beginning of the Christian era and its influence on the order of events in the Gospel of John. This was the subject of her *magnum opus* which appeared some years later: *The Fourth Gospel and Jewish Worship* (1960). During her time as lecturer in the department she married one of our mathematical colleagues. When I left Sheffield for Manchester in 1959 she was appointed to succeed me in the chair (the headship of the department had been upgraded to a professorship in 1955), but unfortunately ill health compelled her to resign after a few years.

For myself, the opportunity of devoting all my teaching hours as well as my hours of private study to Biblical History and Literature was enjoyable beyond words. If I may quote from the inaugural lecture which I delivered on being appointed Professor in the subject, 'to teach this subject of all subjects in the academic freedom which we value so highly, *nullius addictus iurare in verba magistri*,[1] is the most rewarding and exhilarating work in the world'.[2] I still think so. Thrice happy are those who spend their time doing what they would most wish to do in any case, and are handsomely paid for doing it. Such threefold happiness certainly carries with it threefold responsibility.

What is meant by the 'academic freedom' to which I have referred? It means that in the teaching and study of the Bible, as in the teaching and study of any other subject, one is not bound to follow any particular school of thought or promote any particular party line. It means that one's only commitment is to truth, that one is free to follow the evidence wherever it leads, in an atmosphere of free enquiry. There are biblical and theological schools which are instituted to foster one particular system of doctrine or to train men and women for the ministry of one particular denomination. It is natural and proper that such schools should include in their constitution an outline of beliefs or practices to which teachers, if not students, are expected to subscribe. When (as sometimes happens) a member of the faculty of such a school finds that he can no longer subscribe to its constitution, he will probably try to find a more congenial post elsewhere — unless indeed he can persuade the school to modify its constitution. I have friends and colleagues who teach in schools like these, and for the most part they do not appear to be conscious of any limitation on their freedom. But I am thankful that the lines have fallen to me in a university environment and not in that of a theological college.

There are some theological colleges which, in conformity with their constitution, will employ none but conservatives; there are others in which a conservative would be very unlikely to secure a teaching appointment. But in a British university it is quite irrelevant whether a man is conservative or liberal in theology; what matters is his scholarship and his ability to teach. (I know some people who think that even ability to teach is irrelevant, but I do not agree with them.) As I have said before, those members of the Tyndale Fellowship for Biblical Research who hold teaching posts in theological and related subjects in British universities do so simply because they can hold their own academically with scholars whose persuasion is less evangelical than theirs.

I am sometimes asked if I am aware of a tension between my academic study of the Bible and my approach to the Bible in personal or church life. I am bound to say that I am aware of no such tension. Throughout my career as a university teacher I have also discharged a teaching ministry in my local church and occasionally in other churches. Naturally, when I discharge a teaching ministry in church I avoid the technicalities of academic discourse and I apply the message of Scripture in a more practical way. But there is no conflict between my critical or exegetical activity in a university context and my Bible exposition in church; the former makes a substantial contribution to the latter. At the same time, membership in a local church, involvement in the activities of a worshipping community, helps the academic theologian to remember what his subject is all about, and keeps his studies properly 'earthed'. One constantly hears complaints nowadays, among Catholics and Protestants alike, of the widening gap between scholars' understanding of Scripture and the use made of it by 'ordinary' Christians. The gap would not be so wide, I am sure, if more scholars were to involve themselves in the day-to-day life of a local church and communicate the fruits of their scholarship to their fellow church members in a form which the latter could assimilate. I have known some distinguished scholars who did this, to their own enrichment as well as the enrichment of the others.

In fact, I suggest that this is what one would expect in what may be called the Open Brethren tradition. It is part of our heritage that we are encouraged to study the Bible for ourselves and reach our own conclusions about its teaching, without undue deference to one particular school of thought; we are encouraged, in other words, to cultivate a spirit of free enquiry. This free enquiry is the counterpart, in the religious realm, of that free enquiry which has been mentioned already as indispensable to academic life. The Christian acceptance of the Bible as God's word written does not in the least inhibit the unfettered study of its contents and setting; on the contrary, it acts as an incentive to their most detailed and comprehensive investigation.

So, when I took up this new work a few days before my

thirty-seventh birthday, I felt that the whole of my earlier life had been a preparation for this, and that this was the fulfilment. And in 'the whole of my earlier life' I include my twelve years' experience of teaching classics, and the more than twelve years' previous study of them at school and university. I can think of no better foundation than a classical education for the professional cultivation of biblical studies.

Notes to Chapter 18
1. 'Not bound by oath to the teaching of any master' (Horace, *Epistles* i. 1. 14).
2. *New Horizons in Biblical Studies* (Sheffield 1957), p. 1.

19
Church life in Sheffield

When we moved to Sheffield, towards the end of 1947, we transferred our church membership to Cemetery Road Meeting Hall in that city from Fenton Street in Leeds. The designation 'Cemetery Road Meeting Hall' had an uncompromising sound about it; one of its leading members used to speak of it as being in the 'dead centre' of Sheffield. On one occasion, when H. L. Ellison visited it for ministry, he suggested that we change its name to 'Resurrection Hall, Cemetery Road'.

The cemetery which gave the road its name boasted, among the illustrious dead buried there, the hymn-writer James Montgomery, who in his day was editor of the Sheffield *Iris*. A magnificent monument stood over his grave, inscribed with a number of his best known compositions, including the full text of 'Prayer is the soul's sincere desire'. The monument has in recent years been transferred to the precincts of Sheffield Cathedral — a symptom of these ecumenical days, for Montgomery was not an Anglican but a Moravian.

In due course, after we had left Sheffield, the name of the Meeting Hall was changed to Lansdowne Chapel. But before that its legal designation was not the Meeting Hall but the Meeting Room; in fact, some of the older members referred to

Peter Fyvie Bruce, 1874–1955

Mrs. P. F. Bruce, 1883–1965

Elgin High Street

Photo: Elgin Moray District Library, Local Studies Dept.

F. F. Bruce in Miskolc, Hungary, 1935   *Photo: Anni Roth*

King's College, Aberdeen

Edinburgh University

Wedding Day, 19 August 1936

The Parkinson Building of the University of Leeds

Photo: J. Allan Cash Ltd.

The Bridge of Sighs and River Cam, Cambridge

Photo: J. Allan Cash Ltd.

With Fellow-Members of the Scottish Students' Campaign Movement, at Fraserburgh, Easter 1931 (F.F.B. seated at right)

With a group of Honours Graduates in Biblical Studies, University of Manchester, July 1970

Photo: C. J. King

Sheffield University

Photo: J. Allan Cash Ltd

University Buildings, Manchester

Photo: J. Allan Cash Ltd

Betty, with Iain and Sheila, in front of our house in Sheffield, July 1959

With Betty at Regent College, Vancouver, July 1976   *Photo: D. L. N.*

it simply as 'The Room'. Those acquainted with variations of ecclesiastical idiom will recognize from this that it had been formerly an Exclusive place of worship. The particular group that met in it belonged to the Lowe party[1] — the party to which the late Harold St. John belonged at one time. Some of the older members could recall occasions when he came there as a visiting speaker back in his Exclusive days, and described how the place would be filled with people who came from near and far to hear him. But many years before we went to Sheffield the church there had moved from an exclusive to an open position — possibly about the same time as Mr St. John himself did so. During our time in Sheffield the elders of the church included such men of spiritual weight and sound judgment as Ronald Billington (who is still there), Frank Cave (now in Western Australia) and the late Spencer Thomas. For some years Spencer Thomas and I were closely associated as joint-secretaries of the church — so closely, in the eyes of some people, that another church secretary in a place a few miles from Sheffield, having occasion once to write separate letters to each of us, saved paper and postage by writing to me on one side of a sheet and to Spencer on the other side, directing me, when I had read my side, to pass the sheet on to Spencer so that he could read his side, 'as I understand you work closely together'.

A few relics of the church's exclusive past survived. For example, a number of the older members had received 'household baptism' in their infancy, whereas the dominant practice by our time had become baptism on personal confession of faith. But the two understandings of the proper subjects of baptism coexisted peacefully; there was no attempt at coercion of conscience on one side or the other. So it ought to be. I remember one occasion when a number of young girls were baptized in the hall on confession of faith, and one of our older ladies, nearer eighty than seventy, was so impressed that she felt she had missed something in her own youth (she had received 'household baptism' at an earlier age than she could remember) and asked that she

147

might be baptized by immersion. She was a frail little lady, and the elders were not inclined to take the responsibility of acceding to her request, but they had a difficult task persuading her that the Lord would accept the wish for the deed. (I am sure they were right in principle; I have never been an Anabaptist.)

Two very old little ladies, sisters, in their late eighties or early nineties, who belonged to our fellowship, lived in the village of Hathersage, some miles out, and were no longer able to attend the meetings. Occasionally on a Sunday afternoon a few brethren would go out and have a simple communion service with them. They stipulated, however, that at least one of the brethren should be accompanied by his wife, 'because of what the neighbours might think'. They sat stiffly together in their front room for the service, dressed as they had been for meetings half a century before, in hats, coats, outdoor shoes, gloves — and muffs. Christian friends in the village had offered to take them to services in a nearby church. 'But, of course, Mr Cave,' said the older of the two to one of our brethren, 'when one comes out of "system", one doesn't go back into it.' To which he felt like replying, 'Not at the age of ninety.' ('System' was their code-word for the mainstream denominations; in their case it had been Congregationalism, I believe.) But the influence of this dear lady's past came out quite spontaneously one day when she told us of a neighbour, a Christian lady, who had expressed great interest when told that the two sisters were to have a communion service in their home next Sunday. 'I was on the point of asking her to join us,' said she, 'but then I remembered what Mr So-and-so used to say: "I can't very well invite you, being only a guest myself".'

Another Exclusive relic at Cemetery Road was the continued use of *Hymns for the Little Flock*. For some reason the edition used was the 1903 edition, edited by T. H. Reynolds, who belonged to the Raven party. Why a former Lowe assembly should use the Ravenite edition no one seemed to know. In my schooldays a lady, representing some benevolent society, came once to give us a talk on life, and one thing she said stayed with me: 'Every day, do at least one thing you'd rather not do.' So, throughout our twelve years in Sheffield, at every communion service and every prayer meeting at Cemetery Road I did something I'd rather not have done, by using *Hymns for the Little Flock*. It taught me patience; it also provided me with opportunities for theological reflection, as I asked myself time and again, 'What was the reason for this change?' — apart from those changes necessitated by the alteration of 'I' to 'we'. For example, when 'When I survey the wondrous cross' is corrupted to 'When we survey the wondrous cross', a frightful piece of mangling occurs in the last stanza to provide a rhyme for its first line when it is changed to 'Were the whole realm of nature *ours*' — but why introduce a needless piece of mangling into the second stanza by changing its second line to 'Save in the death of Christ, our *Lord*', with consequent mutilation of line 4 for the sake of rhyme? (In so far as I can guess at the reason for the change, it was innocent, though certainly misguided. Once, in those days, I sat in an Oxford college chapel next to a Unitarian theologian, and we were asked to sing this hymn. My neighbour quite distinctly sang 'Christ, my Lord' although the printed text before us said 'Christ, my God' — but I don't think it was familiarity with the *Little Flock* collection that prompted *him* to make that emendation!)

On all such 'editing' of hymns John Wesley said the definitive word in his preface to *A Collection of Hymns for the Use of the People Called Methodists* when he assured those who reprinted hymns by his brother and himself that they were 'perfectly welcome to do so, provided they print them just as they are. But I desire they would not attempt to mend them; for they really are not able'. But the *Little Flock* editors were quite unable to keep their hands off even the hymns of John and Charles: consider, for example, the mess they made of 'Love divine, all loves excelling'.

When some of us from time to time suggested that we switch to a collection which didn't mutilate hymns so ruthlessly, we were told that we should stick to the *Little*

149

Flock because its wording was the only one our older people knew, and they would be put off by any change. That may have been so with some of our older people, but by no means with all. One of our older sisters, whom we came to know very well, could hardly contain her indignation when she talked about the corruptions of the original text of which it was so full. Of these, the corruption of 'When I survey the wondrous cross' was to her the 'head and front of the offending' (and I could not but agree with her). This lady was Miss Jessie Cocker, a retired headmistress, who was possessed of a vigorous personality and an independent mind. On the first occasion when we invited her to have Sunday afternoon tea with us, she told me that she had an old friend who was a former Professor of Oriental Languages. Naturally, I asked his name, and she replied, cautiously, 'S. H. Hooke' — waiting to see how I would react to the mention of such a heretical name (as it was esteemed in some quarters). When my reaction was reassuring, she spoke more freely. She had known Sam Hooke back in the early days when he too had belonged to the Lowe party (and even earlier, before the Raven cleavage). Like Harold St. John, Sam Hooke was in those days a welcome visitor to Cemetery Road; it was there, in fact, that he found his first wife, a fellow-student and close friend of Miss Cocker's. I knew some people, relatives of Miss Cocker's, who had actually been baptized in infancy by Sam Hooke. 'And I have no doubt', said Miss Cocker darkly to me, 'that you hold some queer ideas yourself, if the truth were known.' No doubt she was right. For several years I used to carry messages between her and Professor Hooke, when I met him at academic conferences. Not long after we left Sheffield she died at the age of ninety and I went back to Sheffield to conduct her funeral service. It was the happiest funeral I have ever attended; something of her own cheerful spirit seemed to be present. She bequeathed to me a Sumerian clay seal from Ur, which Sam Hooke had given to her many years before.

There were two 'Open' meetings in central Sheffield, and a few others in the city environs. The other central meeting,

150

now Fitzwilliam Chapel, had also at one time been an Exclusive company (of another connexion than Cemetery Road), and it also used a hymnbook in the *Little Flock* tradition, but the Lowe-Kelly edition,[2] *Hymns Selected and Revised in 1928.* I think perhaps that among some of the survivors from an earlier generation there was still a feeling of reserve between the two meetings stemming from the time when they belonged to two different connexions, but that was fast disappearing. Three of their brethren and three of ours formed an *ad hoc* committee which for some years organized such activities as a joint weekly Bible study and a yearly evangelistic tent campaign, to conduct which we invited such evangelists as Harold German and the late George Grant. The Yorkshire Tent and Bible Carriage Trust kindly put one of their tents at our disposal. On one occasion that comes to mind two senior members of the Trust (both long since departed this life) came to Sheffield to show fellowship with us by attending one of these tent meetings. A senior officer of the local unit of the Salvation Army was present that evening, and he was asked to give the opening prayer. One of the two members of the Trust, referring to this later in private conversation with me, said, 'We were grieved'. But of course they were men of Christian grace: although they were 'grieved' that a believer who did not 'follow with us' should be invited to lead in prayer, they would not have dreamed of causing any unpleasantness about it.

Another joint activity was the Sheffield Christian Rally, held on alternate Saturday evenings in a convenient place in the city centre. This had begun, I think, as a purely 'Brethren' enterprise, but by the time we came to Sheffield it had become more comprehensive, providing a meeting point for evangelical Christians of various traditions.

Then we had our seasonal conferences, which were as much a feature of the Sheffield area as of the Leeds area. Some of them were joint efforts, like the Sheffield and District Missionary Conference and the Sheffield and District Sunday School Teachers' Conference. But those for ministry were organized by local churches independently. It was sometimes suggested by brethren whose roots were not in the area, and who made inadequate allowance for local *amour propre*, that it would be a good thing to have a Sheffield and District Conference for Ministry instead of a multiplicity of small local conferences, or at least for us at Cemetery Road and our friends at Fitzwilliam Street to have a joint one instead of two separate ones. But such suggestions made no headway. And, in view of my own convictions about the autonomy of the local church, why should I find fault with the preference for a multiplicity of local conferences? For many Christians in the Sheffield area, they provided a very enjoyable way of spending their Saturdays throughout the summer.

One argument put forward by those who pressed for a united conference was that better speakers could be secured in this way. But I do not think that experience would support this argument. I recall one small company, about twelve miles from Sheffield, where the effective membership was half a dozen at most. It held an annual conference, and was able to secure well-known speakers. The leading brother, realizing wisely that chairmanship was not his gift, used to invite someone like Spencer Thomas or myself to go along and take the chair on this occasion. At that conference I have listened to ministry from Cecil Howley, Arnold Pickering and F. A. Tatford; and the only time I ever met or heard the late P. F. W. Parsons was when I shared that particular platform with him[3] (Spencer Thomas being in the chair). The leading brother — a rough diamond, but a real diamond — told me bluntly that his policy was: 'Get the best speakers, and pay them well.' (I hope this revelation does not embarrass my friends whose names I have just mentioned!)

My church associations in Sheffield and district were not confined to the circle of the people called Brethren; in particular, one Methodist society had me on its preaching plan for several years on end, right up to my departure from Sheffield. The last time I preached there, one elderly member presented me with a small steel knife, saying, 'When you use it, remember a fellow-believer.' It was very sharp: first time I used it, I cut my finger; but I remembered him gratefully all the same.

Notes to Chapter 19

1. The Lowe party, called after W. J. Lowe, separated in 1890 from the followers of F. E. Raven (see p. 19, n. 3) on the ground of the latter's alleged Apollinarianism (the teaching that in Christ the eternal Logos took the place which in other men is occupied by the human mind or spirit).

2. The Lowe-Kelly connexion was formed in 1926 by the reunion of the Lowe party with the followers of William Kelly, who had separated from the main body of Exclusive Brethren in 1881.

3. Characteristically, Mr Parsons told his hearers why they should not vote in local or national elections; for my part, I put some considerations before them, to be borne in mind 'whether you vote or not'.

20

Ministry here and there

The acceptance of preaching engagements can bring one into unexpected situations. I recall one of my Sheffield brethren telling me how he went to take a Methodist service one Sunday evening, and found himself invited to baptize an infant. (The society had formerly belonged to the Primitive Methodists, who took the line that anything a minister could do, a layman could do better.) Satisfying himself that no essential theological commitment was involved beyond what he was accustomed to at one of our own dedication services, apart from the application of water, my friend rose to the occasion nobly, as though he had been a practising paedobaptist all his life.

I have never been put on the spot in that way. I have found it mildly disconcerting, after accepting an engagement some months in advance, to be told nearer the time that the Sunday in question is 'Flower Sunday', and that an appropriate message will be expected. How does one preach a Flower Sunday sermon? 'Consider the lilies' provides a text, of course, and Sören Kierkegaard's treatise bearing the same title will provide a commentary on it, if preacher and hearers can accept his challenge. A harvest festival service can be taken in one's stride: I have always found 'Except a corn of wheat ...' to be an almost irresistible text for such an occasion.

Perhaps the oddest invitation I have ever received in this way came from the vicar of a Derbyshire parish who was my first Ph.D. student in Sheffield and for whom I sometimes preached. Towards the end of one year he wrote to ask me if I would preach for him on the last Sunday evening in January next — the sermon to be a commemorative one for King Charles the Martyr, on the Sunday nearest the anniversary of his death. Whatever sympathy I might feel for a fellow-Scot, sentenced to death by an English court in circumstances of doubtful legality, I did not consider that he would provide suitable subject-matter for a sermon, so I begged to be excused. I am reminded of another clergyman, a Reformation expert, who told me how he celebrated the anniversary of an important event in the life of Luther by preaching a sermon on that Reformer. At lunch-time in the rectory his young daughter said to him, with that logical severity of which young daughters are peculiarly capable, 'I thought you were supposed to preach about Jesus Christ.' No doubt his sermon on Luther did direct people to Jesus Christ (otherwise it would not have been a sermon on Luther); but the girl had a point.[1] For me, the execution at Whitehall in January 1649, would have afforded no point of contact with another execution, outside the wall of Jerusalem, over sixteen centuries earlier; and Christian preaching is essentially the proclamation of 'the word of the cross'.

One occasion which I remember with special pleasure was a Sunday evening when I went out from Sheffield to preach in Dronfield Baptist Church (between Sheffield and Chesterfield) and was asked to conduct the communion service which followed. This I did, but I was flanked by two deaconesses, one of whom gave thanks for the bread and the other for the cup. When I call them deaconesses, I do so because that was their official designation in the church; but it is a word that I do not care for. I prefer to use the term 'deacon' (or any appropriate synonym) in the common

155

gender, for men and women alike; and I think I could invoke apostolic precedent for my preference.

Another form of biblical teaching in which I engaged during my Sheffield years was under the auspices of the University Department of Extramural Studies. Shortly after World War II this department received a new and vigorous director in my namesake, Professor Maurice Bruce, who developed its activities widely. University departments of extramural studies exist to promote cultural interest in the general area in which the university is situated, and they provide courses of study in any subject catered for by the university, provided there is adequate local demand and support. For several winters on end I conducted such courses on biblical and related subjects, in Sheffield and its environment.

The historical background of the Old and New Testaments was one subject for which there was a recurrent demand. So was the history of the early church. The three works which were in due course combined in one volume under the title *The Spreading Flame* (1958) grew out of such extramural lecture-courses. Interest was shown, naturally, in the content of the Bible as well as in its background. I remember one well-attended course on the Epistle to the Hebrews, which I conducted jointly with the late Douglas Harrison, then Archdeacon of Sheffield and subsequently Dean of Bristol. I think those who attended the course found it specially interesting to have two students of Hebrews leading it, sometimes agreeing with each other and sometimes disagreeing. For myself it was a specially helpful experience, as I indicated some years later in the preface to my commentary on the epistle (1964).

But the subject which dwarfed all others in public interest from 1948 onwards, so far as the biblical field was concerned, was the Dead Sea Scrolls. I cannot begin to count the number of single lectures I gave on this subject to all sorts of audiences, under the auspices of the extramural department and otherwise. These lectures were usually illustrated by slides. Not having in those days visited Qumran, I probably gave the impression of being more knowledgeable than I really was when I showed slides of the area and its caves; however, when at last I was able to inspect the place, I realized with some relief that I had not seriously misled my audiences; the eyewitness descriptions on which I relied were lucid and accurate. No subject drew such large crowds. When I gave an illustrated lecture on it in the village school of Eyam, it seemed to me that the number present exceeded the population of Eyam.

One of the most helpful features of these lectures (as of all extramural lectures) was the half-hour of question and discussion that followed. People's questions can put the lecturer in the picture by revealing their presuppositions. In some places the village atheist would attend and ask what was intended to be a loaded question. For instance: 'Is there any reference to Jesus in the scrolls?' Answer: 'No' (momentary gleam of triumph in the questioner's eye) — 'because all the scrolls thus far published are pre-Christian in date, and so could not mention someone who was not yet born when they were written' (which was true at the time). I might have added that one scholar was quite sure that Jesus *was* mentioned in the scrolls — not by name, but as the 'Teacher of Righteousness'. I suppose that some sort of case could be made out for this unlikely hypothesis, but for the scholar who propounded it the hypothesis carried with it the even more unlikely corollary that the 'Wicked Priest' was Paul the apostle! (This scholar, Dr J. L. Teicher, maintained that the scrolls came from the Jewish-Christian community called the Ebionites, who looked on Paul with disfavour.)

Not only extramural classes but private groups wanted to hear about the scrolls. Within one week I was asked to speak on them to two groups in Sheffield: one a Catholic group and the other a Jewish group. Reckoning that there would be no overlapping between the two groups I gave them both what was to all intents and purposes the same talk. But, as it happened, one lady attended both, so I said to her the second time, 'Well, you heard the same talk twice.' 'Not quite the same,' said she; 'you spoke about "our Lord" to the Catholics but said "Jesus of Nazareth" to the Jews.' (A simple example of adapting one's language to one's audience.)

Then there were opportunities for ministry further afield. Those years saw the beginning of two annual residential conferences which have remained in being to the present day: the Young Men's Bible Teaching Conference and the Conference of Brethren which has now for several years met at Swanwick.

The Young Men's Bible Teaching Conference was first held at Weston-super-Mare in November, 1956. It arose out of a widespread conviction that there was a great need to provide younger men in the Brethren movement with systematic Bible teaching and to encourage them to exercise an expository ministry. The twofold aim of the conference was to instruct them in (i) the basic truths of Holy Scripture and (ii) expository preaching and homiletics. A syllabus of themes was carefully worked out so that, over a period of seven years, the main areas of biblical doctrine might be covered, if only in summary form. In the event, it was surprising how much solid teaching and study could be packed into a single weekend, from Friday evening to Sunday afternoon. A peak attendance of 382 was registered in 1963. From 1957 to 1968 the conference was held at Oxford; in 1969 it moved to King Alfred's College, Winchester, where it has met ever since; in 1971 a revolutionary step was taken when it went co-ed and thus ceased to be the young *men's* Bible Teaching Conference.

The conference owes an immeasurable debt to the late Melville Capper of Bristol. He was its first chairman and was confirmed in that office by his colleagues until ill health compelled him to resign. His enthusiasm, his friendliness, his spiritual insight, his uncompromising ethical standards, his biblical conservatism, his warm-hearted and all-embracing Christian love were just what the conference needed for its guidance and inspiration if it was not to move

158

along narrowly academic lines. Another moving spirit in its earlier years was Dr James Houston, then Fellow of Hartford College, Oxford, and from 1968 onward, first Principal of Regent College, Vancouver (of which he is now Chancellor). Could Regent College be claimed as in some degree one of the by-products of the Bible Teaching Conference? This at least can be said: the vision that led to the establishment of Regent College on its distinctive foundation in 1968 made its invaluable contribution to the inception and development of the Bible Teaching Conference in the preceding years. The Christian Brethren Research Fellowship could also be claimed to some extent as another by-product. More direct by-products were conferences founded with a similar purpose elsewhere in the United Kingdom and overseas.

But the most important effects of the conference should be sought in personal and church life, and these are much more difficult to assess — partly because throughout these years other influences have been at work within the same constituency, tending in the same direction. Much of the ethos of the old MSC conferences was carried over into the Bible Teaching Conference, which is not surprising, when one considers how much the membership of their committees overlapped.[2] The direction of the conference now lies in the hands of men who in 1956 were only just old enough (if that) to satisfy the minimum age qualification for attendance, and perhaps that is as good an index of its impact as any.

The Swanwick Conference began in 1953, in a London hotel, with a small get-together on prophetic interpretation; next year it moved to the conference centre at High Leigh, Hoddesdon, Hertfordshire, and in 1957 it moved again to the more capacious centre at The Hayes, Swanwick, Derbyshire, where it has met annually since then. I participated *in absentia* in the 1954 conference, which dealt with *The New Testament Church in the Present Day*: my paper on 'The Local Church in the New Testament' was read for me. I was able to attend the next year's conference, which dealt with *A New Testament Church in 1955*; my contribution was a

159

paper on 'The Church and its Ministers'. I think all who attended that conference would agree that its most memorable feature was the closing word from the late Harold St. John; it was the last time that most of us heard him speak in public.

The moving spirits in this conference in its early years were men of Mr St. John's generation: one thinks of Montague Goodman, Percy Ruoff and Theodore Wilson. For all their age, they were men who saw visions rather than men who dreamed dreams, and they fulfilled a ministry among the middle-aged comparable to that fulfilled by the Bible Teaching Conference among those in the 18 to 30 age-group. The reports of the conference in the earlier years contained not only the straight addresses but the questions and *obiter dicta* of the ensuing discussions, which may not have been a wise thing — partly because in the informality of the occasion questions or suggestions were voiced which were not intended for the record, and partly because the stenographer (who attended before tape-recorders became so common) could not always catch the precise wording of something that was said in a remote corner of the auditorium.

When more controversial subjects were discussed at these conferences, the reports did not go uncriticized — which was indeed a welcome and healthy feature. From as far away as New South Wales I received a painstaking critique of the 1955 report; but perhaps the report which occasioned most disquiet among some of our brethren was that of the 1964 conference on the subject of *Christian Unity*. The presence at that conference of an officer of the British Council of Churches did not pass unobserved, but his presence did not mean that a plot was afoot to bring the people called Brethren *en masse* into the BCC (as though such a thing were possible). Perhaps the conference influenced him more than he influenced the conference; at any rate, before many months passed he had left the employment of the BCC to serve the British and Foreign Bible Society. The sponsors of the conference, for their part, continue to practise the

160

principles of churchmanship which they held twenty years ago and more.

The Swanwick Conference of Brethren, unlike the Bible Teaching Conference, has not widened its membership to include sisters; instead, a parallel Women's Conference has been held for several years now, but for obvious reasons it can play no part in my reminiscences.

Notes to Chapter 20

1. Sermons have been preached on far less appropriate characters than Luther, or even King Charles. One Saturday in 1961 I travelled north from London in the same railway compartment as a well-known Methodist preacher. (I recognized him, but he did not know me.) On the Monday I asked my Methodist colleague, Gordon Rupp, 'Was So-and-so preaching in the Manchester area yesterday?' 'Yes,' he replied, in a tone of utter scorn, 'preaching on *Lady Chatterley's Lover*!'

2. See p. 119, n. 6.

21
Biblical and theological societies

I

The Sheffield Theological Society met in the University once a month throughout the winter and spring terms, but it was not just a university society. It catered for people in Sheffield and district who had theological interests, ministers and layfolk, and invited eminent speakers from various parts of the country. It was at one of its meetings, shortly after my coming to Sheffield, that I first met and heard Professor H. H. Rowley (of whom more anon). The then Bishop of Sheffield (Dr Leslie Hunter) was its president, and it had two chairmen, one an Anglican and one a Free Churchman. For most of my time in Sheffield Archdeacon Harrison was Anglican chairman; after some years, when a vacancy occurred in the Free Church chairmanship, I was elected to fill it. The Bishop usually took the chair when he was present: I recall that, during my first year in Sheffield, he very graciously took the chair for me when I addressed the society on current problems in the study of Acts. Several years later, he came along to a meeting of the society when the speaker was Dr Michael Ramsey (then Archbishop of York), but insisted in the interests of ecumenicity that the Free Church chairman (myself) should introduce him — which, of course, I gladly did. Dr Ramsey gave a first-rate lecture on the biblical doctrine of sacrifice. (Only a few weeks previously, he had given a lecture in Oxford at which his chairman was the late Cardinal Heenan, then Archbishop of Liverpool. In this innocent fact some serious people discerned a symptom of Romeward tendencies on Dr Ramsey's part. I do not think that any analogous inferences were drawn from his having me as his chairman in Sheffield — but then, his Sheffield lecture was not so well publicized.)

Sheffield Theological Society, I am glad to say, still flourishes healthily, as I was able to see for myself more recently when, after a lapse of several years, I revisited it to deliver a lecture on 'Paul and the Law of Moses'.

II

But there were other societies, more widely based, which came to play an important part in my life from 1947 onwards. These were societies bringing together people who shared an interest in some particular field of study. I had been, from 1935 onwards, a member of the Classical Association; I must now be one of its senior members. In the biblical field I have already mentioned the Tyndale Fellowship for Biblical Research. But two others now enter into the picture — the Society for Old Testament Study and the Society for New Testament Studies. I became a member of the former in 1947 and of the latter in 1948.

The Society for Old Testament Study is a British society, although it has associate members resident overseas and a limited number of honorary members — internationally outstanding figures in Old Testament scholarship. It was founded in 1917, with Principal W. H. Bennett as its first president and Professor Theodore Robinson as its secretary: other founding members were S. A. Cook, T. Witton Davies, R. H. Kennett and A. S. Peake. The basic qualification for membership is the ability to appreciate the Old Testament in

163

Hebrew — such ability to be attested by two sponsoring members of the Society. Early meetings of the Society were modest affairs: the archives contain a photograph of the group that met in Manchester in 1924 under the presidency of A. S. Peake: it comprised less than a dozen. The only survivor of that group, who joined the Society that year at an exceptionally tender age, is the gracious and talented Baroness Eileen de Ward, who was its president in 1975. The Society increased rapidly over the years: its membership had risen above 400 by 1967, when it celebrated its jubilee under the presidency of Dr Donald Coggan, then Archbishop of York (he had been a member since 1932, when he was Lecturer in Hebrew in Manchester University).

For myself, membership of the SOTS was a great help in many ways. In Sheffield I had to spend more than half my classroom time teaching Old Testament — a task for which my formal qualifications were slender indeed — and the proceedings of the SOTS made ample contributions to my Old Testament education. The first meeting of the Society which I attended was held in Manchester, in September, 1948; one of the papers read on that occasion was by Professor John Mauchline of Glasgow, entitled 'Some Observations upon Isaiah 13-23'.[1] Every second year in Sheffield I gave a course of lectures on Isaiah 1-39, and what I said on chapters 13-23 time after time owed much to that paper by Professor Mauchline (to whom, naturally, due acknowledgment was always made). Another illuminating paper was presented at the Society's meeting at Bangor, North Wales, in July 1949: it was read by a distinguished honorary member, Professor W. F. Albright, and dealt with the dating of early Hebrew poetry. In due course I was myself invited to read a paper before the Society, the subject being 'Eschatology in the Prophets of the Persian Period'; that was at its Norwich meeting in July 1951, under the presidency of Professor S. H. Hooke.

The most helpful and delightful aspect of membership of the SOTS, however, was the opportunity which it afforded of meeting scholars and getting to know them. In the early days quite a number of elder statesmen in the Old Testament field were around and attended meetings. There was Professor Theodore Robinson of Cardiff; I remembered hearing him deliver a guest lecture on the prophets in Aberdeen University twenty years before. By 1948 he had reached emeritus status: so had Professors Edward Robertson of Manchester (president in 1948), S. A. Cook of Cambridge, W. B. Stevenson of Glasgow, and S. H. Hooke of London. Among Catholic members the outstanding one was Fr Cuthbert Lattey, S.J., a singularly engaging soul, well known for his works on the Psalter, Daniel and other Old Testament books in The Westminster Version of the Sacred Scriptures. Anyone who was prone to use the term 'Jesuit' or one of its derivatives in a pejorative sense would be cured of any such propensity by getting to know Fr Lattey. Shortly after his death was announced in 1954 I found myself sharing a railway compartment with T. W. Manson, who was a very uncompromising Protestant. 'I see', said he, 'that Cuthbert Lattey has died.' 'Yes,' said I. 'I always felt', said he, 'that if I were to be burnt at the stake, Fr Lattey would find it convenient not to be present.'

Among the most active members of the Society in the later 1940s were two who are no longer with us: Sir Godfrey Driver (as he subsequently became) and Professor H. H. Rowley. There was one occasion when some younger members of the Society were trying to establish whether there was a 'pecking order' within its ranks, and, if so, how it was arranged. It was agreed that those two scholars came at the top: they could peck but not be pecked. 'Yes,' said Professor Bleddyn Roberts of Bangor: 'they're impeccable.' But it was not quite so: even they came in for a measure of criticism. 'Have you seen that last book of Rowley's?' said another elder statesman to me (referring to his Schweich Lectures, *From Joseph to Joshua*, 1950). 'There are two original ideas in it,' he went on. 'They're both wrong.' (But this was an unworthy disparagement of a valuable study.)

Professor Rowley was one of two senior members of the Society who showed me great kindness when I was an inexperienced newcomer to the realm of biblical teaching. He went out of his way to encourage me and to involve me in literary enterprises for which he had editorial responsiblity, such as the Society's annual *Book List*, the *Journal of Semitic Studies*, the second edition of Hastings' one-volume *Dictionary of the Bible* (1963) and of T. and T. Clark's *Companion to the Bible* (1963). He was an effective referee for me when the University of Sheffield was considering my promotion to professorial status in 1955, and I suspect that he was equally influential in my appointment to Manchester in 1959. As I have said before, the deliberations of committees charged with making recommendations for such appointments are confidential, but he was the senior member of the committee concerned with filling the Rylands Chair and he knew me far better than any other member of the committee did. His years of retirement, from 1959 onwards, were filled with activity, even towards the end, when he suffered from a painful and incurable disease. He acknowledged and accepted this state of affairs, but did not regard it as an excuse for inactivity or even unpunctuality. He replied to letters by return of post from his deathbed, as he had done all his life: the last letter I received from him, in September 1969, was written within three weeks of his death. Characteristically, it was written to help a younger scholar, whom our university was considering for promotion. Professor Rowley was in a position to provide supporting evidence which no one else could provide: he had read a work written by the scholar in question for a series which he edited, but as the work was not yet published, no one else had read it. He drove himself harder in scholarly productivity than any other man I have ever known, but he was never too busy to help a younger scholar. His personal faith was thoroughly evangelical: no wonder, for he was converted under the ministry of W. Y. Fullerton as a schoolboy in Leicester. When he became a theological student and was introduced to the current line on Pentateuchal criticism and the like, he consulted his spiritual advisers and was recommended to read James Orr's *Problem of the Old*

Testament (1906). He read it — and was forthwith convinced, 'against his own conservative predisposition', of the validity of the case which Dr Orr controverted! (This information he divulged in a review of the IVF *New Bible Handbook* of 1947.)[2]

The other senior member of the SOTS to whom I owe a special debt was Professor S. H. Hooke. He had been born and brought up among the Exclusive Brethren, and retained vivid memories of some of their early leaders. He could, for example, picture Lord Adalbert Cecil sitting in his parents' sitting-room knitting socks! He also remembered, as a boy, listening to J. N. Darby preaching — and incidentally chaffing a brother in the front row over his gold watch-guard. He recalled how bitterly his father wept the morning news came of Darby's passing. When the Raven division took place in 1890, the Hookes remained with the 'Lowe' party that objected to F. E. Raven's Apollinarianism.

Not until he was in his thirties and married did the opportunity come for him to embark on an undergraduate career. He became a member of Jesus College, Oxford, and gained all the academic honours that were open to him. A college magazine of those days contained the limerick:

> There is a disciple of Mott,
> Who looks like a don but is not;
>   He went in, when at Coll.,
>   For each prize and each schol.,
> And succeeded in bagging the lot.

During his Oxford days he broke with Exclusivism and joined the Church of England, being confirmed by Bishop Gore. But to the end of his days he gave evidence of the rock from which he was hewn — not least in his amazing mastery of the text of Scripture. In this respect there was little to choose between him and Harold St. John, with whom he maintained a warm friendship from their early days until Mr St. John's death in 1957.[3] He remained a layman throughout his life, but this did not prevent his serving as Examining

167

Chaplain to his friend Neville Gorton when the latter was Bishop of Coventry.

From Oxford he went in 1914 to Toronto as Professor of Oriental Languages, and later (1931-45) he occupied the Samuel Davidson Chair of Old Testament Studies in the University of London. Retirement meant no diminution of his activity; from 1956 to 1961 he was Speaker's Lecturer in Biblical Studies at Oxford, at the age of 84 he served an energetic spell as visiting professor in the University of Ghana and four years later he lectured in the University of Rhodesia.

His intellectual powers remained unimpaired to the end, and his spiritual insight seemed to become more penetrating year by year. But at last his exceptional physical strength began to fail: 'I go on working', he wrote towards the end of 1966, 'though longing for the rest that remaineth for the people of God.' He died on 19th January, 1968, ten days short of his ninety-fourth birthday.

Professor Hooke too did his best to bring me into the main stream of biblical activity. He had his eye on me to succeed him in a vacation school of Bible study which he conducted every other year along with the late Dr W. R. Matthews, Dean of St. Paul's, and in 1952 he had me along to Oxford to take part in it; but that scheme came to nothing, for soon after that the ministry which had financed it decided to discontinue its support (reckoning, as Professor Hooke surmised, that he and the Dean of St. Paul's were now too senile to be entrusted with the provision of a refresher course for teachers!). Another enterprise in which he involved me more successfully was the editorship of the *Palestine Exploration Quarterly*, which was transferred from his shoulders to mine in 1957. More will be said about this later.

In two ways I was able to make some small repayment of my debt to Professor Hooke. One was by editing the *Festschrift* (entitled *Promise and Fulfilment*) which was presented to him on his ninetieth birthday in January 1964, and the other (rather oddly) was by being one of his two sponsors in 1950 for election to membership of the Society for New Testament Studies.

III

Whereas the SOTS is a British society, the SNTS has been an international body from its inception on the eve of World War II. It did not really get off the ground until after the end of the war, but then it provided a valuable meeting point for scholars from both sides of the dividing line, as well as from neutral countries. Its terms of membership are more stringent than those of the SOTS: they require such qualities as would be expected in someone holding a lecturing appointment in a university or theological college.

My election to SNTS membership took place (as I have said) in 1948, and I began attending the annual meetings from 1949 onwards. The early meetings were small and informal affairs; they were usually held in the common room of an Oxford or Cambridge college. When the ravages of war in Europe were adequately repaired, meetings were also held on the continent: we have met from time to time in Scandinavia, Holland, Belgium, France, Germany and Switzerland. The Society's first American meeting was held in 1972 in Claremont, California.

The first post-war president of the SNTS was Professor Johannes de Zwaan of Leiden (1947); other presidents in the early years included Professors G. S. Duncan of St. Andrews (1948), T. W. Manson of Manchester (1949), Henri Clavier of Strasbourg (1950), C. H. Dodd of Cambridge (1951), William Manson of Edinburgh (1952) and Rudolf Bultmann of Marburg (1953). I recall how Professor Bultmann, conducting morning prayers as president, expressed himself with the fervour and language of the apostle Paul: one could understand the German students' wisecrack that 'Scripture becomes the Word of God when Professor Bultmann enters the pulpit of Marburg University Chapel at 11 o'clock on Sunday morning'. One among many advantages of meeting such men in the flesh was to learn that you can never adequately judge a man by the books he writes. By reading a book one can judge the book, but to assess men and women as persons one must meet and know them as persons.

Other elder statesmen in the New Testament field who attended those early meetings included Professor R. H. Lightfoot of Oxford; E. G. Selwyn, Dean of Winchester; Henry J. Cadbury and Herbert G. Wood, both eminent members of the Society of Friends (the former American, the latter English); Oscar Cullmann, who for some time occupied three academic chairs concurrently — in Basel, Paris and New York (which involved an exceptional degree of commuting in the year). One scholar whom I do not remember seeing at any of our meetings was Vincent Taylor, although he was a highly esteemed member of the Society. His concern for his health forbade him to move far from his home base; he was absent even from our annual meeting in the year of his presidency (1954). That year we met in Marburg, and the presidential address (on 'The Origin of the Markan Passion Sayings') was read on behalf of the absent president by a fellow-Methodist, C. Kingsley Barrett of Durham. Mention of Professor Barrett leads me on to say that it is good to have regular opportunities of meeting one's own contemporaries who are concerned with biblical studies. From America and Japan, from Australia, Africa and India, we come together each summer, as well as from most of the European countries, on both sides of the Iron Curtain. This enables us to get to know one another and to know what projects others are working on. We no doubt get so used to this that we tend to take it for granted, but I remember G. S. Duncan remarking at an early meeting what a difference it would have made to him and his contemporaries if such opportunities had been available in their young days. It is specially good, too, to meet younger scholars who are beginning to make their names. In the SNTS and SOTS alike there was a time when I felt I did not know many of my fellow-members because I was such a new boy; now I feel I do not know many of them because *they* are such new boys. But so the torch of sacred learning is handed on from one generation to the next.

Notes to Chapter 21

1. The substance of that paper was included in Professor Mauchline's 'Torch' Commentary on *Isaiah 1-39* (London 1962).

2. *Baptist Quarterly* 12 (1947), pp. 286-291.

3. They were 'Harry' and 'Sammy' to each other. A tribute to Samuel Hooke is quoted from an early diary of Harold St. John's by Patricia St. John in her biography of her father: *Harold St. John* (Pickering & Inglis 1961), p. 24. There is a charming reminiscence of the two as young men in Fay Inchfawn's *Those Remembered Days* (London 1963), pp. 77 f.

22

Of making books

An old friend of mine, writing his autobiography, included a chapter which he entitled 'My Books and Battles'. The two were so interwoven that they could not be treated apart. The Lord, as he used to say, has many servants but all too few soldiers, and he wished to be a soldier as well as a servant. I can write about my books but not about my battles. My life thus far has been blessedly free from militant activity; probably (as my old friend would judge) I am not one of the Lord's soldiers. This is not because I am a natural conformist: on the contrary, I have held and expressed over the years a fair number of minority views — not to say unpopular views — in many fields. But I have never thought it my duty to press my views on others; if they differ from me, they could be right. Only, I claim for myself the liberty which I gladly allow them, to hold and express the views which I believe to be justified by the evidence. And such is the free atmosphere encouraged in the churches among which I have moved that I have rarely found it necessary to assert this claim: it has been granted to me as readily as I have granted it to others.

A sense of security with regard to the foundations of faith and life encourages a spirit of relaxation with regard to many other matters. I am sure that an inner insecurity is often responsible for the dogmatism with which some people defend positions which are by their nature incapable of conclusive proof: there may be à feeling that, if those positions are given up, the foundations are in danger. I am sure, too, that a similar insecurity is responsible for the reluctance which some people show to acknowledge a change of mind on matters about which they once expressed themselves publicly: they may fear that their reputation for consistency is imperilled if they do. If I hold today the same conviction about the equality of the angles at the base of an isosceles triangle as I did half a century ago, that is because the argument for it was conclusive then, and nothing that has come to light in the intervening years has modified it. But in the studies which have engaged my attention during the past half-century mathematical certainty is rarely possible. Fresh testimony comes to light; new experiences dictate a change of perspective; what once seemed to be the most probable conclusion may now be ruled out by additional evidence that has become available. Ultimately, the Christian's faith is in a Person: his confession is 'I know *whom* I have believed', not '. . . *what* I have believed'. He has learned, in Sir Herbert Butterfield's words, to 'hold to Christ, and for the rest be totally uncommitted'[1] (or, as I should have preferred to phrase it, to let his only total commitment be to Christ).

With this sense of liberty one can write freely — which is not the same thing as writing irresponsibly. A Christian will consider the probable effect of his words, whether spoken or written. He will respect editorial or publishing policy: if an editor or publisher finds himself unable to publish what he writes, he is free to offer it elsewhere. But in general I have found that the more objective a writer is, the less likely is he to give offence by what he writes. (I say 'in general'; there are some people in whose eyes objectivity is treason.) I have written, without disguising or distorting my views, for the *Bible League Quarterly* and the *Modern Churchman*, for *Precious Seed* and the *Heythrop Journal*, for the IVF *New*

173

Bible Dictionary and the *Interpreter's Dictionary of the Bible*, for the IVF *New Bible Commentary* and the second edition of *Peake's Commentary*. And in each of these pairs, no point of theological principle would have made what I wrote for the one publication unsuitable for the other.

One of my earliest exercises in writing for the public was a letter to the editor of a north-east weekly, the *Banffshire Journal*, whose correspondence columns featured for some weeks an epistolary debate on the nature of baptism. One of the correspondents signed himself 'Historicus', so I, taking issue with him, thought to go one better and signed myself 'Apostolicus'. About the same time, and more seriously, I composed for our school magazine of December 1927 a short biographical article on Professor James Cooper (1846-1922) — one of a series by various writers on distinguished former pupils of Elgin Academy. (Professor Cooper, a native of Moray, occupied the Chair of Ecclesiastical History in Glasgow University from 1898 until a few months before his death. He was a personage of note in the Church of Scotland in his day, leaning as far in an Episcopalian direction as it was possible for a Presbyterian to do.)[2] There lies before me as I write a four-page leaflet entitled *The Proof of God's Love*, reprinted from the *Nairnshire Telegraph* (another northern weekly) of 3rd May 1932. An old friend of mine in Nairn had an arrangement by which he supplied a sermonette to that paper every so often, and he persuaded me to give him one — which I did, taking Romans 5: 8 as my text. In 1933 there appeared in *The Bible Student* of Bangalore (edited by the late Alfred McDonald Redwood), in two instalments, a paper of mine on 'The Early Church in the Roman Empire' which had been read three or four years previously to the Aberdeen University Classical Society. This kind of literary activity only needed a beginning.

My first book, which was published by the IVF in 1943, originally bore the title *Are the New Testament Documents Reliable?* This little work was mentioned in an earlier chapter as being a by-product of my studies in Acts. It was based to a large extent on talks given to students and the like on the historical foundations of the Christian faith: I found (as I still find) that they were readier to entertain seriously the claims of the gospel if they were persuaded that its documentary sources were (contrary to much popular prejudice) historically respectable. Writing in those days as a teacher of classics, I tried to show that the New Testament writings stood up impressively well to the canons of historical and literary criticism which students of Greek and Roman antiquity were accustomed to apply to the writings with which they dealt. The book seems to have achieved its object in successive student generations; it has remained the undisputed best seller among all my writings, not only in English and several other European languages but in Far Eastern languages too. There are many past and present students around the world to whom I am known by name as the author of this work and in no other context.

One reviewer — Professor C. F. Evans of King's College, London (as he now is) — made the pertinent point that the question posed in the title involved another question: 'reliable as what?' I endeavoured to meet this point in the preface to later editions. The review which intrigued me most was one which appeared in instalments in four issues of *The Freethinker* in February and March 1947. The reviewer, who was not convinced that the New Testament documents were reliable, was at pains to emphasize that the length of the review was not an index of the importance of the book; he hoped rather, by demolishing one specimen of this apologetic genre piece by piece, to demolish the whole genre.

A fifth edition, pervasively revised and completely reset, appeared in January 1960 under the slightly altered title: *The New Testament Documents — Are They Reliable?* Since then it has received slight amendments for successive impressions or editions, but it will receive no further pervasive revision. It is not the same book as I should write were I tackling the subject today for the first time; it is probably a better book for its purpose than any that I could write today. I understand perfectly what C. H. Dodd meant when in 1958 he wrote a new preface for a reprint of *The*

Meaning of Paul for Today (a book first published in 1920) and said: 'I have not attempted any such radical revision as would have changed the character of the book. It is a young man's book. The removal of faults of youth might well have introduced the faults of age.'

A commentary on the Greek text of Acts has no chance of being a best seller. This major work, as I have said, took ten years to complete, during the war and after the war, and two more years elapsed between the delivery of the typescript and the appearance of the printed volume in 1951. The dedication to my parents seemed to give them pleasure (as indeed it was intended to do, while at the same time it was intended to acknowledge an infinite debt) — how much pleasure, my wife and I were able to appreciate more personally when in 1967 a commentary on another Greek historical text, the *Hellenica Oxyrhynchia*, was dedicated by our son to *his* parents. It was my work on this Acts commentary, more than anything else, that introduced me to the intricacies of New Testament study and set me on the road which I have travelled for the past thirty years. It bears, I think, clear evidence of being the work of a classical student and not a New Testament specialist. I sometimes wonder what kind of commentary on Acts I should write nowadays, after so many years as a New Testament specialist; more precisely, having first approached Paul through Acts, I wonder how Acts would fare at my hands today if I were now to approach it through Paul. Probably it is good that I wrote it when I did; if ever it receives the pervasive revision that it needs, if it is to take adequate account of recent work, it will be all the better because it received its essential and unchangeable shape in my classical days.

While work on this commentary was approaching its conclusion, I was invited by my late friend Ned Bernard Stonehouse of Westminster Seminary, Philadelphia, to undertake the volume on Acts for the New International Commentary on the New Testament (published by Eerdmans of Grand Rapids), of which he was general editor. I was in two minds about this proposal at first, lest the two commentaries should overlap unacceptably; but the publishers of the commentary on the Greek text granted their *nihil obstat,* and since the second commentary was based on the English text (the ARV of 1901) and was designed to include a large element of general exposition such as the design of the earlier work excluded, I agreed to go ahead. Hardly had I delivered the typescript of this commentary (which was published in 1954) than Dr Stonehouse invited me to tackle Colossians for the same series. For some time he had had in his hands the manuscript of a commentary on Ephesians, by E. K. Simpson, but as the prospectus of the series envisaged the combining of commentaries on Ephesians and Colossians in one volume, the Ephesians commentary could not go forward without its companion. Again I consented: the volume on Ephesians and Colossians appeared in 1957. The two commentaries were in some respects odd companions between the same boards: Mr Simpson's work was a literary masterpiece, but he was such a close student of the Puritans that his style and vocabulary were largely modelled on theirs, and differed markedly from mine. At the same time he had an exceptional knowledge of New Testament lexicography, and his footnotes gave evidence of this. My ties with the New International Commentary were to become closer with the passing of the years, but of that more anon.

When once some people begin to write, they find it difficult to stop: this condition is technically called *cacoethes scribendi* — in plain English, 'scribbler's itch'.

'Well, Mr Gibbon, still at it?' said William Henry, Duke of Gloucester, when the author of the *Decline and Fall* was presented to him. 'Scribble, scribble, scribble!'

What makes a writer write — or, as the Duke might have put it, what makes a scribbler scribble? Scribbler's itch normally does not begin at the start of the process; one must have begun to scribble before the itch comes on. What starts off the process? Economic necessity, as often as anything else. Dr Samuel Johnson is credited with the observation that no one but a blockhead ever wrote except for money. If that be so, I must have been a blockhead when I began my writing career: it was not for money that I wrote *The New Testament Documents*, for in those distant days the IVF publishing department was in no position to remunerate authors.

Nevertheless, one of my publishers — Howard Mudditt, of the Paternoster Press — has gone on record to the effect that it was financial stringency that first made me write for him: far be it from me to deny it, since he confesses that the result was advantageous to him as well as to me. In fact economic necessity had much to do with the writing of two books in the period immediately following my move to Sheffield: *The Books and the Parchments*, published by Pickering & Inglis, and *The Dawn of Christianity*, published by the Paternoster Press, both in 1950. The title of the former work had been given to a series of articles which I contributed in 1946 to the now defunct magazine *The Believer's Pathway*; it gathered together a number of papers and lectures on the languages, canon, text, versions and transmissions of the Old and New Testaments. As a popularization of material usually found in more technical publications it appears to have been found useful over the years. The latter work was also based in part on earlier papers and lectures, but I think one consideration that moved me to write them up in this form was the desire to improve on the work entitled *The Rise of Christianity*, produced in 1947 by the late E. W. Barnes, Bishop of Birmingham. Howard Mudditt was, I think, a little concerned lest one or two rather free expressions of thought might expose him and me to a charge of heresy — he envisaged some readers who knew my father as saying, 'Isn't it sad that poor Bruce's son should go off the rails like this?' — but (bless him) he took the risk, and neither of us came to any harm. I am told that one fellow-Scot described *The Dawn of Christianity* as my contribution to the New Testament apocrypha: I am not in a position to evaluate this judgment.

In the years that followed, two sequels to *The Dawn of Christianity* appeared: *The Growing Day* (1951) and *Light in the West* (1952) — both, as I have said before, the literary

178

deposit of lectures given for the extramural department of Sheffield University, carrying the story of Christian origins from the apostolic age to the conversion of the English. A revised version of the three was published in one volume in 1958 under the title *The Spreading Flame.* I understand that in this form it is widely used as a beginner's textbook in church history and that its name is corrupted by irreverent students. Several years ago in Tiberias, Israel, I was introduced to the young Church of Scotland minister there. 'Ah yes,' said he, ' *"The Flaming Spread"*.'

The discovery of the Dead Sea Scrolls in 1947 and the following years afforded occasion not only for the public lectures mentioned in a previous chapter but in due course also for writing. I wrote an article on them for *The Witness* in April 1950 and gave a lecture on them to the Victoria Institute in that same year which was duly published in its *Journal of Transactions,* but after many people (myself included) had voiced their first thoughts on the subject I found my second (and presumably more mature) thoughts taking shape sufficiently well to make a book: *Second Thoughts on the Dead Sea Scrolls* (1956). In subsequent editions some of the second thoughts became third and fourth thoughts, but so far as the central thesis is concerned I am still substantially of the same mind, so there is no call for a change of title. Later I wrote two monographs on the Scrolls: one on the Teacher of Righteousness and one on their biblical exegesis.[3] I may write more on these topics, especially on the latter, but an important volume of hitherto unpublished exegetical texts from Qumran has been on its way for an unconscionable time, and until it appears I have little more to say than I have said already.

This chapter has been too egocentric by half, but one so subject to scribbler's itch as I am cannot help saying something about his own books. It is much more interesting, for writer as well as for reader, to write about the books of other authors — but that is how it is.

Notes to Chapter 22

1. *Christianity and History* (London 1949), p. 146.

2. In earlier days, when he was minister of East St. Nicholas, Aberdeen, a *double entendre* was discerned in the answer given by an Aberdeen 'wifie' when she was asked in court whether she was a Presbyterian or an Episcopalian: 'I dinna ken; I sit under Jamie Cooper.'

3. The former (*The Teacher of Righteousness in the Qumran Texts*) was the Tyndale Lecture in Biblical Archaeology for 1956; for the latter see p. 194.

23
The editorial chair

My first experience of editorship was gained in the year 1926-27, during which I edited *Elgin Academy Magazine*. The school magazine, which appeared twice yearly, was entrusted to the editorship of a fifth or sixth former; a member of staff acted in an advisory capacity. The member of staff on whose advice I relied was our classics master, J. N. C. Clark. The magazine was printed on the press of one of our two local weekly newspapers, the *Elgin Courant and Courier* (now defunct). The printing manager was the father of one of my classmates. He taught me some of the technical rudiments of the business, such as the importance of submitting copy on one side of a sheet only and the ABC of proof-correcting. I had no further editorial experience until the 1940s.

I have made passing reference in an earlier chapter to the Yorkshire Society for Celtic Studies, to which I belonged during my years in Leeds and Sheffield. This Society published occasional volumes of proceedings, under the title *Yorkshire Celtic Studies*. The earlier volumes in this series appeared under the editorship of Professor Bruce Dickins, of the Chair of English Language in Leeds University; but when he left in 1945 to become Elrington and Bosworth Professor of Anglo-Saxon in Cambridge the office devolved on me, and I retained it for fourteen years. I could not complain of overwork; three slim issues appeared during my term of office, mainly comprising lectures read before the Society by distinguished visitors, covering a wide range of Celtic interests, from modern Ireland to ancient Gaul.

In 1949 Dr R. E. D. Clark, who among his other activities edited the *Journal of Transactions of the Victoria Institute*, found his eyesight seriously affected and had to relinquish this responsibility. (Happily, he was later able to resume editorship of the journal, which is now called *Faith and Thought*.) The Council invited me to take over the editorship. I did so, and continued to serve the Institute in this way until 1956. Whereas contributions to *Yorkshire Celtic Studies* were made exclusively by specialists, the *Transactions of the Victoria Institute* were open to amateurs as well as specialists. The amateurs certainly added liveliness to the pages of the *Journal,* especially in the comments and written communications which followed the main papers and which at one time were reproduced *in extenso.* When the Council, under the wise chairmanship of Air Commodore P. J. Wiseman, decided that — for the sake of the Institute's public reputation, if for nothing else — such comments and communications should be subject to editorial modification, reduction or even suppression, there were natural protests from some who had been accustomed to look upon the *Journal* as a suitable medium for giving publicity to their idiosyncratic views. With the backing of Council, however, the editor's decision was final. Many of the papers and communications, of course, dealt with subjects in which this editor was the merest amateur, but among the members of Council and the Fellows of the Institute there were experts in the various fields whose advice was eagerly sought by the editor and freely given to him.

This editorship was relinquished mainly because another editorship came my way in circumstances which ruled out any refusal. Professor S. H. Hooke had edited the *Palestine Exploration Quarterly* (the organ of the Palestine Exploration Fund, established in 1865) for twenty-three years, and now, at the age of eighty-two, felt that the time had come for him to look around for a successor. His choice fell on me, and the personal bond between us was such that I could not but acquiesce in his choice. At the Annual General Meeting of the Fund in 1956 he accordingly nominated me to take his place; his nomination was approved by the meeting, and I set to work forthwith to prepare the issue for January 1957.

This editorship was most interesting and instructive, for it brought me into touch with many archaeologists and others concerned with the study of Palestine and neighbouring Near Eastern lands — American, European, Jordanian and Israeli as well as British. Although the journal now appeared at half-yearly and not quarterly intervals, it entailed a good deal of work: now for the first time I had to master the art of preparing photographs, line-drawings and maps for the press. Some considerate contributors did this themselves, before submitting the illustrative material with their papers (Dame Kathleen Kenyon was always specially helpful in this regard); others seemed to have no idea about what was required. When the editor directed the printers to reduce by one half a map which had been sent in by an author to illustrate his article, he had to make sure that the indication of scale (one inch to a mile, or whatever it might be) was altered accordingly. Each issue was introduced by a few editorial pages of Notes and News relevant to the readers' interests, which meant that the editor constantly had to keep his eyes open for items which would be useful for this purpose. News-releases from excavation sites and similar pieces of information were always gratefully received and incorporated in these pages.

Having begun this editorial task during my Sheffield days, I continued it after I moved to Manchester in 1959, but as the years went on the mounting scale of commitments arising directly out of my university position meant that I began to feel unable to give to the *Palestine Exploration Quarterly* the time and attention which were necessary to keep its high standard undiminished. Some relief was provided when a review editor was appointed to relieve me of responsibility for the review section, but at last I decided that after fifteen years it would be not unreasonable to give up the editorship. It would have been unthinkable to do so while Professor Hooke was alive, but after his death in 1968 the decision was easier. I demitted what had been a rewarding and enjoyable office with the second issue for 1971; since then, the journal has been in the highly competent hands of Professor P. R. Ackroyd (who, incidentally, holds the chair in the University of London which Professor Hooke once held).

It is with the editorship of *The Evangelical Quarterly*, however, that I have had the closest personal involvement. Other editorships have not been part of me as this one has been. *The Evangelical Quarterly* was launched in 1929 by two Professors in the Free Church College, Edinburgh, Donald Maclean and John R. Mackay, for the 'defence of the historic Christian faith' — the faith enshrined in Holy Scripture and later summarized in the ecumenical creeds and the confessional statements of the Reformation. It was a private enterprise, inaugurated as a venture of faith. The name of a London publisher appeared on the magazine, but the financial backing was provided by the editors and a small group of their friends and well-wishers who had the cause of the historic Christian faith at heart. Professor Mackay's share of the editorial responsibility was terminated after a few years by his illness and death; Professor Maclean remained as editor, with the aid of a few editorial associates, until he in turn died in 1943. Especially after the outbreak of World War II it became clear that more than merely private and personal financial support was necessary if the *Quarterly* and its witness were to continue. I have already mentioned the Kingham Hill conference held in July 1941 by the IVF Biblical Research Committee, at which Professor Maclean invited the IVF or the Committee to assume the ownership of the *Quarterly*. He hoped that thus the witness of the *Quarterly* would be perpetuated, and also that the IVF might be instructed in the way of the Lord more perfectly through this association with such a thoroughly Reformed journal. After careful consideration the IVF accepted his offer, and transference of ownership was effected early in 1942. The IVF nominated two men as additional 'editorial correspondents' — Dr D. Martyn Lloyd-Jones and myself.

Professor Maclean died in January 1943. He had held the Chair of Church History in the Free Church College, Edinburgh, since 1920, and for the last months of his life he was also Principal of the College. He was not only an authority on church history and church polity but a distinguished Gaelic scholar. He was the youngest of the twenty-seven ministers who, with a comparable proportion of elders, preserved the continuing identity of the Free Church of Scotland instead of accompanying the vast majority of that body into union with the United Presbyterian Church to form the United Free Church of Scotland. Firm as his principles were, there was nothing sectarian about his character: he was a man of truly ecumenical spirit. 'He was', wrote Dr Martyn Lloyd-Jones, 'one of nature's gentlemen, with that additional something that can only be supplied by Celtic blood!'[1] When the Scottish Churches Case (1900-1904) was going through the House of Lords, he was entertained by Archbishop Randall Davidson in Lambeth Palace, and a relation of genuine esteem was established between the two men. He was an honoured figure in the World Presbyterian Alliance, and in Holland especially his was a very great name. He was President of the IVF in 1938, and took a keen interest in its welfare and witness. I think with much gratitude of the personal kindness and encouragement which I received from him. To this day I have cause to remember him every time I put on my doctoral hood, for it was once his: his widow most generously presented it to me when I became entitled to wear it in 1957.

On Dr Maclean's death the committee which had been set up for the general management of the *Quarterly* unanimously appointed as his successor Dr J. H. S. Burleigh, Regius Professor of Ecclesiastical History in Edinburgh University, who had served as Assistant Editor since 1938, and I was asked to become Assistant Editor in his place. This arrangement continued for seven years, until in May 1949 the General Assembly of the Church of Scotland elected Professor Burleigh as Convener of its Church and Nation Committee. This weighty administrative responsibility impelled him to relinquish the editorship of the *Quarterly*, and the committee of management appointed me editor from January 1950 onwards.[2] The late Professor Alexander Ross of the Free Church College was appointed Associate Editor at the same time; the link between the *Quarterly* and the Free Church of Scotland was thus maintained until his death in 1965.

Every editor, I suppose, imparts something of his own character and interests to the journal which he edits. If an objective assessor found that in the last thirty years or so the *Quarterly* has contained less systematic and apologetic theology and more exegetical material, I should not be surprised. Some of the older readers were conscious of a change in emphasis, and a few of them would write in to ask what had become of the godly men who had contributed to its pages in earlier days. The answer frequently was that they had departed this life. But the readers who appreciated their writings have largely been replaced by younger readers who find that the present emphasis of the *Quarterly* speaks to their condition; there must be few readers today who have been readers from its inception in 1929.

At the beginning of 1954 the IVF became publishers as well as owners of the *Quarterly*. Under its tendance in this twofold capacity, the child whose chance of survival was so precarious in 1942, when the IVF adopted it, made such rapid strides towards vigorous health that by the end of two years the time seemed ripe for the *Quarterly* to make arrangements for its own future. Thanks to the ready co-operation of The Paternoster Press, these arrangements were quickly and happily made, and remain in being to this day. When Howard Mudditt came to Edinburgh to meet the committee of management and discuss the transfer of ownership, he made quite an impression on them: after he had left to give the members an opportunity to discuss what he had put before them, one of the committee (Professor A. M. Renwick) said, 'He reminds me of Cromwell' — presumably because of his combination of spiritual faith and sound practical judgment. Before these arrangements could be publicized, one Christian journal, unaware of what was afoot, published the *Quarterly's* premature obituary — in time for the editorial in our October 1955 issue to include a note of assurance, added at the last minute, that we 'shall not die, but live, and declare the works of the LORD'.

Since the beginning of 1956, then, the path of the *Quarterly* has been smooth. It was not always so. The IVF, by reason of its constitution and clientéle, has always had to be specially sensitive to the climate of opinion in the evangelical world, and the editor had to bear in mind that the sins of the *Quarterly* would be visited not on his own head but on that of the IVF. Sometimes, however, he did not realize that something would be reckoned a sin until it had been committed. Two occasions of this sort come to mind.

One of these was the most unpleasant experience I have had in my whole literary career. Some time in 1952 or 1953 H. L. Ellison gave me a paper which had been prepared for another purpose and which he hoped might be of use for the *Quarterly*. It was a helpful study entitled 'Some Thoughts on Inspiration' in which he insisted, *inter alia*, that 'the inbreathing of the Holy Spirit into the reader is as essential for the right understanding of the Scriptures as it was in the original writers for their right production of them'. What is wrong with that? 'What indeed?' you may ask. I found Mr Ellison's thoughts very much in line with my own, as they were then and as they still are, so I published his article in the *Quarterly* for October 1954 — and almost immediately afterwards I wished I had suppressed it. I was as flabbergasted by the sequel as he himself was, although it was infinitely more painful for him. In the first place, he found himself obliged to resign from the very congenial teaching post which he had filled acceptably and to the great profit of his students. That was bad enough, but worse was to follow. Worst of all, I think, was a public attack by a senior Christian leader — not, I am happy to say, one of the people called Brethren — which could have had no other effect than to bring Mr Ellison into serious disrepute in the eyes of the evangelical public. When Mr Ellison sent him a well-justified letter of protest, all the reply he got was (in effect): 'That's no way to speak to a man old enough to be your father.' Mr Ellison refers to this incident in *From Tragedy to Triumph* (1958), p. 61 (in a comment on Job 15: 10); and in the preface to that work he refers movingly to the 'period of suffering and distress' which broke over him when he had just begun the studies in the book of Job which it contains and gave him a deeper appreciation of its message than would otherwise have been possible. If anyone still asks what error he was charged with, the answer (believe it or not) is — 'Barthianism'. Comment, as they say, would be superfluous.

The other occasion I can recall more light-heartedly, because no one took any harm from it. In July 1955 we had an issue devoted to sanctification, one of the articles being an extended and critical review of Professor Steven Barabas's book *So Great Salvation* (1952) by Dr James I. Packer of Bristol, under the title ' "Keswick" and the Reformed Doctrine of Sanctification'. Accepting Professor Barabas's exposition as an authentic account of the Keswick doctrine of sanctification, Dr Packer compared it, to its great disadvantage, with the historic Reformed teaching on the same subject. Whether Dr Packer's treatment was well-founded or not, it evoked some very unsanctified reactions from those who disagreed with it, but the author's tenure at Tyndale Hall[3] was not imperilled. In an odd kind of way, however, I think his article was even more embarrassing to the IVF than Mr Ellison's had been the year before; it must have been a real relief to the IVF to be quit of responsibility for the *Quarterly* so soon afterwards.

Let me conclude this chapter with a digression. When a man's standing in the constituency which he serves, not to speak of his livelihood, depends on his reputation for fidelity to the truth of Scripture, it is a very serious matter for anyone else to broadcast doubts about his fidelity or orthodoxy. If he himself statedly renounces something which is of the essence of the historic Christian faith, he will be prepared for the consequences, but he should not be held responsible for the inferences which other people may draw from his statements. Most deplorable of all is the launching of a whispering campaign to the effect that So-and-so is 'going off the rails' or is 'getting away from the Lord'. I say this the more freely because I am myself invulnerable in this regard; my livelihood has never been dependent on my reputation for orthodoxy and I am under no subtle pressure to toe any party line or to pronounce 'shibboleth' in one approved way. But I have great sympathy for my friends who *are* vulnerable, and to those whose zeal is over-prone to find grounds for attack one may recommend the noble words of Harold St. John (who himself was a target for such assaults from time to time): 'Should a man not lay his hand upon his mouth before he criticizes his brethren?'[4]

Notes to Chapter 23

1. Foreword to G. N. M. Collins, *Donald Maclean, D.D.* (Edinburgh 1944), p. ix.

2. The last issue of 1980 marks my resignation from the editorship of the *Quarterly*; my successor is Professor Howard Marshall of Aberdeen.

3. Tyndale Hall, Bristol, is now merged with two other Anglican colleges in that city to form Trinity College.

4. *A New Testament Church in 1955* (Report of the High Leigh Conference of Brethren 1955), p. 91.

24
In foreign parts

For eighteen years (1936-54) I had not set foot outside the United Kingdom, partly because of the restrictions of wartime and partly because of limited resources which were fully utilized in bringing up a young family. My first post-war visits to the Continent took place in the context of the Society for New Testament Studies. The Society was international, so there was no reason why it should always meet in one country. For several years in succession after the war, however, its meetings were held in Britain by general agreement: for one thing, I suppose it was psychologically easier for (say) French and German colleagues to meet here than in each other's countries. But as painful memories were eased with the passing of time the Society decided to hold every second meeting on the Continent, so in 1954 we met at Marburg, Germany; in 1956 at Woudschoten, near Zeist, Holland; in 1958 at Strasbourg, France, and in 1960 at Aarhus, Denmark.

These were very pleasant occasions: for one thing, they made it possible to meet European colleagues (some from beyond the Iron Curtain) who for one reason or another had not found it convenient to come to the meetings in Britain. On the journey to Marburg in 1954 I found myself sharing a railway compartment with T. W. Manson of Manchester (that was the occasion when he passed his obituary comment on Cuthbert Lattey which I quoted earlier). At a later stage in the journey we were joined by Dr and Mrs Henry Chadwick and by Professor and Mrs C. K. Barrett and their two children. The post-war 'economic miracle' in Germany was just getting under way: the material havoc wrought by the war was still evident in every city through which we passed. Marburg itself was relatively unscathed: the local belief was that Marburg, like Tübingen, another university city, had been spared in order to provide convenient headquarters for the armies of occupation. Perhaps comparable beliefs were entertained on our side in Oxford and Cambridge.

Because this was my first visit to the Continent after so long an interval, it stands out vividly in my memory. It was specially good to meet so many German colleagues for the first time. Rudolf Bultmann, as I have said before, had attended one or two of the English meetings of the Society; by this time he had attained his seventieth birthday and ranked, beyond dispute, as the grand old man of Marburg — a rank which he maintained for a further twenty-two years. Otto Michel of Tübingen was there (a patron of the SMD,[1] the German counterpart of the IVF) and Joachim Jeremias of Göttingen. Among men who were more or less my own contemporaries were W. G. Kümmel (Bultmann's successor in Marburg), Kurt Aland, Günther Bornkamm, Walther Eltester, Ernst Fuchs, Heinrich Greeven, Ernst Käsemann, Karl Georg Kuhn and Anton Vögtle. From Aarhus in Denmark came the late Johannes Munck with his German-born wife, Elisabeth, who speedily became a lasting friend to many of us.

We held our morning prayers in the building which, over four centuries earlier, had provided the setting for the Marburg Colloquy between the Lutherans and Zwinglians. One morning our prayers were led by Professor Jeremias, who thought we ought to sing a hymn together. But, because of the lack of suitable hymnbooks, the hymn had to be one which was known — and known by heart — in a German and an English version. 'Now thank we all our God' commended itself. So it was duly given out — but there was no instrument or else no instrumentalist. The Bishop of Leicester (the late Dr Ronald Williams), one of the English members present, proved equal to this emergency and acted as our precentor, and our bilingual praise was sustained successfully to the end. ('He was the right man to do it,' said one of the Bishop's friends; 'he has no inhibitions.')

Of the lectures given at that Marburg meeting, I remember two in particular. One was given by K. G. Kuhn on 'The Two Messiahs of Aaron and Israel'; it showed how the recently discovered Qumran texts revealed that the community expected two Messiahs — one priestly and the other royal and military. During the following discussion George Beasley-Murray (then of Spurgeon's College) recalled how, seven years before, he had argued for the same dual expectation on the basis of the 'Testaments of the Twelve Patriarchs' in the *Journal of Theological Studies 48* (1947), pp. 1-12, but had not found much readiness on the part of others to accept his conclusions. But these conclusions were now powerfully reinforced by the new evidence. When Professor Kuhn's lecture was published shortly afterwards in *New Testament Studies* (the journal of our Society), it carried a footnote pointing out that 'this presentation of the two Messiahs was demonstrated convincingly by Beasley-Murray as early as 1947'.[2]

The other Marburg lecture which remains vividly with me was given by Henry Chadwick, then Dean of Queens' College, Cambridge (later Dean of Christchurch, Oxford, and now Regius Professor of Divinity in Cambridge). It was a most valuable study of Paul's procedure in apologetic and debate, entitled 'All things to all men'. In it he showed (convincingly, to my mind) that Paul regularly goes as far as he can with those with whom he argues, whether judaizers or hellenizers, until he reaches the point where he says *'but . . .'* — and sometimes the qualification which follows the *'but . . .'* is so far-reaching that it cuts the ground from under the feet of the other side. Dr Chadwick's illustrations were drawn chiefly from 1 Corinthians and Colossians. This lecture, too, appeared later in *New Testament Studies*; I have had recourse to it time and again in my own Pauline studies.[3]

Two years later the Society met in Holland, at the Woudschoten conference centre. On this occasion I was accompanied by my wife; she had not visited the Continent since our honeymoon twenty years before. The neighbouring University of Utrecht played host to the party. The papers read at that meeting do not stick so clearly in my memory as do those of the Marburg meeting, although I can call them to mind by looking at the programme. That year's president was the late E. G. Selwyn, Dean of Winchester, whose presidential address dealt with 'The Authority of Christ in the New Testament'. There seemed to be a greater concentration of Scandinavian — especially Swedish — members at that meeting than at any of the previous ones. That was the first occasion, too, that I met the late Henry J. Cadbury, a veteran Quaker scholar from U.S.A., and a world-famous authority on the Acts of the Apostles, of whose works I had made ample use in writing my own commentary on that book. (He became president of the Society in 1958.) Another veteran Quaker scholar present there was the late Herbert G. Wood of Woodbrooke, Birmingham; he indeed had been at several of our earlier meetings in England (and served as president in 1957). On the morning after the Woudschoten conference ended, as we were queuing for customs and immigration inspection at Harwich on disembarking from the night ferry, J. A. T. Robinson (now Dean of Trinity College, Cambridge), who had shared a cabin with Dr Wood, came hurrying up to the front of the queue looking for him and thrust a washbag into his hands: Dr Wood had inadvertently overlooked it when packing.

About five months later (in February 1957) I was back in Holland on another errand. The Free University of Amsterdam had invited me to spend a few days there as a guest lecturer under a scheme sponsored by the British Council; I was able in addition to give one lecture apiece in the Universities of Leiden and Utrecht. These lectures were duly published in book form under the title *Biblical Exegesis in the Qumran Texts* (1959-60).

Next year I paid another lecturing visit to a more distant land and for a longer period. I have visited America frequently in the years that have intervened since then, but my first visit (mid-March to mid-April 1958) left specially clear impressions with me, no doubt because it was the first. The primary purpose of my going was to deliver two short series of lectures — one (the John A. McElwain Lectures) in Gordon Divinity School, Wenham, Massachusetts (now Gordon-Conwell Theological Seminary) on Paul and the Old Testament, and the other (the Calvin Foundation Lectures) in Calvin College and Seminary, Grand Rapids, Michigan, on Christian Apologetic in the New Testament. The former series remains unpublished, apart from one lecture, 'Promise and Fulfilment in Paul's Presentation of Jesus', which I contributed to the presentation volume for S. H. Hooke a few years later; the latter was published under slightly different titles in America and Britain, the British title being *The Apostolic Defence of the Gospel* (1960).[4]

But I had a number of other engagements to fulfil during those weeks. My first night on American soil, I am happy to remember, was spent in the 'prophet's chamber' of Union Theological Seminary, New York (thanks to the good offices of Walter Liefeld, who was then a graduate student there); I was greatly impressed by the long list of distinguished names in the guest-book under which I was invited to sign my own much less distinguished one. Next morning I had breakfast with the late Dr Henry P. Van Dusen, then President of the Seminary, and his wife and family, and afterwards gave a brief talk (on Hebrews 2:10) at morning prayers in the Seminary chapel. I was then whisked away to a weekend conference for theological students, organized by the Inter-Varsity Christian Fellowship, at Upper Nyack, where I spoke on such subjects as form criticism and the messianic hope. On the Sunday afternoon I flew from New York to Boston, where I had to give an after-church talk to students in Park Street Church (the church where Dr Harold Ockenga ministered), and then was driven out to Gordon Divinity School, ready to give my first lecture there early next morning. I was quickly introduced to the pace of American life!

One afternoon Dr Glenn Barker, then Professor of New Testament at Gordon (now at Fuller Theological Seminary, Pasadena), took me to a seminar at Harvard Divinity School (where he was registered as a graduate student). The seminar was presided over by the two New Testament professors at Harvard, Amos Wilder and Krister Stendahl, a Swedish scholar whom I had met at Woudschoten but who had since then crossed the Atlantic to take up the Harvard post which he still holds.

One specially pleasant evening during that week I spent as the guest of Mr and Mrs Edwin J. Tharp at Rockport, Massachusetts. Mr Tharp, with whom I had had some occasional correspondence arising out of *The Harvester* question page, was an Englishman by birth who had spent nearly forty years as a missionary in China. Mrs Tharp was a daughter of Philip Mauro, and needed little prompting to talk about her father, especially when she learned that his writings had been read with appreciation in my parental home. She plainly had great love and admiration for him — 'but he made a mistake when he started to fight,' she said.

On the Friday of that week (28th March) I had the one free day of my whole visit: Dr Roger Nicole, Professor of Systematic Theology at Gordon (French Swiss by origin), and his wife took me for a drive through Massachusetts and New Hampshire, to see such varied places as Lexington, where the first shot was fired in the American War of Independence; Concord, also the scene of much fighting and the birthplace of Louisa May Alcott (author of *Little Women*); and Salem, infamous for the witch-hunt of 1692. Next day I took the train to Philadelphia, and beguiled the journey by marking a pile of answers to an examination which I had set as part of my Gordon assignment.

In Philadelphia I was the guest of Westminster Theological Seminary. I was to have stayed in the home of my friend Ned Bernard Stonehouse, who had stayed with us in Sheffield some years previously, but his wife died suddenly a few days before my arrival. Other members of the faculty whom I had met in England were Cornelius Van Til and my fellow-Scot John Murray; among those whom I had not previously met were Edward J. Young, Old Testament professor, and Paul Woolley, church historian. Dr Young had such a reputation for biblical conservatism that others measured themselves by him: 'I'm conservative, of course,' said more than one theologian to me, 'but not like E. J. Young.' But there were limits even to Dr Young's conservatism: some American conservatives thought he had sold the pass by dating Ecclesiastes about the time of Malachi. Dr Young was too sound a Hebraist to date it earlier. But he was sensitive to criticism on this score, and said once that if he believed the book claimed to be by Solomon, he would accept the claim. As it was, he believed that the author was someone 'who lived in the post-exilic period and who placed his words in the mouth of Solomon, thus employing a literary device for conveying his message'.[5] But he could be quite severe on those who used the same argument with regard to the date and authorship of other Old Testament books.

In addition to lecturing at Westminster I went one day from Philadelphia to Princeton, to give a lecture in the famous Presbyterian seminary of that city, from which Westminster had broken away in 1929-30. My chairman at Princeton Seminary was the President, Dr John A. Mackay, a distinguished Invernessian whom (as I have said earlier) I had met in Aberdeen twenty-eight years before.

Dr Bruce Metzger, Dr Mackay's son-in-law, whom I knew as a fellow-member of SNTS, was (and is) Professor of New Testament in the Seminary. Before my lecture he and Mrs Metzger entertained me in their home. Dr Metzger showed me his books, and took down from the shelves Tischendorf's eighth edition of the Greek Testament — a rare enough treasure then (a reprint is now available at an enormous price). But this particular copy had once belonged to F. J. A.

Hort, and was inscribed and annotated in Hort's hand. 'How did you get this?' I asked. 'Well,' he replied, 'I saw it listed in a catalogue of secondhand books which I received from Britain, so I sent for it and got it.' I could only conclude that some British catalogues of secondhand books are mailed to the United States before they are released over here!

On my first Sunday in Philadelphia I preached in Tenth Presbyterian Church. The minister, the famous Dr Donald Grey Barnhouse, was away from home. The collection that Sunday morning was for a fund set up by Dr Barnhouse to augment the resources of some British ministers known to him; I wondered idly if some of the congregation supposed that they had one of the beneficiaries in the pulpit! After the morning service one lady shook my hand with special warmth and said, 'I do want to thank you for your book *The Training of the Twelve*' (by another Bruce). How could I explain that that book was written in 1877 without making her feel abashed?

One afternoon in Philadelphia I visited the home of Joe Bayly, then editor of *His* magazine and later to gain fame as the author of *The Gospel Blimp*. His wife and he expected me to involve them in some deep theological debate, but were relieved to find that I preferred to relax with their delightful children.

On Good Friday I flew from Philadelphia to Chicago; next day a theological students' conference had been arranged for me in one of the lecture-rooms of the Chicago Faculty of Theology, on the same lines as the one at Upper Nyack a fortnight before. While in the Chicago area I stayed with my wife's cousins, the late Ernest and Mae Bendelow. On Easter Day I had been booked to speak in Norwood Chapel, one of the Brethren meeting-places in the area, and very much enjoyed fellowship with the friends there. Next day I visited Wheaton College, at the invitation of Dr Merrill Tenney; on the Tuesday morning I gave a lecture at Emmaus Bible School, Oak Park, Illinois, and spent that afternoon with the late Mr and Mrs John Duff; on the Wednesday I gave a lunchtime talk to a group of Christian Reformed ministers,

197

after which I was taken to the airport and put on board a plane for Grand Rapids.

Calvin College and Seminary provide liberal arts and theological education respectively for the constituency of the Christian Reformed Church — a vigorous body of Dutch origin. My lectures there were well attended, not only by that particular constituency. Among others who came along I met the Pell brothers of the Folio Press and the veteran evangelist Hugh K. Downie, who spent his closing years in Grand Rapids. There too I met Mr and Mrs Norman F. Douty, who drove in each evening from East Lansing, where they then lived — quite a long way off. But one man, who had corresponded with me off and on, hitch-hiked 500 miles from Ontario to spend the week in Grand Rapids and attend the lectures. He hoped, I think, to kill two birds with one stone: he brought with him a hefty manuscript which he submitted to the late William B. Eerdmans, Senior — but it has remained unpublished, probably because it was unpublishable.

Grand Rapids is best known in the Christian world as the home of great publishing houses. I cherish a memory of Mr Eerdmans standing at the entrance to Calvin Christian Reformed Church, Grand Rapids, where I had been preaching that Sunday evening, with one of his arms round Herman Baker and the other round the late Bernard Zondervan, saying, 'I don't regard these men as *competitors*; I regard them as *colleagues!*' I cherish the memory of Mr Eerdmans; he showed me much kindness. 'Ask what you will,' he said to me in an expansive mood; 'the sky's the limit.' I took him at his word — almost; I didn't quite ask for the sky.

One day during my time in Grand Rapids I was taken to Hope College, Holland, Michigan, to give a potted, single-lecture version of the course I was giving at Calvin College. On Thursday, 17th April, I was taken by road to Kalamazoo, Michigan, to speak to a meeting of churchmen. Then I took the night train to New York, from which I took flight for Manchester Airport on the Saturday evening, reaching

Sheffield on the Sunday afternoon, in time for the new term, which opened next day. Quite a full month: I shouldn't care to repeat it nowadays.

During my visit, and afterwards, I was frequently asked what my dominant impression of the United States was. I had no hesitation in replying, 'The overwhelming hospitality of the American people.' I have paid many visits to the United States since then, but that remains my dominant impression.

Notes to Chapter 24
1. Abbreviation for *Studentenmission Deutschlands*.
2. *New Testament Studies* 1 (1954-55), pp. 168-179 (p. 172, n.1).
3. *New Testament Studies* 1 (1954-55), pp. 261-275.
4. A revised edition appeared in 1977 under the new title *First-Century Faith* (Inter-Varsity Press, Leicester).
5. *An Introduction to the Old Testament* (Grand Rapids 1949), p. 340.

25

I cross the Pennines

Less than two weeks after my return from that American trip T. W. Manson's death (on 1st May, 1958) was reported. For twenty-two years he had occupied the Rylands Chair of Biblical Criticism and Exegesis in the University of Manchester, which now became vacant. ˙

Between 1880 and 1903 there had been a federal university in the north of England — the Victorian University — comprising three constituent colleges in Leeds, Liverpool and Manchester. In 1903 the federation was dissolved, and each of the three colleges was elevated to independent university status, the title 'Victoria University' being retained by Manchester. One of the first moves made by the newly constituted Victoria University of Manchester was to establish a Faculty of Theology, which came into being in 1904. In the climate of that day, this was a venturesome thing to do. The denominational strife in the English educational world at the beginning of the century frightened other new secular universities off the very idea of including such controversial subjects in their curriculum: the University of Liverpool, indeed, wrote into its charter a clause prohibiting the teaching of theology in any form.[1] Manchester, however, saw no need to be alarmed by such a chimaera, and its enterprise was justified by the result. Ecumenical co-operation is taken for granted today, but it was a reality in the Manchester Faculty of Theology from 1904 onwards, and no doubt, in this respect as in others, what Manchester did today, other places did tomorrow or the day after.

When the new Faculty was established, Mrs Rylands, third wife and by that time widow of the Manchester industrialist John Rylands, endowed a Chair of Biblical Exegesis in his memory. (Already, in 1899, she had founded in his memory the great Library bearing his name in Deansgate, Manchester, which more recently, in 1972, was merged with Manchester University Library to form the John Rylands University Library of Manchester.) To the newly endowed Rylands Chair the University in 1904 appointed as its first occupant Arthur Samuel Peake, who twelve years previously had left Oxford in order to train men for the ministry of his own denomination, the Primitive Methodists, in Hartley College, Manchester. He continued to serve Hartley College concurrently with his tenure of the Rylands Chair, which he held with distinction for twenty-five years.

When he died in 1929 the University invited Charles Harold Dodd, then Yates Professor of New Testament in Mansfield College, Oxford, to succeed him. By this time the title of the Chair had been expanded from 'Biblical Exegesis' to 'Biblical Criticism and Exegesis'. This did not mean that criticism was now in practice added to exegesis as a subject of instruction; it simply meant that the actual scope of the work of the Chair was recognized in its title. Peake placed exegesis above criticism. 'Criticism', he said, 'has never attracted me for its own sake. The all-important thing for the student of the Bible is to pierce to the core of its meaning.'[2] Professor Dodd enhanced the high reputation of the Chair during the few years that he occupied it, but in 1935 he was lured away to Cambridge, to succeed F. C. Burkitt as Norris-Hulse Professor of Divinity. Once again Manchester University turned to Mansfield College to fill the vacancy, and appointed Thomas Walter Manson, who had succeeded Professor Dodd in the Yates Professorship there, to be his successor in the Rylands Chair. Comparisons are

201

proverbially odious, but Professor Manson brought at least as much distinction to the post as his two predecessors had done, and my private opinion is that he was the greatest man who has ever filled it, or is ever likely to fill it. He may have lacked Professor Dodd's scintillating brilliance and quicksilver intellect, but made up for it in reliable solidity and soundness of judgment. This does not mean that where he and Dodd differed I should always agree with him and not with Dodd: on the question of the destination of Romans 16, for example, I agree completely with Dodd against Manson.[3] But I am thinking of the all-round quality of the man, as shown, for instance, in his first and greatest book, *The Teaching of Jesus* (1931), still the best study of that important subject.

When his death was reported, I wondered (as many others must have done) who his successor would be. I thought of one scholar of my own generation who seemed to be specially well fitted for the post: the same thought perhaps occurred to this man's own university, for it promptly elevated him to professorial status. As I have said before, the deliberations of university appointment committees are confidential, so I do not know all the steps taken by the committee set up to make arrangements for the succession to Professor Manson, but from the fact that a full year elapsed before they made contact with me, it might be inferred that by that time they had begun to scrape the bottom of the barrel.

Be that as it may, in May 1959, I had a letter from the Vice-Chancellor of Manchester University inviting me to come to Manchester to meet the committee, 'without commitment on either side'. I accepted his invitation in quite a relaxed frame of mind: I had no desire to leave Sheffield, but I thought it would be interesting to meet the committee and see what they had in mind. Some of the committee members were fairly well known to me; others I met for the first time. H. H. Rowley was there, characteristically the most vocal member present; he was within a few months of his own retirement from the Hebrew Chair. The Professors of Greek and Latin I also knew: the former (H. D. Westlake) remembered meeting me at Cardiff in 1946, when we were both unsuccessful applicants for the Greek Chair there. One interesting member of the committee was John Cohen, Professor of Psychology, who expressed some disappointment that I laid no claim to competence in rabbinical literature. Two theological professors were there: Gordon Rupp (Ecclesiastical History) and S. G. F. Brandon (Comparative Religion), whose book *The Fall of Jerusalem and the Christian Church* (1951) I had reviewed with some severity in *The Evangelical Quarterly* seven years before. At the interview he said he was surprised that in my Acts commentary I had not said more about the first mention of James the Lord's brother (Acts 12: 17); to him the brevity of Luke's reference to James at that point suggested an underlying hostility to him. It all goes to show that one's interpretation of Scripture can depend on the presuppositions which one brings to the reading of it. He asked in what area of New Testament study my future research was likely to be conducted: I said it would probably lie in the history of non-Pauline Christianity. This was because I was then engaged on the exposition of Hebrews for the New International Commentary. In fact, however, my research has been more and more concentrated over the subsequent years on Paul himself.[4]   The whole interview was a pleasant occasion, but while it was going on I could not judge what impression I was making on the committee. It was plain to me that I had at least one friend at court, for more than once when I was asked a question Professor Rowley answered it for me before I could do so for myself — but such zeal can sometimes be counter-productive! However, after the interview I walked back to the station, as I had plenty of time to catch the next train to Sheffield, and was overtaken on the way by the Professor of Mediaeval History, another member of the committee, who told me that the committee had unanimously agreed to recommend my appointment to the Chair. I was thus not unprepared for a letter from the Vice-Chancellor a day or two later, inviting

203

me to accept nomination. I asked for a few days to reach a decision. The following weekend was Whitsuntide (I spent that Whit Monday, 18th May, at a conference in Banbury, where I shared the ministry with the late H. J. Brearey), and when the Vice-Chancellor reached his desk on the Tuesday morning after the bank holiday he found my letter of acceptance.

My churchmanship and my theological stance (e.g. my association with the IVF) were perfectly well known to the appointment committee, but were academically irrelevant. This is something which certain people find it difficult to understand. For example, some years ago a columnist in a Belfast newspaper made some reference to me, and commented that the tenure of the Rylands Chair by a person of my brand of churchmanship was a source of unending wonder. I wrote him a letter in which I expressed polite surprise at his comment: didn't he know, I asked, that in a secular university a man or woman's denomination was irrelevant in the making of any appointment, theological or otherwise? He sent a reply saying that if I lived in Northern Ireland I would know what he meant! (What, I wonder, was I expected to make of that?)

To sever my connexion with Sheffield was not easy. I felt (as I still feel) immense gratitude to the University of Sheffield for making it possible for me to devote my whole time to the study and teaching of the Bible, and I had forged ties of strong affection with many of my colleagues and students there, as well as with our friends in Cemetery Road Meeting Room. As for the university department which I had built up from the foundation, I had developed an almost proprietorial relation with it, but I suppose that for that very reason it was good that there should be a break.[5] From early October to mid-December 1959 I served both Sheffield and Manchester. On Tuesdays, Wednesdays and Thursdays I functioned as Rylands Professor in Manchester, but on Mondays and Fridays Manchester lent me to Sheffield, where I helped out in my former department as acting head until mid-November, when Aileen Guilding was appointed to the

Chair in my place, and then as her part-time assistant until just before Christmas. That term did not allow me much leisure for extra-curricular activity! And all the time the Lutterworth Press was waiting for the delivery of my manuscript on *The English Bible,* promised for 31st December, 1959, so that it could be published immediately after the appearance of the New English Bible (New Testament) in March, 1961; but delivered it was by the stipulated date.[6]

One pleasant memory which I retain from those days is of the extraordinarily warm and friendly welcome I received from my new colleagues in Manchester — first in personal letters when I was appointed, and then in actual co-operation when I arrived to take up my duties in the Faculty of Theology. It was a small, closely-knit faculty, with a kind of family atmosphere, and I was immediately made to feel one of the family. I once heard a member of the faculty describe it as a mutual admiration society, and he meant that by way of praise, not blame — 'long may it be so,' he added.

To join a much larger theological team than I had ever belonged to before was an experience both helpful and challenging. My colleagues set a standard which it was for me to emulate. But this was not such a challenge as the thought of maintaining the standard set by my predecessors in the Rylands Chair. 'I think', said the Vice-Chancellor in a letter to me, 'you will find that the Faculty and the University will give you all the support that it possibly can and for our part we have no doubt that you will do everything possible to extend the power and influence of what we believe to be a great Chair.' These, rather than the words in the formal contract of appointment, were my real terms of reference, and the attempt to fulfil them has been a gratifyingly mind-stretching experience.

Happily, I had always found myself in agreement with T. W. Manson over such a wide area of biblical study that students were not conscious of any such abrupt change of course as sometimes takes place with a new appointment. Whereas in Sheffield in 1947 and the following years I had to construct syllabuses, in Manchester I inherited well-established syllabuses which provided a suitable framework within which I could do the sort of thing I wanted to do. Again, whereas in Sheffield I had found it necessary (because of staffing limitation) to teach more Old Testament than New, in Manchester I was able to concentrate for the most part on New Testament teaching, for which I was better qualified. (I continued, throughout my Manchester years, to lecture on Septuagint texts, on the text and canon of the Old Testament, and on the book of Daniel.) Of my predecessors, Peake had taken both Testaments for his province and demonstrated his equal competence in both, but Dodd and Manson had both specialized in the New Testament, and so did I. Even so, my business was not to imitate them but to be myself and promote the interests of the Chair by pursuing my own interests — a congenial task indeed.

The scope of my Manchester department was practically identical with that of my Sheffield department, but whereas the Sheffield department was designated in terms of its subject-matter (Biblical History and Literature),[7] the Manchester department was designated in terms of the academic treatment of that subject-matter (Biblical Criticism and Exegesis). A word about the two terms of this designation may be apposite here.

Biblical exegesis is more important than criticism, but biblical criticism embraces a variety of disciplines necessary to lay the ground-work for exegesis. First there is textual criticism: that is the business of establishing the original wording of written documents, as far as one can, with the aid of the best available witnesses to the text. Because this is a foundation discipline, it was at one time known as 'lower criticism' and distinguished from 'higher criticism'. 'Higher criticism' was a comprehensive expression used to cover the study of the composition (including, where appropriate, the sources), authorship, constituency and date of written documents. Anyone, for example, who examines the Epistle to the Hebrews in order to ascertain its structure, the character and outlook (if not the identity) of its author and addressees, and the probable date at which it was written, shows himself thereby to be a higher critic in the only proper sense. (This is worth saying, because at times the expression has been used as a kind of religious swear-word, to designate attitudes and techniques which may indeed be deplorably *uncritical* — such as an approach to Scripture which dogmatically rules out in advance the possibility or relevance of supernatural factors.) In more recent generations there have been further refinements. There is 'form criticism', for example, which studies the literary and pre-literary 'forms' in which various kinds of material (both narratives and sayings) have been preserved and communicated. There is 'tradition criticism', which is specially concerned with material which has been transmitted for shorter or longer periods by word of mouth before being written down. And there is 'redaction criticism', which studies the way in which the final author arranged and presented the material which had been transmitted to him. If we are studying the Gospel of Luke, for instance, we can consider (i) the nature of the accounts which he received, as he tells us, from 'those who from the beginning were eyewitnesses and ministers of the word' (that is tradition criticism) and (ii) the principles on which he organized these accounts into the highly individual masterpiece which now lies before us (that is redaction criticism). In more recent years we have been introduced to a further discipline called 'structural criticism' or 'structuralism', which I have not studied and have no thought of studying. (I have more important things to study in the days that remain to me.) The structuralist is concerned with the written product in its final form, as a literary or textual phenomenon, without regard to its historical setting or transmission or to the author's intention.[8]

When the groundwork has been laid by such studies as these, the student can proceed to the exegesis of the text — that is, to consider two important questions: (i) What did the speaker or author mean by what he said? (ii) What did his original hearers or readers understand by what he said?

207

Exegesis is thus narrower than exposition. Exposition considers these questions, but considers the further question: (iii) What do these words mean for us today? Because of our different situation, they may not have precisely the same meaning as they had for their original constituency, but if their meaning for us today is to be valid at all, it must be logically related to what they originally meant. The question of the meaning of Scripture for men and women of today is actively canvassed by many European theologians under the heading of 'hermeneutics'; it is certainly an important question, but has not traditionally been part of the curriculum of the Manchester Department of Biblical Criticism and Exegesis. In our Faculty of Theology at present it seems to be most actively explored by Dr David Pailin, Senior Lecturer in Philosophy of Religion — but that is largely because of his personal interest in the subject.

Notes to Chapter 25

1. This clause was later removed from the charter, so that the University of Liverpool is now free, if it wishes, to institute theological teaching; but so far it has not done so.

2. *The Bible: Its Origin, its Significance and its Abiding Worth* (London 1913), p. 455.

3. That is to say, I hold that chapter 16 is an integral part of the original letter and was intended (as Dodd argued) for Rome, not (as Manson believed) for Ephesus.

4. There have been occasional incursions into other areas, especially the Johannine; cf. 'The Revelation to John' in *A New Testament Commentary* (Pickering & Inglis 1969), pp. 629-666; *The Epistles of John* (Pickering & Inglis 1970); *Men and Movements in the Primitive Church* (Exeter 1980).

5. It was good indeed for the Department. Since my departure, and especially under the twelve-years' leadership of James Atkinson, it has advanced from strength to strength. Nowadays it enjoys worldwide esteem among biblical scholars because of the two quarterly journals which it publishes — the *Journal for the Study of the Old Testament* and the *Journal for the Study of the New Testament*.

6. I recall with gratitude that it was Professor C. H. Dodd who recommended me to the Lutterworth Press when they consulted him about a suitable author for such a book.

7. More recently its name has become simply the Department of Biblical Studies.

8. See A. C. Thiselton, 'Structuralism and Biblical Studies: Method or Ideology?' *Expository Times* 89 (1977-78), pp. 329-335.

26

Manchester colleagues

When I went to Manchester in October 1959 I was the junior professor in the Faculty of Theology — in actual age as well as in seniority of appointment. For the last six years of my tenure I was the senior professor in both respects, so the change of perspective enabled me to look back and take stock of personal relations as they were at the beginning.

I have mentioned the very warm terms in which my new colleagues welcomed me. From Professor Rowley, whose retirement took effect the day before I entered on my appointment, I received a very cordial letter which concluded by saying that his only regret was that he would no longer be at the university to be my colleague. He did, however, stay on in Manchester for a few years before he moved to Stroud, so I saw quite a lot of him. His successor, Dr Edward Ullendorff, who entered on his office on the same day as I entered on mine, was a pure Semitic philologist. After five years with us he went to the University of London, where a new Chair of Ethiopic Studies had been specially created for him in the School of Oriental and African Studies. In his place we secured Professor James Barr, eminent alike as philologist and theologian. He moved to Oxford in 1976 as Oriel Professor of the Interpretation of Holy Scripture; two years later he was translated to the

Regius Chair of Hebrew there, in succession to W. D. McHardy.

The Chair of Semitic Languages and Literatures, however, is more closely attached to the Faculty of Arts than to the Faculty of Theology. In the Faculty of Theology I was associated very closely with the Professors of Comparative Religion (S. G. F. Brandon) and Ecclesiastical History (Gordon Rupp).

Professor Brandon was a polymath with an unusual career. He was appointed to his Manchester Chair in 1951, at the age of forty-four, having spent the twelve preceding years as a regular army chaplain. Yet throughout those twelve years he had pursued his studies unremittingly, and shortly before his appointment to the Chair he had published within one year (1951) two major works: *The Fall of Jerusalem and the Christian Church* (an expansion of his B.D. dissertation for Leeds University, his *alma mater*) and *Time and Mankind* (for which he was awarded the D.D. degree by the same university). It was these two works which brought his name to the notice of the committee charged with making a nomination to the Chair; the invitation to meet the committee and to accept the appointment came to him out of the blue. Two areas of his special study were religious iconography (from prehistoric cave-paintings to stone carvings in mediaeval cathedrals) and ancient Egyptian myth and ritual. He was also intensely interested in Christian origins, a field in which he maintained a thesis with which I found it impossible to agree — that our Lord, if not actually a Zealot, was certainly a Zealot sympathizer, and that the Jerusalem church had close affinities with militant nationalism.[1] Yet his scholarly integrity was such that when I published my *New Testament History* (1969), in which I did not conceal my complete dissent from these views, he reviewed it most generously. He got me from time to time to contribute to enterprises for which he had some responsibility, such as his own *Dictionary of Comparative Religion* (1970) and that odd encyclopaedia of the supernatural, *Man, Myth and Magic* (1970-71); and when in

210

1960 the Modern Churchmen's Union chose Christianity in history (past and present) as the theme for its annual meeting, he persuaded me to address it on the significance of the Dead Sea Scrolls in this regard — the only occasion on which I have been in direct contact with that interesting survival from a past age. To work together for twelve years with such a man was an enriching and challenging experience; 'as iron sharpeneth iron', so contact with him greatly stimulated my thinking on the subject of common interest on which we held such divergent opinions. When he died unexpectedly as the result of an infection caught in Egypt in 1971, all his colleagues felt his loss keenly, and when it fell to my lot to deliver the memorial address for him in Manchester Cathedral, my tribute to him was full and heartfelt.

With Gordon Rupp, Professor of Ecclesiastical History, on the other hand, my agreement was as near total as makes no practical difference. In him I found a man who, for all his involvement in high-level ecclesiastical politics, lived by the uncomplicated gospel of Luther and the Wesleys. Indeed, he caught me out once by observing that my comment on Hebrews 7: 25 in my work on that epistle should have been more evangelical than it was: how could I be content with adducing our Lord's prayer for Peter (Luke 22: 32) as an analogy for his present intercession and not mention his atonement: 'Five bleeding wounds he bears . . .'? The main complaint that Professor Rupp's friends would make of him would be Samuel Johnson's complaint about John Wesley: that he was always too busy to fold his legs and have his talk out. But, busy as he might be, we knew that when he was in Manchester we could never get him to attend a Thursday evening occasion at the university: that was the evening when he conducted a Bible class in his local church. He left us in 1968 to become Principal of Wesley House and then Dixie Professor of Ecclesiastical History in Cambridge (he retired from the latter post in 1977). For all his learning, his chief end in life can be summed up simply in words of Charles Wesley which come readily to his lips:

> 'Tis all I want, this,
> To administer bliss
> And salvation in Jesus's name.

He was succeeded by Basil Hall, another kindred soul, as devoted a student and admirer of Calvin as Gordon Rupp is of Luther. He came to us from Westminster College, Cambridge (the theological seminary of the Presbyterian Church of England, as it was then). But while he came a Presbyterian minister, he took Anglican orders during his time with us, judging (as he said) that the Church of England was in fact, if not in name, more reformed than the English Presbyterians (or even the United Reformed Church). He left us in 1975 to become Dean of St. John's College, Cambridge (from which post he has lately retired).

Manchester University has another appointment in ecclesiastical history, much more ancient than the professorship in that subject — the Bishop Fraser Senior Lectureship, established last century at Owens College. When I arrived in Manchester this post was held by Dr Arnold Ehrhardt, a most exceptional man. He had been Professor of Roman Law in the University of Frankfurt, but was evicted from his chair by the Nazis. I think he had some small measure of Jewish ancestry, but even apart from that they could not easily have tolerated a man of his enlightened outlook. He enrolled as a student of theology in Basel, under Karl Barth, crossing the Swiss frontier daily to attend his classes, until the day when he crossed it and did not return (having been tipped off by a friendly informer). It was said that, mounted on a motor cycle, he beat the Gestapo to the frontier by half an hour. In due course, reunited with his wife and family, he came to England, took a higher degree at Cambridge and was ordained in the Church of England. For some years he had a living in downtown Manchester and endeared himself to his working class parishioners by his sheer friendliness and lack of pomposity. To his studies in early church history he brought his unsurpassed expertise in Roman law: the breadth and depth of his learning were prodigious, and he has been justly described as a twentieth-century Erasmus. He was the most lovable and charitable of men, but found it very difficult to re-establish amicable relations with German colleagues who, in his opinion, had compromised the faith under Hitler. The University of Frankfurt rehabilitated him, gave him the status of honorary professor and voted him a pension in consideration of wrongful dismissal, but it was only with a struggle that he brought himself to accept these amends. For some years he and I jointly conducted a seminar in New Testament and early church studies;[2] when he died in 1965 Mrs Ehrhardt kindly allowed us to call it the Ehrhardt Seminar in his memory. His place was taken by Benjamin Drewery, a well-known Methodist scholar.

Another refugee from Hitler's Germany who enriched the life of Manchester University was Dr Günther Zuntz, who taught Hellenistic Greek as successively Senior Lecturer, Reader and then as the holder of a personal chair. Professor Zuntz, who now lives in retirement in Cambridge, is an illustrious textual scholar, equally expert in the manuscripts of Euripides and of the New Testament as witness his Schweich Lectures, *The Text of the Epistles* (1953), the most thorough and careful study of the text of the Pauline writings and Hebrews which had been undertaken up to that time, with special reference to three important witnesses — Papyrus 46 (one of the Chester Beatty collection and our oldest witness to the text of the epistles), Codex Vaticanus (B) and the tenth-century minuscule manuscript 1739. A classical philologist, he said, while making no claim to be a theologian, 'cannot exclude from his interest what is perhaps the most influential book written in the Greek language'. For 1 Corinthians and Hebrews his examination of the text is particularly thorough and indeed indispensable to the careful student of either of these epistles. But Professor Zuntz is equally at home in Byzantine musicology and in the interpretation of the murals of the Villa dei Misteri at Pompeii. It must have been a sore trial for a man of his learning to try year by year to impart the rudiments of Greek culture to some of our pass-degree candidates in theology, whose scholarship was not commensurate with their godliness. But he applied himself seriously to this task and devised a new scheme for teaching elementary Greek, in which tape recordings played a substantial part.

On his retirement he was succeeded by Dr John Kane, a graduate of Keele University, who, over and above his expertise as a teacher of Hellenistic Greek, is an authority on Palestinian archaeology in the Graeco-Roman age.

There was one gap in the teaching curriculum of the Faculty of Theology: the university appointed no one to teach History of Doctrine, although the subject was included in the examination syllabus. This was because of an understanding between the university and the denominational colleges in Manchester, which were associated with the Faculty. When the Faculty was founded, practically all its students were also students in one or another of these colleges, and the colleges undertook the responsibility of teaching History of Doctrine. In those days the colleges were well equipped in staff and other resources. But with the passage of years the balance changed: the colleges depended more and more on the university's resources, and there was a rapidly increasing number of students who were not candidates for the ministry of any church and who were registered in the university only, not in the colleges. It therefore became more and more necessary for the university to make its own provision for the teaching of History of Doctrine, and during my two years' stint as Dean of the Faculty of Theology (1963-64) I had to make representations for the establishment of a chair in this subject. The representations were successful, thanks (it is interesting to recall) to the support of one or two agnostics in the Faculties of Science and Medicine, who, because of their seniority and sound judgment, carried weight in the counsels of the university and who were persuaded that a strong academic case had been made out for the establishment of this new chair. The subject is now called Historical and Contemporary Theology. The first professor was Dr Hubert Cunliffe-Jones, who had been Associate Principal of the Congregational College in Manchester; when he retired we were fortunate in securing as his successor Dr Richard Hanson, who after holding chairs in the Universities of Durham and Nottingham had served for three years as Bishop of Clogher in the Church of Ireland, endeavouring to fulfil a ministry of conciliation in a diocese which straddled the frontier between Northern Ireland and the Republic. No doubt he was glad to return to the calm of academic life.

In the Department of Biblical Criticism and Exegesis my predecessor had relied on part-time help from members of the staffs of the theological colleges, and I inherited their help. George Farr, of Manchester Baptist College, was (until 1980) part-time lecturer in Old Testament and Owen Evans, of Hartley-Victoria Methodist College (now Director of the New Welsh Bible), performed the same service for the New Testament. When Mr Evans left to take up an appointment in the University College of North Wales, Bangor (teaching Greek New Testament in Welsh), he was replaced in our department by Eric Hull, of the Congregational College, who died with tragic suddenness in November 1977, only a few weeks after becoming Principal of his College. But in 1959 our department was beginning to expand rapidly, owing particularly to a recently instituted Honours School of Biblical Studies, and in my first two years two new full-time lectureships were instituted — one in Old Testament and one in New Testament. To the Old Testament lectureship came Arnold Anderson, who has since made his name as author of the excellent two-volume commentary on the Psalms in the New Century Bible (1972). He was a Latvian by birth, and after adventurous vicissitudes came to this country after the war as a 'displaced person'. He went to Spurgeon's College and then Oxford University (where he was a pupil of G. R. Driver); after that he held an assistantship in Hebrew in Edinburgh University. From 1960 onwards he was my right-hand man in the department. Two or three years later the frontiers between our department and that of Near Eastern Studies were redrawn, and in consequence we acquired John Allegro as an augmentation to our strength on the Old Testament and inter-testamental side. He became widely known in the early 1950s as a member of the international team of scholars charged with the assembling and editing of the Dead Sea Scrolls, and earned the gratitude of his colleagues in many lands for the promptness with which he published some of the most important texts with which he had to deal. When he left us in 1970 he was succeeded by Adrian Curtis, one of our own honours graduates in Biblical Studies.

On the New Testament side we have had a more rapid overturn of successive lecturers. First we had Robert Kraft, who came to us with a brilliant record from Wheaton and Harvard; we knew that we could not hope to hold him for long, and after two years he was offered a professorship in the University of Pennsylvania, where he still is. In his place we appointed Clark Pinnock, a Canadian scholar who had just completed his Ph.D. with us; he also stayed for two years and then accepted a professorship in New Orleans Baptist Seminary (from there he moved successively to Trinity Evangelical Divinity School near Chicago, Regent College, Vancouver, and McMaster Divinity School, Hamilton, Ontario). Then came Ralph Martin, himself a Manchester graduate and sometime pupil of T. W. Manson, who had been for some years on the staff of London Bible College; after four years he was called to a chair in Fuller Seminary, Pasadena, California. America's keenness to have them certainly bears witness to the quality of the men whom we appointed! In Ralph Martin's place we secured Stephen Smalley, a Cambridge graduate who had spent eight years lecturing in the University of Ibadan, Nigeria. He stayed with us for eight years, and we thought that he was the more securely anchored because his wife Susan, whom he married in 1974, was herself a lecturer in the Department of Historical and Contemporary Theology. But in 1977 he accepted an invitation to go to Coventry Cathedral as Canon Residentiary and Precentor. In his closing months in

Manchester he had been hard at work on his book *John: Evangelist and Interpreter,* which The Paternoster Press published in 1978 as an addition to its series of volumes on the four Gospels. As a temporary replacement for him the University appointed Colin Hemer, who had taken his Ph.D. with us a few years previously with a thesis on the Seven Churches of Asia.

Among my departmental colleagues I must include, for highly honourable mention, the secretaries with whom the University of Manchester generously provided me. For my first four years I had as my secretary Miss June Hogg, a gifted young lady to whom I was indebted for the typing of *Israel and the Nations* and my Tyndale commentary on *Romans* (both published in 1963). Then she married a lecturer in the Department of Mathematics and left England with him soon afterwards when he took up an appointment in an Australian university. But I was supremely fortunate in securing the services, in her place, of her sister Margaret, who remained as my secretary for the remaining fifteen years of my tenure of the chair. Thanks to her, the phrase 'the perfect secretary' in my mind does not express an unattainable ideal; it is the natural and proper way to describe Margaret. When people asked how I managed to maintain my literary output during those fifteen years, the answer in large measure was to be found in her help: not to mention a host of minor works, she typed my *New Testament History* (1969), my New Century volume on *1 and 2 Corinthians* (1971), and *Paul: Apostle of the Free Spirit* (1977). Not only is she an excellent typist; she is a vigilant proof-reader, and as for her competence in the compiling of indexes, I have known professional indexers who did not reach her standard of efficiency. It was by way of a small, but well merited, tribute to her co-operation that I dedicated to her the last book that she typed for me: *What the Bible Teaches about the Work of Jesus* (1979). My successor now profits by her expertise as I formerly did.

Both in the Faculty of Theology, then, and in the more intimate fellowship of the Department of Biblical Criticism and Exegesis I was exceptionally happy to have such colleagues. When I retired in 1978 I was succeeded by my friend Barnabas Lindars, of the Society of St. Francis, who had been Dean of Jesus College, Cambridge; and I have good reason to believe that he finds as much happiness among his Manchester colleagues as I used to do.

Notes to Chapter 26

1. Cf. his *Jesus and the Zealots* (Manchester 1967).

2. He acknowledged that it was this seminar that encouraged him to publish the volume of his collected papers entitled *The Framework of the New Testament Stories* (Manchester 1964). Some material which he left in manuscript at the time of his death was subsequently published, including a series of lectures on *The Acts of the Apostles* (Manchester 1969), which I prepared for the press. Another posthumously published volume of his is entitled *The Beginning* (Manchester 1968), a study of the background to John 1: 1 and 1 John 1: 1; it was edited for the press by Dr John Heywood Thomas (then Lecturer in Philosophy of Religion in our Faculty and now Professor of Christian Theology in the University of Nottingham), who prefaced the work with a biographical sketch of the author.

27

New home and new church

I

A shift of work from Sheffield to Manchester meant that we had to think of a shift of domicile. There was no great urgency about this: as I have said, I had university duties in Sheffield as well as in Manchester from October to December 1959, and commuted by train between the two cities. But from January 1960 onwards I was to give my undivided attention to the University of Manchester, and there was no point in staying on in Sheffield. But where should we go to live? The time was past when proximity to schools played an important part in a choice of residence. Moreover, ever since our marriage we had lived in large cities, and we saw no reason for going to live in Manchester, if we could find a smaller place with ready access to it. We thought of Buxton, equidistant from both Sheffield and Manchester (25 miles distant from each), but enjoying much better communications with the latter city than with the former.

One factor which pressed Buxton on our attention was that our daughter Sheila, who was at that time a student in St. Andrews, had a university friend who lived in Buxton. Sheila went to visit this girl in the course of one vacation, and the girl and her parents urged the advantages of Buxton on her, and through her on us. (As it turned out, soon after we went to live in Buxton, the girl's father was moved to another place, so the family left Buxton.) In September 1959 my wife and I visited Buxton one afternoon to spy out the land, came upon a house we liked which was marked 'For Sale', procured an order to view and found it to be as attractive inside as outside, made an offer and reached agreement with the owner and his agents. The occupants planned to move out on 25th March, which suited us very well, so as soon as they left, we moved in. One of our neighbours in Sheffield, hearing that we were likely to leave soon, asked if he might have first refusal of our house there, so we were able to sell it to him with effect from the same day as we took possession of 'The Crossways' in Buxton.

On the distant horizon of our thinking at the time was the consideration that we might as well decide to live somewhere which would not involve another move when retirement came along: that consideration has now justified itself.

Buxton in those days had good communications with Manchester (to which indeed there were two alternative routes by rail — the former LNW and the former Midland) and with London. At least one train leaving St. Pancras each day for Manchester Central had a through coach for Buxton which was detached from the other coaches at Miller's Dale and completed its journey on a short branch line. As a result of the more recent dismantling of much of the Midland track, communication with the east is now more difficult, but it is still easy to get to London Euston via Stockport and Inter-City train, and communications with Manchester by road and rail remain good. Road communications may be complicated in winter by overnight snowfalls, but I have never been unable to get to the university by train. From time-to-time my colleagues who lived nearer Manchester listened to the news at breakfast and heard that Buxton had been 'cut off'; then they made their way to the university to find that I had got there before them!

Buxton is a town of just over 20,000 population, situated in the High Peak district of Derbyshire. It lies between 1,000 and 1,100 feet high, but the surrounding area is even higher, for one comes down into Buxton from every point of the compass. It is famed chiefly for its spa waters, which are believed (with reason) to be specially helpful to sufferers from arthritis, whether taken internally or externally. Its natural baths were known in Roman times, and gave the place the name of *Aquae Arnemetianae*. Until fairly recently Buxton was one of the fashionable watering places of England, but has begun to change that role for others. It is still a popular conference centre, and is becoming increasingly a dormitory town for Manchester. To us one of its great attractions was (and is) the beautiful countryside around it.

II

If it was no longer necessary to have our choice of residence dictated by proximity to schools, we did have some regard to accessibility to a suitable church. For many years there had been a meeting of brethren in Buxton, but not long before we went there it had disbanded because it had dwindled numerically to a point where it could no longer maintain itself. (Some of the older people remembered how many years ago a young man named Donald Coggan visited the meeting with his fiancée, who had relatives in Buxton, and broke bread with them.) But we had our eye on Crescent Road Hall in Stockport, not because it was the nearest brethren's meeting to us (there were — and are — at least two others which are nearer) but in part because it was most accessible. In fact, it was doubly accessible: lying near the main route by road and rail between Buxton and Manchester, it was conveniently accessible from Buxton on Sunday and from Manchester on a week night. Another thing which attracted us to Crescent Road was the fact that we already knew a number of the friends who met there, having been associated with them in our young people's Easter holiday conference — among these Arnold Pickering is the most widely known.

The church at Crescent Road Hall traced its origins back

221

to 1900. It made two or three moves in the first ten years of its existence, but in 1910 it took up a more durable residence in a new corrugated iron building at the corner of Crescent Road and Dawson Street, in the Lower Brinnington district of Stockport. Its notice-board, in unsectarian terms, proclaimed it to be 'A Centre for Christian Worship and Witness' — a most accurate description. Shortly after we joined it, a special conference was held to celebrate the fiftieth anniversary of the opening of the hall. By that time it was becoming clear that more commodious premises would soon be necessary to maintain and extend the church's activity. Various explorations were made, but all led into blind alleys, until in 1973 we learned that a Methodist society on the Brinnington housing estate, about a mile farther out from the centre of Stockport, was likely to disband shortly and that its premises, which were modern and convenient, were likely to be up for sale. Our church agreed unanimously that we should move there, if we could acquire the building, and after about a year of negotiations (at every stage of which we had ample evidence of the guidance of God) the building became ours and we moved in on 28th July, 1974. As the 'Crescent Road' designation was no longer applicable, we renamed ourselves Brinnington Evangelical Church.

In earlier chapters I have said something about churches to which I belonged in other places where we have lived. When one has been away from a church for a number of years, one acquires the necessary perspective from which to view and assess it objectively. It is more difficult to view and assess objectively a church to which one belongs and in whose life one is very much involved. But, avoiding all odious comparisons, I can say that we have never been in a more congenial fellowship than that which we have found in Stockport.

It may be asked, of course, why in our successive changes of abode we have always thrown our lot in with a church of this particular order. That is a question which may be taken up later.[1] But let me quote here something that I wrote a number of years ago in an issue of the *CBRF Journal*. Issue

222

No. 8 of that journal (June 1965) featured twelve contributions on the theme 'Why I left the Brethren' (and two on the theme 'Why I joined the Brethren'). To present a more complete and better balanced picture, the editor included in a later issue (No. 10, December 1965) six contributions on 'Why I have stayed with the Brethren' (with four others on 'Why I joined the Brethren' and four 'On returning to the Brethren'). I began my contribution on 'Why I have stayed . . . ' by saying: 'Ecclesiastically speaking, I belong (1) to the Church Universal and (2) to the local church which meets in Crescent Road, Stockport; and ecclesiastically speaking I belong to nothing else. The only alternative to staying in the Church Universal would be to renounce the faith once delivered; and if I am asked why I stay in the church at Crescent Road, Stockport, my reply must be: "If you only knew that church, you would have no need to ask why I stay in it!" ' That remains true; the church has changed its location and its name, but it has not changed its identity or its character.

It has, however, seen considerable changes in its membership over the years since we joined it. Some ten years ago we lost twenty of our members who left us to establish a new church, together with some Christians from other places, some miles distant from Stockport — Marple Independent Evangelical Church. This move was made in full agreement with ourselves, although our strength was sorely depleted by their departure. They aimed at starting their new church life with Holy Scripture as their sole authority, in complete freedom from tradition of any kind. Although our church at Brinnington would be reckoned liberal by some standards, it is positively conservative in comparison with the sister-church at Marple. A year or two ago our Marple friends celebrated the completion of some extensions to their building with a special meeting at which I was invited, as guest speaker, to expound the New Testament teaching about the local church. Representatives of neighbouring churches attended as a token of fellowship, from a Salvation Army officer to the local Catholic priest, so

I had a more diversified audience than I usually find before me when I speak on church doctrine!

Happily, this loss was largely offset less than a year before our move from Crescent Road to Brinnington when Hope Hall Evangelical Church in Manchester decided to disband itself. About fourteen of its former members came to join our fellowship, adding very substantially to our strength not only in numbers but in quality as well.

At the last Sunday morning communion service in Brinnington Methodist Church, just before the disbanding of the society and the transfer of the property to us, a deputation of members of the Crescent Road church joined them at the Lord's Table in token of fellowship. The Methodists were glad that the building would continue to be used for the preaching of the gospel, and at the end of the service the superintendent minister of the circuit symbolically handed over the keys to me, and I accepted them as a representative of the Crescent Road church, the occasion being appropriately sanctified by the word of God and prayer. (The symbolism was not really impaired by the fact that I handed back the keys after the service, in the privacy of the vestry, because the legal formalities of the sale had not yet been completed.)

After we moved in, a good deal of installation and decoration had to be undertaken, but on 5th April, 1975, when the first and most necessary stages of this work had been completed, we held a special meeting at which our friends from elsewhere were invited to join us in returning thanks to God for his good hand upon us.

When we first joined the church at Crescent Road in April 1960, we were given a warm welcome by all its members, and felt at home there from the outset. Before long, the church invited me to accept the title and function of 'teaching elder' — a high honour indeed. To quote the distinction which G. V. Wigram made in his tract on *Ministry in the Word* (1844), this title implies a *stated* ministry but not an *exclusive* ministry. Perhaps the church recognized that I was not likely to be much good at anything other than teaching, whereas some of my brethren have the ability to 'rule well' and perform other valuable services as well as to 'labour in the word and in teaching'.

We were conscious immediately of an atmosphere of spiritual freedom in our new fellowship — which is not to say that it was absent from our previous associations. The meetings were marked by a sense of relaxation, with no feeling of 'uptightness' such as manifests itself in some places if someone suddenly departs from tradition or deviates from a party line. (Some 'lines' are good lines, but party lines are almost always bad lines.) No one was liable to be upset if a member, or a visitor, did or said something on Sunday morning (or at any other time) which had never been done or said before. Arnold Pickering has been known to quote the closing words of 2 Corinthians 3:17 in a revised version which runs: 'where the Spirit of the Lord is, there is flexibility'. There is more to liberty than flexibility, but flexibility is an essential element of spiritual liberty. If any one doubts this, let him try replacing 'flexibility' in that quotation by its opposite, 'rigidity', and see how it fits. Rigidity and spiritual liberty are incompatible; rigidity, indeed, can prove to be *rigor mortis*. When *rigor mortis* affects a church (like the church of Sardis), it is in a desperate state indeed. Happily, the Spirit of liberty is also the Spirit of life: he can raise a church from death and restore it to life and liberty. Henry Barrow (one of the radical reformers, who was executed under the first Elizabeth in 1593) described 'a true planted and rightly established church of Christ' as 'a brotherhood, a communion of saints, each one of them standing in and for their Christian liberty to practise whatsoever God has commanded and revealed unto them in his holy word'.[2] Spiritual liberty is never divorced from acknowledgment of the authority of the word of God, for the word is the primary vehicle of the voice of the Spirit. But 'a true planted and rightly established church of Christ' will always be prepared to accept and obey that further light which (in the words of John Robinson of Leiden) God may yet cause 'to break forth out of his holy word', and will indeed *expect* such light to break forth. Such an attitude of expectancy, my experience suggests, is by no means rare among churches of our order. We are as prone to be influenced by tradition as our neighbours are, but we know that tradition is not the ultimate authority, and that 'This is what we have always done' or 'This is what we were always taught' cannot be the most conclusive argument.

The fact that we find our regular church fellowship twenty miles away from the place where we live does not (and, of course, should not) mean that we play no part in church life in Buxton. Individual churches in the neighbourhood, as well as the local council of churches, soon discovered that we were available for occasional services. For six consecutive Wednesday evenings before Easter 1974, for example, I gave a series of Lenten talks for our council of churches on 'St. John's Passion Narrative'. My membership of the Manchester Faculty of Theology has similarly involved me from time to time in church activities in that city, and I welcome every such opportunity of wider fellowship. I recall in this connexion another series of weekly Lenten talks, given in 1978 at midday services in St. Ann's Church (in the city centre) on 'Jesus Christ: who is he?' The rector was anxious that some more positive teaching should be given on this basic theme than the negative treatment offered some months earlier in *The Myth of God Incarnate*.[3]

As for 'para-church' bodies, there is none with which I co-operate more happily or more frequently than the British and Foreign Bible Society, especially its local Associations. I have for many years taken part in the Annual Meetings of a large number of these Associations in the part of England where I live. I enjoy doing this primarily because of my unqualified support of the purpose and ministry of the Bible Society — the production and circulation of the Scriptures worldwide. But I find in these occasions a secondary cause for enjoyment. Some of the most desirable things in life come as by-products of other activities. Christian unity is one of these most desirable things, but it is best promoted not by organizations set up specifically in order to foster it but in the process of Christian co-operation in causes which all Christians cherish in common. The Bible Society represents such a cause, and I have been gratified to see Christian unity in action at grass-roots level wherever I have found a local Association (or, in some places, an 'action group') of the Bible Society bringing together on a practical footing members of all the churches in a district. It is indeed only natural that this should be so, for the British and Foreign Bible Society, from its inception in 1804, was a pioneer in what would nowadays be called ecumenical action.

Notes to Chapter 27

1. See pp. 282 ff.

2. Cf. F. J. Powicke *Henry Barrow, Separatist, 1550?-1593 and the Exiled Church of Amsterdam, 1593-1622* (London 1900).

3. I have often thought that if this symposium had been produced under some such title as *Ten Essays in Christology*, it would not have created the stir it did. The inclusion of the emotive word 'myth' in the title was more responsible for the stir than the contents of the book.

28

Pupils, past and present

As children are to a parent, as converts are to an evangelist, so are pupils to a teacher. As I look back over forty-three years of teaching, there are few things that give me such undiluted joy as the contemplation of my pupils, past and present. Not every teacher might be happy to be judged by his pupils, I suppose. Seneca cannot be held entirely responsible for the way that Nero turned out, and even Aristotle could have had misgivings about some features of the career of his former pupil Alexander. Other teachers find their pupils disconcerting in other ways: we have recently been reminded, for example, that Bertrand Russell was not only dissuaded by the devastating criticisms of his most illustrious pupil, Ludwig Wittgenstein, from writing any more of his *Theory of Knowledge* (which had been designed as the sequel to *Principia Mathematica*) but was even reluctantly persuaded by him that mathematics, the art in which he really shone, was nothing but tautology.[1] None of my pupils has tried to convince me that my lifetime studies have been futile or that I would have been more usefully employed breaking stones by the roadside; some of them, indeed, have gone on to show how these studies can be more fruitfully pursued than they have been pursued by me.

I shall be well content to have the quality of my teaching assessed by the quality of my students. As I used to tell them year by year in our Pauline studies, Paul's readiness to have his apostolic ministry judged by the quality of his converts finds an appreciative response in my mind (to compare great things with small) in respect of my teaching and their achievement. Not that I can claim credit for their achievement, but it is pleasant to enjoy something of their reflected glory. Nor am I thinking only of those who have attained high academic distinction: I think of many who work faithfully and effectively as teachers, preachers and missionaries in many parts of the world. I have sometimes thought of getting a large map of the world and sticking coloured pins or flags in here and there to show where former students are living and working, from the far east to the far west.

Of some of my Edinburgh students, not much junior to myself, I have said something already. Of my Leeds students, the most outstanding academically was Olwen Parry, who succeeded me in my lectureship there. Another was Dr Catherine Alder, who was for many years head of the department of Religious Knowledge in Goldsmiths' College, London. I remember her as one of a class of two with whom I read New Testament texts in Greek. She had some experience of Modern Greek, the other member of the class had done a little classical Greek, so New Testament Greek helped to bridge the linguistic gap between them. (From Leeds she went to St. Andrews to take her B.D. and Ph.D. degrees.) Of my men students from those days, most went into parishes, while most of the girls went into school teaching — although some of the latter, after a year or two, married some of the former. This reminds me that a few years ago, one of my external examiners in New Testament, observing the marked difference in attainment between two groups of Manchester students, asked, 'What do your B.A. (Honours) girls think when they sit in the pews and listen to your B.A. (Theol.) men in the pulpits?' to which I replied: 'Sometimes they marry them, and presumably write their sermons for them.' Some of them, I am happy to add, occupy pulpits themselves.

When I went to Sheffield in 1947, my new department taught courses for the pass degree of B.A. only, but I made it my business as soon as possible to have an Honours School of Biblical History and Literature instituted, in which both Hebrew and Greek would be taken for three years. It was inaugurated in 1949, with one student applying to enter it — one only, but one who established its academic prestige from the outset, David Payne by name. When he graduated in 1952, he was not only awarded first class honours in his chosen field of study but also the Gibbons Prize, awarded that year to the most distinguished graduating student in the whole Faculty of Arts. No one did more than he to set the stamp of intellectual respectability on a department on which some had looked with misgivings when it was set up. From Sheffield he went on to further studies in the University of Glasgow and the Hebrew University of Jerusalem, and he is now Head of the Department of Semitic Studies in the Queen's University of Belfast.

Among other students whom I taught in Sheffield I think of Dr Paul Garnet, now teaching in Concordia University, Montreal; Anthea Cousins, who became headmistress of The Park School, Yeovil, and now, with the publication of *Centurions and Sinners* (1979), seems to have embarked on a new and promising career as an author. I think also of Elizabeth Johnston (née Ward), who became Lecturer in Biblical Study in Aberdeen University and then exchanged an academic career for a domestic way of life; and Margaret Howe, who came back for a further spell of study with me at Manchester, where she took her Ph.D., and now teaches in Western Kentucky University.

Some of my former Manchester students are now in various areas of the foreign mission field. Sylvia Hedinger (née Hales-Lovell) is with the Wycliffe translators in Cameroon, and Rosemary Foster (née Chapman) is a missionary teacher with OMF in Indonesia, while Donald Horsfield was for some years a missionary teacher with the

London Missionary Society in Papua New Guinea. I remember going to Westhoughton in Lancashire, his native place, one evening many years ago to attend his ordination service: he was ordained directly into LMS. I have attended other ordination services and taken a minor part in them, such as reading the Scripture lesson or leading in prayer, but on this occasion I gave him his charge (by his own invitation) and shared in the act of ordination, which was performed, at his request, not by the laying on of hands but by the exchange of the right hand of fellowship. I did so, the chairman explained, as a representative of 'the wider church', a form of words which, while not chosen by me, was by no means unwelcome. The wider the church, the better pleased I am to belong to it, provided it acknowledges Jesus as Lord — and if it does not, then, of course, it is no church.

It was a thoroughly ecumenical service: greetings were conveyed from the local Catholic congregation and the nearest Brethren assembly, as well as from several other companies betwixt and between. Some years later, Donald put down deep roots into his new homeland by marrying a Papuan girl. When I gave this news to Professor Cunliffe-Jones, another of his former teachers, he said, 'Ah well, Donald was always a pioneer.'

My students have been drawn from a wide denominational range, embracing most of the main-line varieties of Christian fellowship, from Rome to Plymouth (so to speak), and a number of others. Those from Rome have been more numerous since Vatican II. Catholic educational authorities in this country prefer nowadays to expose their prospective teachers to a regular university course, and indeed frequently second some who have been teaching for quite a time to come and study with us for two or three years. Our Faculty of Theology thus has a small, but regular, contingent of priests, teaching brothers and nuns among its students, and these are in many ways an asset to our community. I had among my students in Sheffield one Mormon (who was always careful to insist that he belonged to the *Reorganized* Church of Jesus Christ of Latter Day Saints) and one

Christadelphian girl, who knew the text of Scripture inside out but of all the students whom I have ever taught was most impervious to the historical-critical method. In Manchester we had a succession of Seventh-day Adventist research students, most of them (interestingly enough) from Australia. They liked to make a critical assessment of themes which have played their part in Adventist theology: I had from three of them successful Ph.D. theses on 'The abomination of desolation', 'The day of the Lord' and 'The day of atonement in the New Testament'. (One of them, I gather, has incurred suspicion in his denomination for being over-enthusiastic in expounding justification by faith alone: some of his critics have discerned my influence here — but I think he was firmly established in this truth before ever he met me.) Over the years I have also had a few Jewish students, some of whom have shown an interest in the New Testament as well as the Old, and one year a mature Hindu student sat politely through a course of mine on the Apostolic Age.

Most of my research students had taken their first degrees elsewhere. In my Sheffield days they included Dr Maurice Barnett, later minister of Westminster Central Hall, whose thesis dealt with the social aspect of biblical holiness; another Methodist scholar, Dr Cyril Powell, who studied the biblical concept of power; and a younger man of exceptional promise, Dr Ronald Clements, who while he was pastor of a Baptist church in the Sheffield area wrote a thesis on the dwelling-place of God in the Old Testament. He now lectures in Cambridge and is well known as a leading scholar in Old Testament circles. When his subject of research came up for approval by the Sheffield Faculty of Arts, someone asked if it should not have been sponsored by the Department of Architecture rather than by mine! In a revised form his thesis was published as a monograph, *God and Temple* (1965).

Mention of this volume reminds me that my shelves are enriched by a succession of books on which I look with special affection and pride because they started life as theses prepared under my supervision. Picking out some at random (with apologies for the omission of others), I mention *The Holy Spirit in the Acts of the Apostles* (1967) by J. H. E. Hull; *The Use of the Old Testament in St Matthew's Gospel* (1967) by R. H. Gundry; *The Use of the Old and New Testaments in Clement of Rome* (1973) by D. A. Hagner; *A History of the Criticism of the Acts of the Apostles* (1975) by Ward Gasque; *Paul: Libertine or Legalist?* (1975)[2] by John Drane; *A History of Interpretation of Hebrews 7: 1-10 from the Reformation to the Present* (1976) by Bruce Demarest, and *Introductory Thanksgivings in the Letters of Paul* (1977) by P. T. O'Brien. More are in the pipeline. Colin Hemer's thesis on the letters to the seven churches of Asia, for example, which was based on study *in situ* as well as in ancient literature, will be seen, when it is published, to have superseded Sir William Ramsay's book on the subject.

My only share in the production of these works has been to help their authors to decide on a subject adapted to their interests and qualifications and then say 'Go to it'.

Murray Harris, of Auckland, N.Z., now Professor in the Bible College of New Zealand, completed a thesis on the interpretation of 2 Corinthians 5: 1-10 which his Cambridge external examiner pronounced to be the best Ph.D. thesis he had ever read. (That examiner had himself written on the problems of 2 Corinthians 5: 1-10, and Dr Harris had argued against him, but that enhanced, rather than diminished, his appreciation of the thesis.) Another Ph.D. student, Ronald Fung of Hong Kong, secured the degree for a thesis in two volumes on the relation between righteousness and faith in the thought of Paul, on which his examiners commented that, when once it is published, it may well be greeted as the definitive work on the question whether justification by faith is the central motif in Paul's understanding of the gospel or only a 'subsidiary crater' (to borrow Albert Schweitzer's expression).

My former research students are now teaching or otherwise engaged in Christian activity in many parts of the world. I have just mentioned one in Hong Kong; my last

Ph.D. student in Manchester, Che-Bin Tan, teaches in the same school (the China Graduate School of Theology). Two other Chinese scholars who studied with me (Swee-Hwa Quek and David Wong) teach in Singapore. One of my ablest students was a Korean, Seyoon Kim, who now teaches in Seoul. Peter O'Brien and David Peterson teach in Moore College and the University of Sydney; Desmond Ford and Norman Young in Avondale College, Cooranbong, N.S.W. David Wenham was on the staff of Union Biblical Seminary, Yavatmal, South India, and is now at Tyndale House, Cambridge. René Padilla has made a name for himself in Latin America and beyond as a leader in the International Fellowship of Evangelical Students and similar causes in that area. Donald Hagner and George Gay teach in Fuller Seminary, Pasadena; Robert Gundry and Moises Silva in Westmont College, Santa Barbara. Bruce Demarest teaches in the Conservative Baptist Seminary, Denver, Colorado; Alex Deasley in the Nazarene Theological Seminary, Kansas City, and Kent Brower in the Nazarene College, Winnipeg. Julius Scott teaches in Wheaton Graduate School. Howard Andersen is President of the North-Western Baptist College, Vancouver, and Ward Gasque is on the staff of Regent College in the same city (although he has been seconded for two years to become first President of New College, Berkeley, California).

This is a form of name-dropping in which I can indulge with no sense of shame: I have good reason to be proud of my students. And it gives me real satisfaction to find that there are those who still count themselves my students, if no longer in any official sense.

What do I try to do for them? Well, teach them, of course — which does not mean simply feeding them with facts, much less indoctrinating them. Naturally, to some extent I *can* feed them with facts. For example, I have been studying Greek for a longer time than they have, and can tell them, as we read the Septuagint or Greek New Testament, that a certain form is the aorist infinitive passive of such-and-such a verb. That is the kind of statement which can be accepted without much disputation. But most of my teaching deals with matters which call for the exercise of personal judgment. If we are discussing (say) the date, authorship and purpose of a particular biblical document, I can put all the evidence before them and tell them in which direction I think the evidence points, but I cannot force my conclusions on them: they must make their minds up for themselves. This means that they must be taught how to evaluate the kind of evidence on which conclusions of this character are based. The same is true when we are studying the exegesis of a passage on the text or meaning of which editors, translators and interpreters differ. I can tell them my own view, and why I hold it, but I cannot impose it on them. What I do impose is the duty of knowing clearly, and stating clearly, their reasons for holding their own preferred view, whether it coincides with mine or not. If pupils turn out to be carbon copies of their teacher, it says little for his qualities as a teacher.

No student of any subject will get real satisfaction out of it unless he is in sympathy with it. If I can help them to sympathize with (say) Isaiah or Paul, to see why he addressed himself as he did to his constituency and what he was aiming to achieve, then I have succeeded in something. It would be disastrous if I myself treated my subject so unsympathetically that, fascinating and exciting as it is in itself, I put them off it. Although my business is to expound Scripture objectively, there is no reason why I should exclude a note of animation from my voice when expounding Romans 3: 21-26 or Hebrews 9: 11-14.

I was (mercifully) never paid to teach dogmatic theology, but experience has shown me that when students are exposed to the word of God, it confronts them with its innate authority without any help from me. Some of them may have had little previous conception of its authority; others have been brought up to accept a package deal in which biblical authority is wrapped up with a good deal of expendable luggage, and need to be helped to distinguish what is essential from what is not. The gratitude of those who have received this particular form of help is sufficient in itself to make a Bible teacher's work rewarding.

Notes to Chapter 28

1. R. W. Clark *The Life of Bertrand Russell* (London 1975), pp. 169 ff., 203 ff., etc.
2. If any reader wonders what the answer to this question is, it is 'Neither'.

29
East Africa and North America

The sixties brought with them further opportunities for us to pay visits overseas. Not only were there international conferences and foreign lecture tours, but in 1963 both our children settled in other parts of the Commonwealth and provided us with the incentive to visit their new homes. Iain, with his wife and two children, went to St. John's, Newfoundland, where he took up an appointment in the Memorial University of Newfoundland. Sheila went to lecture in a teacher's training college in Uganda. There she married in 1965 and continued to live until 1974, when she and her husband, James Lukabyo, with their family of five (plus one adopted daughter), emigrated to Australia and took up residence in the neighbourhood of Sydney. So family visits to Newfoundland, Uganda and now Australia, were woven into the pattern of the years.

I

Uganda, which we visited twice, has a charm peculiarly its own. An illuminated sign at Entebbe Airport proclaims the nearby capital, Kampala, to be 'the friendliest city in Africa'. Not having seen all the cities of Africa, we could not underwrite this use of the superlative, but it would be difficult to find anywhere in the world friendlier people than the Ugandans. We were greatly impressed by the vitality of Christian life and witness in Uganda, at all levels of society. I recall a meeting with the Graduates' Fellowship group in Kampala, at which I was glad to mark the high proportion of Ugandan members who were employed in the civil service or occupied comparable positions of public responsibility. At grass roots level (literally) we recall a morning communion service which we attended on Christmas Day, 1965, in a bush church near Kamuli, in the north of the province of Busoga. The service was conducted according to the order of the (Anglican) Church of Uganda, but for the greater part of the time there was a free-and-easy degree of spontaneous audience participation which would have been thought excessive in most Brethren churches back home. The service was attended by the Kyabazinga (king) of Busoga (then Vice-President of Uganda), accompanied by his resplendently dressed bevy of wives. Although he was a professing Christian, he was, as a polygamist, debarred from communion; I think one of his wives (presumably his first one) did communicate. Next day, which was a Sunday, I preached at a much more decorous evening service in Jinja, in the church where Sheila and James had been married some months previously by Noel King, Professor of Religious Studies in Makerere University.

On a later visit to Uganda I gave a lecture in Makerere University: by that time Noel King had left Uganda to take up an appointment in California, and my lecture was delivered on the day when it was announced that he was to be succeeded by John Mbiti, a native of Kenya and graduate of Cambridge (who later became Director of the Ecumenical Institute at the Château de Bossey near Geneva).

One incident which has stuck with me and which I have frequently mentioned relates to a visit we paid to the home of a Uganda Asian, a neighbour of our daughter's, in Kamuli. As we sat at tea, the conversation turned to a mission hospital run by a Catholic sisterhood a mile or two away, which we had been shown round a few days before. 'It's impossible to speak too highly of the good that these women have done for this neighbourhood,' said our host, a Hindu — 'and they do it all for Jesus Christ.' Talk about 'adorning the doctrine'!

The people of Uganda certainly did nothing to deserve the reign of terror under Idi Amin or the near-anarchy which, in some parts of the country, followed his expulsion. All the friends of Uganda must wish her a happy issue out of these afflictions and a stable and prosperous future.

II

Invitations to deliver short courses of lectures in North America came along every now and then. In 1961 Betty and I spent a month at the Summer School of Theology in Winona Lake, Indiana (which at that time was affiliated to Fuller Theological Seminary, Pasadena, California). This attracted visiting lecturers and students from over a wide area, and we made several good friends among both groups. Among the visiting lecturers was the late Dr J. Oliver Buswell, Jr., one of America's best known evangelical theologians. My assignment was to give two lecture courses — one on Acts and one on the Dead Sea Scrolls.

One of the Saturdays during the Winona Lake summer school was our silver wedding anniversary: we celebrated it by taking a long walk round the lake after which the town of Winona Lake is named and treating ourselves to a meal in the neighbouring city of Warsaw — previously known to me only as the birthplace of Theodore Dreiser. (I could remember, some thirty years before, reading his *Dreiser looks at Russia*.) The difficulty about going for a long walk in America, we found, was that practically every motorist who overtook us stopped and offered us a lift; it was difficult to convince them that we were really walking for the enjoyment of walking. They probably thought we were slightly round the bend. Even our friends on the summer school campus expressed surprised incredulity when we announced our

239

intention of walking round the lake, and even greater incredulity when they were told that we had carried out our intention. It was the sort of thing Dr Buswell did, but then he was known to be an exceptional kind of person, with a most un-American taste for physical exercise!

That was the only occasion on which we went to North America and returned by sea: we went out on the *Queen Elizabeth* and came back on the *Queen Mary*. On our arrival at New York we were met by Walter Liefield (now of Trinity Evangelical Divinity School, Deerfield, Illinois) and entertained by him and his wife Olive; we had also the opportunity of fellowship with friends at Sea Cliff Gospel Chapel, Long Island, where Walter was at that time fulfilling a pastoral ministry. From there we flew to Chicago, where we spent some days before the summer school with our cousins Ernest and Mae Bendelow; this meant a renewal of fellowship with brethren in the Chicago area (especially at Woodside Bible Chapel, Maywood, Illinois) and an opportunity to sample the ministry provided at a residential conference at Lake Geneva, Wisconsin. We returned to Chicago for a few days after the summer school and then flew to New York, where we spent the last night of our trip in the (now defunct) Biblical Seminary on East 49th Street, as the guests of our friends Dewey and Marion Beegle (now of Wesley Theological Seminary, Washington, D.C.).

Later visits to North America were undertaken to deliver the Payton Lectures in Fuller Theological Seminary, Pasadena, and the Norton Lectures in the Southern Baptist Theological Seminary, Louisville, Kentucky (February-March 1968), the Smyth Lectures in Columbia Theological Seminary, Decatur, Georgia, and the Earle Lectures in the Nazarene Theological Seminary, Kansas City (April 1970), the Lund Memorial Lectures in North Park Theological Seminary, Chicago (November 1970), and the Thomas F. Staley Lectures in Ontario Bible College, Toronto (March 1973). Some of these courses of lectures have already provided material for books: the Payton Lectures were published under the title *This is That* later in 1968. The title

— a very appropriate one (drawn from Acts 2: 16) — was chosen by my British publisher, Howard Mudditt; the publisher of the American edition, however, reckoned that this title would be meaningless to the American Christian public, so he produced it under the rather clumsy title (based on the sub-title of the British edition): *The New Testament Development of Old Testament Themes*.[1] The Norton Lectures appeared as *Tradition Old and New* (1970); one reviewer suggested that this was the most 'autobiographical' thing I had written to date. He got this impression, no doubt, because I was largely moved to deal with that subject by my personal experience of the working of tradition in some communities which imagined that they were quite uninfluenced by any such thing. The lectures delivered in Toronto were published in America as *Paul and Jesus* (1974).

On another visit to America I participated in the twenty-fifth anniversary conference of the Evangelical Theological Society, held in Wheaton College, Illinois, in the last week of December 1973. For its silver jubilee the Society invited two foreign guests — Dr Howard Marshall of Aberdeen and myself. Our contributions were published in the proceedings of the conference, *New Dimensions in New Testament Study*, edited by R. N. Longenecker and M. C. Tenney (1974) — his on ' "Early Catholicism" in the New Testament' and mine on 'New Light on the Origins of the New Testament Canon'. The Evangelical Theological Society strikes me as being a more conservative body than the Tyndale Fellowship in this country, but there is a maturity of scholarship in the twenty-odd papers in this volume which augurs well for the progress of the Society during the next quarter of a century.

Unpublished yet are my lecture-courses at Decatur, on 'Pillars for a Life of Jesus Today' (a title which will be intelligible to readers who know the article 'Gospels' in the *Encyclopaedia Biblica*),[2] and those given in Kansas City, on 'Jesus and His Contemporaries'. Both of these may one day be included in a more comprehensive work. Unpublished

241

also in their entirety are my Lund Memorial Lectures on 'The Beginnings of Bible Interpretation'; they may take their place in a wider survey of the history and principles of biblical interpretation.

These lecturing visits made it possible for me to fit in a few other minor engagements which would not in themselves have justified a crossing of the Atlantic. For example, between my visits to Pasadena and Louisville in 1968 I spent a weekend on the campus of Oral Roberts University, Tulsa, Oklahoma. This was in response to an invitation from my friend Dr J. Harold Greenlee, who was at that time Professor of New Testament there. It was in prospect of this visit that I said to my fellow-elder Arnold Pickering, 'I am to pay a visit to Oral Roberts University; I shall probably come back speaking with tongues' — to which he replied, 'We shan't mind if you come back speaking with tongues; we *shall* mind if you come back and divide the church'. Arnold not only has his priorities right; he has the gift of expressing them with a simplicity which makes them quite obvious once he has put them that way — a contrast to the heavy weather which elders of some other churches make of such issues. (As it happened, I heard no speaking with tongues throughout my visit.)

On the Sunday morning there I attended a communion service at the University Chapel where I saw (and heard) something which I have not come across elsewhere. The bread was distributed in the form of unleavened biscuits, which were retained by the communicants until the chaplain recited the words of institution. When he came to the clause, '... which is broken for you', they all simultaneously broke their unleavened bread, with a crack which could be heard all over the chapel, and ate it.

The campus is dominated by the high prayer-tower, reached by an electric lift. Here prayer requests from Oral Roberts' worldwide radio and television congregations are received and answered. I met Dr Roberts briefly and appreciated his attending a lecture which I gave in the chapel on the Sunday afternoon. I had more prolonged fellowship with the School of Theology, some members of which were interested to know how far I regarded the Acts of the Apostles as normative for today. What I did not realize was that tensions were building up between the School of Theology and the university administration which led soon afterwards to the resignation of the dean and several other members of the School.

During the week of my Norton Lectures in Louisville a parallel series of practical lectures on the ministry was given in the Seminary by a Southern Baptist preacher, Dr J. P. Allen. He was the first living instance I ever came across of a man whose Christian names consisted of initials only — the J.P. stood for J.P. and nothing else. At the same time a Church of Scotland minister, Dr S. J. Knox, was a visiting lecturer in church history in the Presbyterian Seminary in the same city. Although he lived next door to my brother-in-law in Aberdeen, we had to go to Louisville to meet each other for the first time.

Columbia Seminary, Decatur, which I visited in 1970, trains ministers for the Southern Presbyterian Church. Decatur is on the outskirts of Atlanta, a city full of memories and memorials of the War between the States of 1861-65. My friend Ludwig Dewitz, Professor of Old Testament in Columbia Seminary, acted as my guide around the area; I had known him many years before when he was working in Sheffield for the Mildmay Mission to Jews. But my most moving experience in Atlanta was to stand before a much more recent memorial — that to Martin Luther King.

Between Decatur and Kansas City I spent a long weekend in Jackson, Mississippi, with my former research student Julius Scott and his wife and family; he was then on the staff of Belhaven College in that city. I gave a lecture in the college and also conducted a seminar on the Greek text and exegesis of Galatians 2: 1-10. In Kansas City it was my pleasure to make the acquaintance of the Williams brothers of the Walterick Press, who attended some of my lectures in the Nazarene Seminary.

My lecturing visit to North Park Seminary in Chicago

later in 1970 gave me an opportunity to visit also Trinity
Evangelical Divinity School in Deerfield, north of Chicago,
which had on its teaching staff at that time five men who had
done research in our Manchester Faculty of Theology.

Of all the academic centres which I have visited in North
America, I suppose my closest association has been with
Regent College, Vancouver. For a time I seemed to be
engaged as a summer school lecturer there on a triennial
cycle — in 1970, 1973 and 1976. Regent College has
continued to grow in staff and student numbers and has now
for some years been housed in property of its own (to begin
with, it rented premises from the Vancouver School of
Theology); it has also received the academic recognition
implied in affiliation to the University of British Columbia.
Once or twice in my journeys in North America I have come
across a curious rumour to the effect that Regent College was
founded to teach amillennialism. To anyone who knows the
truth of the matter this is odd indeed; it is difficult to imagine
how such an idea could have been launched. The doctrinal
basis of Regent College is as close to that of the IVF/UCCF as
makes no material difference; the Second Advent is confessed
along with the other foundation articles of the Christian
faith, but no particular line of eschatological interpretation
is laid down. Perhaps in some people's eyes this in itself is
ground for suspicion, but I suppose that within the staff and
student body of Regent College one would find the same
wide spread of eschatological views as is to be found in most
evangelical groupings.

Notes to Chapter 29

1. Sometimes there are reasons not immediately apparent on this side of the
Atlantic for title changes in American editions. For example, my carefully chosen
title *Paul: Apostle of the Free Spirit* (1977) was judged inappropriate in the United
States because the term 'free spirit' is associated there (I am told) with (*a*) a brand of
gas (petrol) and (*b*) a brand of hippy, so the work was re-christened *Paul: Apostle of
the Heart Set Free*. When a distinguished American reviewer criticized this title
because it used the word 'heart' in an unPauline sense, I reflected with
complacency that the responsibility was not mine.

2. In that article P. W. Schmiedel isolated nine passages, of indisputable
authenticity in his eyes, which 'might be called the foundation-pillars for a truly
scientific life of Jesus' (column 1881).

30

A visit to New Zealand

One prolonged overseas visit which my wife and I greatly enjoyed was to New Zealand, in July and August 1966. This visit was paid at the invitation of two groups — the New Zealand Inter-Varsity Fellowship and the Wellington Assembly Research Fellowship. The latter group is now called the Christian Brethren Research Fellowship (N.Z.), taking over the name from the British CBRF, but under its old name (abbreviated WARF) it was in existence before the British CBRF, and in fact provided a precedent for our CBRF to follow. The two groups worked together in arranging our itinerary, and the efficiency of their collaboration in this was seen in the smoothness with which the programme developed, although I had the impression that each group put on a full-time schedule for me in one place after another, so that at the end I felt as if I had said everything I knew at least four times over!

On our way to New Zealand we spent a couple of hours between flights at Sydney. We were met at Sydney Airport by Mr T. Carson and another friend, who took us for a short motor run along the coastal road. Mr Carson and I had been in communication with each other about our contributions to *A New Testament Commentary*, which was published by Pickering & Inglis three years later; it was good to meet him personally. He mentioned that at that very time a meeting was being held to elect a new Archbishop of Sydney in succession to Dr Hugh Gough. The churchman elected, as we learned a day or two later, was Dr Marcus Loane — to whom, some years later, our Ugandan family was to be deeply indebted for very special and timely help in its emigration to Australia.[1] When we spent those two short hours in Australia we could not have guessed at a future turn of events which would bring us repeatedly to Australia and provide an opportunity not only of seeing our family but also of making the acquaintance of many more friends in that country and participating in various forms of ministry.

Our time in New Zealand was spent for the most part in the four main university cities: Christchurch, Dunedin, Wellington and Auckland. In each of the four I had a midday series of open meetings arranged by the IVF, in which I spoke on such subjects as Jesus and the Gospels, Christianity in the Roman world, and the New Testament canon. The meetings arranged by the WARF, in consultation with the local brethren, were normally held in the evenings, on a wider variety of subjects — all of which must have been settled in advance, for I find them all listed on a duplicated copy of the itinerary with which we were presented at the beginning of our tour. On three Sunday evenings I addressed special meetings of students on the relevance of the Bible — in Christchurch Cathedral, Knox Presbyterian Church, Dunedin, and Elizabeth Street Chapel, Wellington. There were addresses to church elders under the auspices of WARF, and conferences for ministers under the auspices of the National Council of Churches. In Dunedin there were three lectures (on the life and thought of the Qumran community) in Knox College, the seminary of the Presbyterian Church of New Zealand. There were two residential weekend study conferences organized by WARF — one at Marton and the other at the New Zealand Bible Training Institute near Auckland. In Auckland there was the first New Zealand Tyndale Lecture (on 'Paul and Jerusalem'), and my records show that I gave a talk to the Classics Department of

Auckland University on the Epistles of John — treating them, presumably, as Hellenistic documents.

The head of the Auckland University Classics Department at that time was Professor E. M. Blaiklock, which explains sufficiently my being invited to address it. During our ten days at Auckland we were the guests of Professor and Mrs Blaiklock in their beautiful home at Titirangi, overlooking the Manukau harbour on the west and the Waitemata harbour on the east.

Another Auckland engagement was a television appearance with Professor John Morton, of the Chair of Zoology in Auckland University, during which we discussed the theme of resurrection. This was the subject of lively debate in New Zealand church circles at that time, because of some not very original (but, to many, revolutionary) remarks about the nature of our Lord's resurrection which had been recently published by a Presbyterian leader. My discussion with Professor Morton was not at all a confrontation: he led off by saying that, as a scientist, he found nothing incredible in bodily resurrection, and my contribution was simply to say why, in my judgment, the resurrection of our Lord to which the apostles bore witness was inevitably a *bodily* resurrection. Some years later Professor Morton issued a very helpful book entitled *Man, Science and God* (1972). I am sure that many viewers were interested to find an Anglican scientist expressing much less scepticism on a cardinal point of Christian doctrine than a Presbyterian theologian.

Both in the universities and in the churches which we visited it was good to meet old friends whom we had known in the U.K. In Dunedin, for example, we stayed with Professor and Mrs Ian Breward of Knox College: three years previously, as Dean of the Manchester Faculty of Theology, I had presented Professor Breward for his Ph.D. degree.[2] In the University of Otago (in Dunedin) my chairman was Harry Thornton, Professor of Philosophy: in our undergraduate days in Scotland he and I had been members of the Scottish Students' Campaign Movement. In the Victoria University of Wellington my chairman was Hugh A. Murray, Professor of Classics: we had been fellow-students at Aberdeen, where he was two or three years senior to me.

Again, both in the universities and the churches there were other visiting speakers from this country during those weeks, but we avoided getting in one another's way. In South Island we met the late E. W. Rogers (a veteran teacher among the Brethren in the U.K. and overseas), who did me the honour of attending one of my talks to theological students at Dunedin, and was present at the airport to bid us Godspeed when we flew from Dunedin to Wellington. In North Island it was a special pleasure to meet the late Robert Auld, with whom I had maintained correspondence for over twenty years, ever since he invited me to contribute a series of articles on 'The Gospels and the Apostolic Preaching' to his short-lived journal, *The Bible Expositor*, launched in 1945. This was a journal of high quality, but I suppose it was not sufficiently popular to be economically viable, especially with its limited base in New Zealand. Robert Auld had paid visits to this country in the course of those twenty years, but we had never seen each other until we met in Marton, in the home of my old friend the late John Stewart, who with his wife extended hospitality to us when we went there for the weekend study conference arranged by the WARF. He participated in that conference and in the similar one later convened in Henderson, near Auckland. This personal contact confirmed the impression formed through correspondence: here was a man whose ideas on the principles and substance of biblical interpretation were largely identical with my own: our minds seemed to work the same way. This was not due entirely to the fact that we were both Scots! Indeed, I had been agreeably surprised twenty years before that he found some of my material for *The Bible Expositor* so acceptable. It was more heavily influenced by C. H. Dodd's *The Apostolic Preaching and its Developments* (1936) than anything which I wrote on the same subject today would be, and it would not have been so congenial to editors of certain evangelical journals in Britain as it was to him. I am glad to have had the opportunity of meeting him even briefly: I imagine that his last illness was already upon him then.

One of my academic colleagues from Britain, Dr Robert Leaney of Nottingham University, was giving a course of lectures in St. John's College, Auckland, while we were there. And from one city to another we seemed to follow, with about a week's delay, in the footsteps of Canon Hugh Montefiore, Vicar of Great St. Mary's, Cambridge (as he was then), now Bishop of Birmingham (and best known nowadays for his vigorous application of biblical principles to 'environmental' issues). Dr Montefiore, as usual, was hitting the headlines in each place he visited with his radically unconventional way of putting things; according to my informants, he told people here and there that I would come along a week later and clear up the mess he had left (his words, not mine). And indeed, in one place after another, I found myself invited to answer questions arising out of his utterances. But one thing impressed me (although it did not surprise me):[3] I found that he was severely criticized by people who had not heard him, but formed their opinions on the basis of newspaper reports: many people who actually had heard him expressed positive appreciation of much that he had said.

For my own part, I have always thought it best to avoid saying things in public which might provide material for sensational headlines. But one never knows. One morning during our week in Dunedin I opened the daily newspaper and my eye was caught by a headline: 'Pictorial views of Bible recommended'. 'This looks interesting,' said I to myself, and read on — only to find that this was a report of an interview I had had a day or two before with a representative of that paper. I suppose I had said that some things in the Bible were to be understood pictorially rather than literally, and I had no cause for complaint, but this saying went abroad among the brethren in North Island as well as South Island, and some of them must have wondered what could have possessed the WARF to invite such a heretic to New

Zealand. On the other hand, I have a cutting from the *Auckland Star* for 11th August, 1966, which bears the headline, 'Resurrection was physical, says theologian', and then begins with the sentence: 'Intensive study has led Professor F. F. Bruce, of Manchester University, to believe that actual physical resurrection was meant by the Gospel stories of the empty tomb.' That, I suppose, settled it — save the mark!

One issue that had been exercising the Brethren churches of North Island shortly before my visit was the charismatic movement. I had been warned that I might find myself involved in this issue, and that some were hoping, while others were fearing, that I might prove to be a dove rather than a hawk. In fact, the controversy seemed to have died down by the time of our visit; in any case, my complete lack of experience in such matters would have disqualified me from giving any advice, even if I had been asked for it. The hopes and fears I have mentioned were aroused by answers I had given on the subject from time to time in *The Harvester*, but there can be a hiatus between the objective exposition of Scripture and the giving of advice in an actual situation — and that not only with regard to speaking in tongues.

In spite of the heavy programme, our friends went out of their way to provide some relaxation when it was possible. We have very happy memories of a trip from Auckland to the Bay of Islands which we made as the guests of Charles and Elva Grey; and George and Kath Stevenson of Upper Hutt entertained us royally during our week of Wellington engagements. But really, it is invidious to mention names when so many friends lavished such kindness and hospitality on us. To recall the whole period of our New Zealand visit is an undiluted pleasure. Another powerful impression was made on us by the scale of the missionary interest and activity of our New Zealand brethren, unsurpassed anywhere in the world, I should think, in proportion to their strength and numbers.[4]

From Auckland we took flight for North America, touching down on the way at Papeete, Tahiti. We spent two or three days in Vancouver as guests of Mr and Mrs E. M. Sheppard. It was good to meet for the first time friends such as these who had been only names before; two others whom we got to know then were Wemyss and Anne Reid. I had a couple of evening addresses in Granville Chapel and a lunchtime talk to local ministers, as well as a meeting with the committee concerned with the establishment of what was soon to become Regent College. Whereas New Zealand reporters wanted to know whether our Lord's resurrection was physical or only 'spiritual', Vancouver reporters, living in a continent where theological radicalism had reached a more advanced stage, wanted to know what I thought about the death of God — a fantasy which was enjoying a brief vogue at that time. I could not conceal my conviction that this was about as silly a question as could well be conceived: since God is, by definition, the living God, to talk of his death is a contradiction in terms. (I can readily understand, of course, that some people's consciousness of God may fade and die; and I heartily agree that certain other people's God is better dead, because he is no true God but an idol of the imagination. But Christians worship the Creator of the universe, the Father of our Lord Jesus Christ; and he is the living and true God.)

From Vancouver we flew to St. John's, Newfoundland, where we spent a fortnight free from any kind of public engagement with Iain and Pam and their two children. One evening during that fortnight we went along to the University to see the Archbishop of Canterbury, Dr Ramsey, receive an honorary degree. In this country I had heard the Archbishop (mindful of his own academic career) begin an address to university people with the words: 'Once I was a *real* turtle.' Sure enough, this was the gambit with which he opened his speech of thanks to the Memorial University of Newfoundland. Lewis Carroll's *Alice* provides a text for all seasons!

From Newfoundland we flew home, thus completing a round-the-world excursion. Apart from internal flights in

251

New Zealand, it had been mapped out for us in advance by our local travel agents in Buxton, and the whole journey went like clockwork.

Notes to Chapter 30

1. It gave great pleasure to all Archbishop Loane's friends when he was awarded the K.B.E. in the New Year Honours for 1976.

2. In 1976 Dr Breward served as moderator of the General Assembly of the Presbyterian Church of New Zealand.

3. It did not surprise me, because I knew him. He had been Dean of Caius College for some years (including the years when our son was an undergraduate there), and gave great help to its junior members, some of whom remember him with gratitude to this day.

4. A very enjoyable second visit to New Zealand, from 29th February to 22nd March 1980, under the auspices of CBRF (N.Z.), provided a welcome opportunity to renew old friendships and to forge new ones.

31

The Holy Land

Mention has already been made of the opportunity for foreign visits provided by meetings of the Society for New Testament Studies. My wife and I still avail ourselves of this opportunity: we have attended meetings during the past twenty years in Münster and Heidelberg, Germany; Gwatt, Switzerland; Louvain, Belgium; Nordwijkerhout, Holland; Sigtuna, Sweden; Claremont, California; Durham, North Carolina; Paris and Toronto. But the high spot of all the foreign visits organized by this Society was an archaeological study tour of Palestine in the summer of 1969.

I

For such matters as travel and accommodation the Society enlisted the expertise of Inter-Church Travel, who also provided us with one of their most experienced guides, a man who had spent some years in and around Jerusalem and was now rector of a Surrey parish. He was accustomed to leading parties of pilgrims among whom he was the undisputed expert; it must have been a gruelling experience for him to act as guide to a crowd of disputatious scholars and their wives, who treated the most confident identifications of sacred sites with deep scepticism. When we came to Caesarea Philippi one of the party, perhaps with memories of the 'Hill of Precipitation' at Nazareth in his mind, pointed to the cliff-side out of which the Nahr Banyas (one of the sources of Jordan) emerges and said to our guide in mock-serious tones, 'And this, I suppose, is the Rock of Interrogation?' Our guide took this and much more in good part: indeed, he acknowledged afterwards that this study tour had been an education to him. But his knowledge of people and places was exceptional: on the way from Jerusalem to Bethlehem, for example, we made a detour in order to see a cave doing duty as a stable which gave a better impression of the *kind* of setting in which our Lord was born than could be had in the Church of the Nativity.[1] But he was the sort of man who knew where this cave was and knew the humble family who occupied the place.

We flew from London to Frankfurt to pick up some of our colleagues who had been attending a conference there and a number of continental participants in our tour, and then from Frankfurt to Athens, where we spent the night. That evening some of us sat on the slopes of the Pnyx to view and listen to a *son et lumière* production from the Parthenon, on the summit of the Acropolis to the east of us. Next day there were optional trips to Delphi and Corinth: we went to Delphi, and got back just in time for our Olympic Airways flight to Lod, from which we were taken by coach to Jerusalem. It was Saturday evening, 16th August.

Next morning we were up before breakfast and went to the Church of the Holy Sepulchre to join briefly in Syrian and Greek services which were going on there; then back to our hotel for breakfast, after which some of us went to St. George's Cathedral, where the preacher, as it happened, was Dr Coggan. In the afternoon we went to Bethlehem, calling on the way at Rachel's Tomb.

During our week in Jerusalem we stayed at the Hotel Panorama on the slope of the Mount of Offence (the southern extension of Olivet on which Solomon built shrines for foreign deities). The hotel was well named: from

254

the window which extended the full length of the west wall of the dining room one had a magnificent panorama of the Old City with the temple area in the foreground. Some of our party, who sat there at breakfast on the morning of 21st August, had a front-seat view of the flames ascending from the silver-domed el-Aqsa mosque and of the arrival of the fire engines to deal with the conflagration. Fortunately it was soon brought under control, but the 800-year-old wooden pulpit, which we had admired during a visit to the mosque three days previously, was practically destroyed.

Hardly had the flames been quenched when the national radio of a neighbouring Arab state broadcast a report of the incident, adding that the Israeli cabinet had unanimously resolved, at a meeting held a few days before, to burn the building down. It seems incredible that any listener could have been expected to treat this calumny seriously (the Israeli authorities have an excellent record of impartial respect for the holy places in the territory under their control): the Arabs in the Old City, at any rate, knew who the incendiary was, for they caught him and handed him over to the police. He was a crackpot Australian, said to be a member of what was then called the Radio Church of God, who had rather crudely assimilated that body's doctrine about the future of Jerusalem and the temple area, and thought he might begin clearing the ground for the installations of the new order. I have met some Bible students in Britain who envisaged the erection of Ezekiel's temple on a coming day within the precincts of what is now the Haram esh-Sherif, but theirs was an academic interest, expressed in carefully argued exposition and the drawing of ground-plans; none of them imagined, as this unfortunate Australian did, that the divine programme might be expedited by a helping hand. Providentially, the repercussions of his criminal action were not so serious as they might easily have been.

I said that some of our party saw the fire; others, including my wife and myself, missed it, because we had got up at 2 a.m. to set out for Masada. The idea of getting up so early was to be able to explore the top of the rock in comfort, before the sun was too high — and a good thing too. There is a convenient chair-lift to the summit now, but in 1969 we climbed up (and down) on foot. It was well worth the effort, to see the remains of Herod's palaces and the Zealots' last stand. The Zealots' synagogue and ritual bath, pronounced kosher by modern rabbis, provided evidence that, far from being the godless miscreants of Josephus's account, the Zealots were scrupulously observant Jews.

From Masada we returned to Jerusalem by a circuitous route which took us through Beersheba and Hebron.

Since ours was an archaeological study tour we were provided with specialist guides to the various sites; our Dominican brethren of the Ecole Biblique were particularly helpful in this regard. It was a treasured experience to be conducted over the site of Qumran by the late Père Roland de Vaux, who in his animated way re-lived his original excitement as he took us from point to point of the buildings which he had excavated thirteen to sixteen years before. Jericho, Samaria-Sebaste, Hazor, Megiddo and Caesarea (on the Mediterranean) were among the other archaeological sites we visited.

As for sacred sites, those in Jerusalem are less certain than those (say) in Rome, because the destruction of Jerusalem in A.D. 70 and the foundation of a pagan city on the site in A.D. 135 meant not only the obliteration of landmarks but a hiatus in local memory. The pools of Bethesda and Siloam are reasonably certain, and even more so, of course, is the temple area. To walk the short distance from the Dome of the Rock to the east side of the sacred enclosure is to have the assurance that here, in what was then the Court of the Gentiles, our Lord walked and taught when he visited Jerusalem.

One of the most memorable occasions of our tour was a communion service arranged for our party, by courtesy of our sisters of Zion, on the site of the courtyard of what was in New Testament times the Antonia fortress — widely identified with the 'Pavement' of John 19: 13 on which Pilate set up his judgment-seat and pronounced our Lord's death sentence. It was no ordinary experience to remember our Lord on the very spot, perhaps, where

> Bearing shame and scoffing rude,
> In my place condemned he stood.

(It may be, indeed, that Pilate's praetorium in Jerusalem should be located not in the Antonia fortress but in Herod's palace on the western wall of the city. Even so, the pavement on which the service was held is certainly a relic of the Roman military regime under which Jesus was condemned and executed.) The service was beautifully informal: several men and women of our group took audible part in it, and the thanksgiving for the bread and the cup was said by the then Archbishop in Jerusalem, George Appleton. We had another communion service the following week, on the verandah of the Church of the Adolescence at Nazareth.

There is always a special joy in sharing in such communion services, for they provide an opportunity of fellowship with brothers and sisters of the most diverse Christian traditions and associations. Such fellowship is no broader in principle than what we maintain in Brinnington Evangelical Church, but the opportunities for such simultaneous width of fellowship are naturally rarer in a local church.

Our Galilean base for the second week of our tour was the Ganei Hamat hotel, on the southern outskirts of Tiberias. Much of the accommodation of this hotel took the form of chalets, each providing living-space for a couple. Across the road from the hotel was the Lake, in which morning bathing was very popular. One day we crossed the Lake from Capernaum to Ein Gev, where we enjoyed a meal in the kibbutz. A squall sprang up as we returned, but as our boat was propelled by an internal combustion engine, we could not enter into the disciples' experience of 'toiling in rowing'.

On our way north from Jerusalem to Tiberias we visited several places of interest, sampling the water from Jacob's well, for example, and being shown by the priest in the

257

Samaritan synagogue of Nablus what he assured us was 'the oldest book in the world' — the Abisha scroll[2] in its silver container.

From first to last, it was a fascinating tour, in which we were able to survey the land, if not from Dan to Beersheba, at least from Beersheba to Dan.

II

Ten years later we took part in another archaeological study tour of the Holy Land, organized this time by the Society for *Old* Testament Study. We concentrated more on sites of Old Testament interest, and this involved the climbing of numerous *tells,* from Tell Lachish and Tell el-Hesi in the south to Tell Acco and Tell Dan in the north. There was thus no lack of strenuous physical exercise! The mention of some of these *tells* provides an example of the Israeli tendency, in providing Hebrew names for ancient sites, to express greater certainty about identifications than is always warranted. When Arabic names were used, one could be cautious and say 'Tell Duweir, probably the site of ancient Lachish' or 'Tell el-Qadi, almost certainly the site of ancient Dan (previously Laish or Leshem)', but the question is foreclosed by the names Tell Lachish or Tell Dan.

Among many things that impressed us after ten years was the extension of Israel's excellent road system all over the West Bank. We were taken by coach up the steep ascent from Jericho to Ai, by a new road consisting largely of hair-raising bends of 'devil's elbow' dimensions, but with a firm metal and tarmac foundation. We thought of Joshua's followers advancing up the wadi below. On the other hand, we sampled what was very much the kind of road that Joshua's followers and their successors for many centuries must have used, when our party walked along the three-mile path from Ai (actually from Deir Dibwan, near the site of Ai) to Michmash, escorted for the first part of our way by youngsters who reminded us of those who escorted Elisha on his way to Bethel.

Other sites which we had not visited before included Shiloh and Gibeon, where we were impressed by the great pool (2 Sam. 2: 13; Jer. 41: 12). On our way to the north we stopped for refreshment at the place where the Wadi Baida joins the Wadi Fara'a, and contemplation of the abundant supply of fresh water confirmed in my mind the belief that this is Ainon near Salim, where John baptized 'because there was much water there' (John 3: 23). We drank the water from Elisha's fountain near Jericho, and can confirm that it is 'wholesome to this day' (2 Kings 2: 22).

It was good to revisit Masada and Qumran: whereas in 1969 we climbed Masada on foot, this time we went up by the cable-car which has been installed since then. The new road west of the Dead Sea gave us the opportunity to visit Engedi and Ain Feshkha. The latter place (renamed Enot Zuqim) is now a national park, where bathers in the Dead Sea can wash off the salt in fresh-water pools.

In Jerusalem itself we could see evidence of the unremitting tempo of archaeological research over the ten years. We could admire the tasteful rebuilding of the Jewish quarter of the Old City (which in 1969 was still derelict) and the careful landscaping of the area round the walls, which is being made a national park. The holy places and other monuments from earlier days, of which Jerusalem is so full, have never been more conscientiously safeguarded.

Notes to Chapter 31

1. Similarly, for many visitors to Jerusalem the Garden Tomb gives a much better impression of the *kind* of setting in which our Lord was buried and raised again than could be had in the Church of the Holy Sepulchre.

2. Cf. *The Books and the Parchments* (Pickering & Inglis [3]1962), p. 128.

32

In the Mediterranean World

Apart from overseas trips undertaken to see members of our family, no form of travel has given my wife and me more satisfaction than our visits to the central and eastern Mediterranean.

I

Historical and geographical landmarks in early Christianity are of special interest to us both. Our visits to Rome have given us outstanding pleasure. The first time we spent some days in that city was for a meeting of the International Organization for the Study of the Old Testament (April 1968). Most of my time was taken up listening to lectures, but Betty was free to explore the city either alone or with other ladies of the party. Even so, I recall brief visits to the Forum Romanum, to St. Peter's and St. Paul's, a late bus ride one evening along the Via Appia (I still remember how beautiful the façade of the basilica of St. Sebastian was in the moonlight) and an afternoon walk along the Via Salaria, during which it occurred to me that we might have a chance of seeing the Catacombs of Priscilla.

And so we had. Earlier that day, we had seen a coach load of British ladies enjoying a tour of Rome sponsored by a women's weekly magazine well known in the U.K. As we arrived at the entrance to the Catacombs of Priscilla, there was this coach parked outside, and we were just in time to tag ourselves on to the end of the party as they were taken on a conducted tour by an English-speaking guide.

In no city in the world, I imagine, is there such a concentration of authentic monuments of early Christianity as one may find in Rome. Our short taste of what it had to offer made us resolve to go back and spend a longer time there with nothing else to do than to explore its antiquities; the opportunity came in April 1973, when we spent a fortnight there. There has been no hiatus in the history of Roman Christianity from apostolic times to the present day, as there was in Jerusalem after its destruction by Titus; the sense of continuity is too powerful to be put into adequate words.[1]

Among the catacombs on or near the Appian Way we visited the cemeteries of Callistus and Domitilla — the latter perhaps providing a link with the princess of that name who was exiled by Domitian about A.D. 95, the former providing evidence of the Christian allegiance of some members of the Pomponian family in the second century, which makes us wonder if the 'foreign superstition' with which a lady of that family, Pomponia Graecina (wife of Aulus Plautius, the conqueror of Britain), was charged in A.D. 57 might not have been Christianity. The catacombs beneath the basilica of St. Sebastian on the Appian Way preserve ample evidence of the association of that site in popular piety with the memory of Peter and Paul in the third and fourth centuries. Among the early churches in the city itself the basilica of San Clemente is specially fascinating: beneath it lies a fourth-century church, which was built partly on top of the house of Clement (hence the name of the church) and partly on top of a Mithraic temple next door to the house of Clement. The original church on the site may have met in a room in the house of Clement — 'the church in his house'. As we stood down there, listening to the rushing water which is carried through an underground tunnel into the Cloaca Maxima, we realized that this was the scene of the murder in Ngaio Marsh's detective story *When in Rome* — although she exercised a fiction-writer's licence and changed the name of the church. In all our explorations in Rome we learned to rely with confidence on Georgina Masson's *Companion Guide to Rome:* a young Welshman attached to the basilica of St. Sebastian, seeing her book in our hands, remarked that she 'ought to be canonized'.

Our programme permitted us to make trips to Ostia and Tivoli — the latter trip was made under the guidance of a taxi-driver who had a standard supply of jokes: 'Free hotel', as we passed the jail; 'Last hotel', as we passed the cemetery.

My own particular interest in Rome and the Eastern Mediterranean is in the footsteps of Paul. If Rome is largely dominated by Peter, Paul has not been forgotten. During the morning of the last day of our Roman fortnight in 1973 there was a bus strike, which threatened to disrupt our plans for the day; but after lunch the buses were running again, so we went first to St. Paul's Outside the Walls, to pay our respects at the apostle's traditional tomb, and from there by another bus to the Trappist settlement at Tre Fontane, farther along the Ostian road, to see the reputed site of his execution, known in antiquity as Aquae Salviae.

II

Other visits to the Mediterranean world have been facilitated by Swan's Hellenic Tours. Under their guidance we have visited the Christian chapel on the first floor of the 'Bicentenary House' at Herculaneum, contemplated the breath-taking wealth of mosaics in the ancient churches of Ravenna, stood in the arena at Carthage where Perpetua and Felicitas were martyred in A.D. 202, viewed the Pyramids of Giza and the tombs of the Pharaohs at Thebes, visited the headquarters of the Knights Hospitallers in Rhodes and Malta, climbed to the summit of Santorini (Thera) and descended into the cave at Patmos where John (reportedly) received the Revelation, and inspected the ancient church of St. Titus at Gortyna in Crete, dedicated to the first missionary to that island. 'He made a good job of it too,' said our Cretan guide; 'to this day 98 per cent. of the people of Crete are Christians.'[2] We have read the text of Paul's Athenian address inscribed on bronze at the foot of the ascent to the Areopagus (Mars' Hill) and the text of 1 Corinthians 13 on a wall in the neighbourhood of Roman Corinth. In Corinth we have stood before the tribunal (*bema*) from which Gallio ruled (in effect) that what Paul was preaching was a variety of Judaism and thus entitled to the protection of Roman law so long as no 'wrongdoing or vicious crime' was involved, seen the piece of inscribed lintel which stood above the entrance to the 'Synagogue of the Hebrews' and walked along the Lechaeum road past the probable site of the meat-market (A.V. 'shambles') where the Christian housewife was encouraged by Paul to buy her Sunday joint, 'asking no question for conscience' sake'. In Ephesus we have contemplated the fragments of the once magnificent temple of Great Artemis, visited the ruined basilica of St. John, and sat high up on the steps of the theatre, listening to Dr Henry Chadwick reading from the orchestra beneath us Luke's vivid description of the riotous assembly in that same place over 1900 years ago. The acoustics are perfect, and a further advantage of climbing to the top of the steps is that one can trace from there (almost as by aerial photography) the outlines of the ancient harbour, long since silted up, so that Ephesus now stands seven miles inland. We have even driven up the steep ascent to the 'House of the Virgin Mary' — no tradition from antiquity this, but identified from the detailed description of a building seen in vision by a Westphalian nun at the beginning of the nineteenth century. We have considered which of the ancient sites at Pergamum was responsible for the apocalyptic designation of that city as the place 'where Satan's throne is'; from Pergamum we have gone by Turkish coach across the lower slopes of 'many-fountained Ida' to explore 'the ringing plains of windy Troy' and, on another occasion, to look down from the citadel of Assos to the harbour (with its ancient breakwater) where Paul re-embarked on his last voyage to Palestine. In Istanbul we have thought ourselves back into the era of Byzantine pomp and piety in the former Church of the Holy Wisdom. To visit such places with even a modicum of historical imagination is to find Christian and non-Christian antiquity come alive.

During one of Swan's Hellenic cruises (in the summer of 1975) we disembarked at Alexandria and spent three very full days in Egypt. We joined other members of the party who elected to spend two nights in Luxor, so as to pay brief visits to the Valley of the Kings and the temples of Karnak and Luxor. This experience whetted our appetite for more, so we celebrated my first year of retirement by taking part in one of Swan's Nile cruises in late January and early February, 1979. It was the first time that we had ever been able to take a holiday at that time of year, and those who remember what the English winter of 1978-79 was like will appreciate what a welcome break it was. Now we were able to explore and digest at greater leisure what we had covered so hastily on the earlier occasion, cruising up the Nile to Aswan, spending the nights on board and the days in visiting temples and tombs and other antiquities, now on the one bank and now on the other. From Aswan some of our party flew to Abu Simbel; we preferred to spend that day in a more relaxed manner, sailing on the Nile in a felucca and visiting the islands of Elephantine and Seheil. A few days previously the Shah and Shahbanou of Iran had stayed on Elephantine, on the first stage of their journey into exile; banners welcoming the Shah still lined the main roads of Aswan, but they soon began to come down. More durable were the banners all over the country proclaiming 'Sadat is our hope'; we were left in no doubt about the popularity of his peace agreement with Israel.

Was Rameses II equally popular? Certainly he seems to have been one of the greatest megalomaniacs of all time, having his colossal likeness reproduced in stone all over his

264

kingdom, from Memphis and Heliopolis to Abu Simbel. On seeing the fallen fragments of his gigantic statue in the Ramesseum near Thebes, we could not help recalling Shelley's lines:

> My name is Ozymandias, king of kings;
> Look on my works, ye mighty, and despair!

(Ozymandias is the Greek form of one of the names of Rameses.) Rameses may or may not have been the Pharaoh of the Oppression, but if his achievements are compared with those of Moses, the comparison is thought-provoking. It is to his son Merneptah that we owe the first reference to Israel outside the Old Testament: he had made sure, he boasted, that Israel would have no future. 'Israel is desolate; it has no more seed.'

From the perspective of my own studies, I was specially interested to visit the ancient synagogue in Fustat (Old Cairo) whose *genizah* or store-room yielded up so much unsuspected literary treasure at the end of the nineteenth century, and the relics of early Egyptian Christianity in the Church of St. Sergius and the Coptic Museum in that part of the old city which in Roman days was called Babylon on the Nile.

The seventeen days passed quickly, and the English winter was still there to greet us on our return; but we brought back a store of rich and enduring memories.

Notes to Chapter 32

1. Further reflections on this theme are expressed in my contribution to the symposium *In God's Community*, edited by D. J. Ellis and W. W. Gasque (Pickering & Inglis 1978), pp. 153-168.

2. But in the period between the Turkish conquest of Crete in 1669 and the liberation of the island in 1898 there was quite a high proportion of Muslims, many of whom had apostatized from Christianity.

33
Other literary work

Over and above the editorship of journals, of which some account has been given in earlier pages, there has come from time to time the editorship of composite volumes or series of volumes. Among the latter I recall the Lutterworth Press series of *Bible Guides*, twenty-two paperbacks published between 1961 and 1965, for which I figured as one of the two joint-editors — albeit in an extremely nominal role (the real, but unacknowledged, editor was Dr Cecil Northcott, then editorial secretary of the Lutterworth Press). Not at all nominal has been my general editorship of the New International Commentary on the New Testament (the earlier volumes of which were published in the U.K. as the New London Commentary), in which I succeeded the late Ned Bernard Stonehouse on his death in 1962. The first volume to appear under my editorship, as it happened, was my own commentary on Hebrews (begun at my predecessor's invitation); it was dedicated, as was fitting, to Dr Stonehouse's memory. At the time of his death all the commentaries had been assigned to authors. He had reserved two books of the New Testament — Matthew and Revelation — for himself; these had to be reassigned. Several substantial contributions to the series (assigned by Dr Stonehouse) have appeared since I took over the general editorship — the second part of the commentary on Romans, by John Murray; the commentaries on Mark, by William L. Lane; on John's Gospel, by Leon Morris. Among those which I have assigned there are in circulation the commentaries on James, by J. B. Adamson; on 1-3 John, by Howard Marshall; on Revelation by R. H. Mounce. Others are still awaited; an editor sometimes feels that it would be more expeditious to undertake an assignment himself than to wait for another writer to complete it. But patience is fostered in this and in other ways in the course of literary work. Apart from contributors who are engaged on the task of filling the remaining gaps in the series, there are others who are busy writing commentaries to replace earlier contributions to the series which, having served their generation, have now earned honourable retirement. So there is no discharge in this editorial war.

Then there was the Paternoster Church History, for which I had a modicum of editorial responsibility (mainly in deciding on appropriate writers and inviting them to contribute the volumes falling within their special field of study). This series really developed out of my own work, *The Spreading Flame* (1958). That volume carried the story of early Christianity down from its beginnings to the conversion of the English in the sixth and seventh centuries; the subsequent volumes dealt with further phases reaching on to the twentieth century. The luminous titles were devised by the publishers, not by the editor or the contributors. One gap in the series remains — the volume dealing with the Puritans (*The Refining Fire*) — but it may be filled one day. Some reviewers thought that Scottish nationalism had exercised an undue influence on the series when there was added to it a volume on the Scottish Covenanters — *Light in the North* (1964), by Jimmy Douglas. But the true reason for its inclusion was that, despite the limited canvas on which the Covenanters operated, their experiences highlighted certain fundamental and permanently relevant principles of church life, especially with regard to the relation between church and state. Several of the volumes in this series are widely used as college textbooks on the periods of church history with which they deal, both in the British Commonwealth and in America (where the series is published by Eerdmans under the title 'The Advance of Christianity through the Centuries').

As for individual volumes for which I have had editorial responsibility, I have already mentioned the *Festschrift* presented to S. H. Hooke on his ninetieth birthday, *Promise and Fulfilment* (1963). There is a polite fiction by which someone who is being honoured in this way is supposed to know nothing about it until, to his delighted surprise, he is presented with it at the appointed time. But Professor Hooke took the liveliest interest in the inception and progress of this work, even suggesting the names of a number of people whom he would like to be invited to contribute to it. Then there is a symposium entitled *Holy Book and Holy Tradition* (1968), edited by Gordon Rupp and myself, which contains the papers read at an international colloquium held in our Manchester Faculty of Theology in November 1966. We had as participants scholars from Sweden, France, Germany, Holland and the Republic of Ireland as well as from the United Kingdom, and the treatment spanned the millennia from cave drawings of the Upper Palaeolithic period to the relation between Scripture and tradition in modern ecumenical debate. My share in this colloquium and in the editing of its proceedings stimulated my further interest in the subject of tradition and was responsible, in part at least, for my own *Tradition Old and New* (1970).

There is another form of editorship which does not carry with it the labour and responsibility associated with ordinary editorship. That is consulting editorship. A consulting editor may be asked for his advice, or may volunteer his advice, but the real editor or the publisher is not obliged to accept that advice when given.

My first experience of consulting editorship, so far as I remember, was for a series of slim volumes entitled 'Pathway Books' published by the house of Eerdmans between 1956 and 1960. There were three other consulting editors for this series: Leon Morris, Bernard Ramm and Edward J. Young. Each of us contributed a volume to the series; others were contributed by S. B. Babbage, G. C. Berkouwer, E. M. Blaiklock, G. W. Bromiley, L. DeKoster, C. F. H. Henry, H. Ridderbos, N. Ridderbos, J. A. Thompson and L. D. Twilley. The Ridderbos brothers, Herman and Nicolaas, are twins, born in the same year as myself: Herman was for many years Professor of New Testament in Kampen Theological Seminary and Nicolaas Professor of Old Testament in the Free University of Amsterdam. How nominal this consulting editorship was may be gauged from the fact that when Nicolaas Ridderbos's little book, *Is there a Conflict between Genesis 1 and Natural Science?* (1957), appeared in the series, Edward J. Young, consulting editor though he was, published an adverse review of it. I say, 'consulting editor though he was', but perhaps I should have said, '*because* he was a consulting editor'; he may have felt it necessary for that very reason to make his position clear, and his position was that the 'framework hypothesis' by which Professor Ridderbos interpreted the creative week of Genesis 1 did less than justice to the text. Since I do not teach in a confessional situation myself, I am sometimes slow to appreciate the pressures which affect a number of my colleagues who do teach in such a situation.

The next consulting editorship which came my way was a much more demanding one. I was one of four consulting editors for the IVF *New Bible Dictionary*, which appeared in 1962. The others were Jim Packer, Donald Wiseman and the late R. V. G. Tasker. We were fortunate in the editor-in-chief (technically 'organizing editor') with whom we co-operated — the same Jimmy Douglas who has just been mentioned as author of *Light in the North*. His editorial ability is superb, but his academic expertise is in church history, and most of the contributions to the *Dictionary* lay in other fields than that. The consulting editors therefore were expected to give advice within their specialist fields — Donald Wiseman in archaeology, Jim Packer in theology, and Professor Tasker and myself in biblical matters. This involved (so far as I was concerned) the reading in manuscript and proof of all the articles on biblical subjects and checking them not only in respect of scholarship but also (and this was a more delicate business) to make sure that they did not conflict with the doctrinal basis of the IVF. Since the IVF is a confessional body, its publications are expected to conform with its confession of faith. At the same time, since it exists primarily to serve the academic world, its publications are expected to maintain a standard of unexceptionable scholarship. There is no incompatibility at all between confessional fidelity and scholarly integrity, but those responsible for such publications, whether in an executive or a consulting capacity, must bear both ideals in mind simultaneously.

On the whole I think our efforts were successful. Inevitably, we did not please everybody. One reviewer (the church affairs correspondent of the *Daily Telegraph*) regretted that the work laboured under 'the handicap of such avowed partisan bias' as was involved by its evangelical sponsorship, but conceded that the editor had the assistance of certain 'well-known biblical scholars' and that the work was 'strong in its archaeological contents'. 'Used with caution,' he concluded, 'the Dictionary offers a valuable compendium of background information.' The caveat 'used with caution' is particularly rich, because it was also employed by some reviewers who criticized the work from the opposite extreme and thought (mistakenly) that, apart from its purely theological articles (which were unexceptionable), its contents frequently fell below the desirable level of orthodoxy. Yet reviewers at either extreme united in praising its high standard of up-to-date archaeological information — and rightly so. It was this feature, no doubt, that moved the late W. F. Albright, then the greatest living biblical arachaeologist, to speak of it as the best one-volume Bible Dictionary available.

When tributes are being paid, it is but fitting to include one to a man whose work was done unobtrusively in the background — Ronald Inchley, then the IVF Publications

Secretary. Only those most closely involved with the Dictionary can appreciate the vast amount of technical skill which he and his staff devoted to preparing the edited material for the press and seeing it through the press.

As these words are written, a new and revised edition of this *Dictionary* is now in its final stages of production: for this too I have served as a consulting editor, along with Donald Wiseman, Jim Packer, Donald Guthrie and Alan Millard, with Norman Hillyer as organizing editor.

Another major work for which I was enlisted as a consulting editor was the *New Testament Commentary* published in 1969 by Pickering & Inglis and edited by Cecil Howley. This work proved to be the first instalment of *A Bible Commentary for Today* (American edition entitled *The New Layman's Bible Commentary*), published in October 1979. For both parts of the work I shared the consulting editorship with H. L. Ellison. But whatever consulting aid he and I have given is but a drop in the bucket compared with the editor's indefatigable and meticulous work. Of the *Commentary*, as of the IVF *Dictionary*, it could be said that they marked the coming of age of the respective sponsoring bodies. Both works owed a great deal to the contribution of younger contributors who had only very recently passed through their formative years: neither work could have achieved such a high standard ten years earlier.

Reactions to the *New Testament Commentary* were in a way comparable to reactions to the *New Bible Dictionary*. There was a wide central area of positive appreciation; at one extreme there were those who found both works too conservative, and at the other extreme there were those who found in them too radical a departure from what was believed to be the path of truth and safety. Since all contributors to the *New Testament Commentary* were associated, as the preface pointed out, 'with the churches of the Christian Brethren',[1] the response within those churches was especially interesting. Where the response was more critical, this was not so much (I think) because of specific passages to which objection was taken. Such passages indeed

271

there were — the section on 'The Revelation to John' was, as one reviewer put it, 'surprisingly disappointing' — but the real basis for uneasiness, I suspect, was that the tone and idiom of the whole work differed so widely from what had traditionally characterized much expository writing within the Brethren movement. In America particularly the lack of consistent dispensationalism was felt to detract from the value of the work. In fact, no consideration was taken in the choice of the contributors to their outlook in this regard: some held dispensational views; others did not. The general outlook of the work, indeed, is more or less that with which we are familiar in such periodicals as *The Witness, The Harvester* and the *CBRF Journal.* This whole issue of a shift in perspective in Brethren exegesis of Scripture, which is reflected in the shift in tone and idiom, is something that might well be the subject of a separate study in another context.

Another literary activity during those years was the answering of questions in certain periodicals. There was a period in the mid-fifties when I answered questions in the *Life of Faith* 'Christian Workers' Forum': this was one of two responsibilities which I found it necessary to relinquish on becoming editor of the *Palestine Exploration Quarterly* (the other, as I have said before, was the editorship of the Victoria Institute's *Journal of Transactions*). But my main effort under this heading was the conduct of the 'Answers to Questions' page in *The Harvester* month by month from July 1952 to April 1975 inclusive. I was invited to take on this task by the editor, Dr F. A. Tatford, when H. P. Barker, who had conducted this page for many years, died suddenly in his early eighties. Responsibility for this page was for me in many ways an enriching, and sometimes exhilarating, experience. The area of subject-matter was as wide as can well be imagined, ranging from the ridiculous to the sublime — e.g. from the propriety of miniskirts to the ontological argument for the existence of God. (For a brief observation on the former subject I was awarded the *Buzz* badge of honour for August 1968.[2]) In 1972 a selection of the less ephemeral contributions to this page was published in the volume *Answers to Questions.* I demitted this office when I had answered 2,000 questions partly because that was a good point to stop and partly because I had no intention to go on so long that the present editor would find himself left in the lurch without warning and have to lay hands suddenly on the first person who came to his mind. The present editor had been given ample notice of my retirement, so when the time came Peter Cousins had been carefully chosen and was ready to take over the responsibility, to the great profit of *Harvester* readers. He can speak to the condition of today's generation far better than I.

Thus far, I have not found his answers so disturbing as many of my seniors found mine twenty-odd years ago. Perhaps in those days I was over-prone to stick my neck out. But no doubt there are some advantages in sticking one's neck out earlier rather than later: people soon get tired of running up to it with their little axes. There may be some disadvantages too: if one becomes associated with radical views, such views, when expressed, tend to be dismissed as predictable. Some months ago a conference in London debated a controversial issue of church practice, and a spokesman for the more liberal side is said to have quoted some statement of mine in support of his own argument. But the reaction was: 'O, he *would* take that line!' — and so my quoted statement merited no lengthy consideration. But all this adds to the interest of 'the living of these days'.

Notes to Chapter 33
1. The contributors to the Old Testament part of the work have been drawn from a wider field.
2. *Buzz* is a British Christian youth magazine; this is the only occasion, I think, on which it has taken cognizance of me.

34

Collaboration and criticism

An editor can exercise some control over the contents of what he edits and over the maintenance of his time-table: contributors whose material does not come up to standard can have it returned to them for revision or for submission to some less exacting editor, and those who do not deliver their material by the stipulated time cannot complain if they miss the boat. But one who writes for another editor is subject to factors over which he has little control. Over the years I have written many contributions for symposia and dictionaries of various kinds: so far as Bible dictionaries are concerned, I suppose that if all my contributions to these were brought together, they would almost make up a Bible dictionary by themselves.

One of the earliest works to which I made a modest contribution was the *Oxford Latin Dictionary*. It had long been a reproach to British classical scholarship that the tradition which could produce such a superb work as Liddell and Scott's *Greek-English Lexicon* should be content for so long with such a second-rate production as Lewis and Short on the Latin side. Alexander Souter used to tell us that Lewis and Short contained an average of sixty errors to the page; he had compiled a list of them which began to rival the Dictionary itself in length. It was fitting, then, that when the Delegates of the Oxford University Press decided to publish a completely new Latin Dictionary he should be appointed editor — a post which he held from 1933 to 1939. At his instance I excerpted the works of Fronto for the new Dictionary between 1933 and 1936. He gave up the editorship in 1939 in order to concentrate on the production of *A Glossary of Later Latin to A.D. 600,* which was published in 1949, the year of his death. From 1939 onwards the work was held up by the war and a number of lesser frustrations, and it was not until 1968 that the first fascicle of just over 250 pages was published (covering *A-Calcitro*), to be followed by a further fascicle every second year (the sixth, carrying the record forward to *Qualitercunque,* appeared in 1977). Contributing to composite works of this kind teaches one patience, although, happily, excerpts from the writings of a second-century Latin author do not date as quickly as some other contributions which suffer from a delay of several years between composition and publication — and of these I have a larger number than I like to contemplate. There is an encyclopaedia for which I wrote several New Testament articles fifteen years ago; the carbon copies make strangely dated reading now, and will seem still more dated by the time they are published.

Promptness is specially important in *Festschriften,* composite volumes presented to one whom it is desired to honour on a significant birthday or comparable milestone (like retirement). The point of such a presentation volume is lost if its publication is delayed beyond the occasion which it is intended to commemorate and its editor must be quite ruthless in refusing late submissions. In recent years I have spent a good part of my writing time in composing articles for *Festschriften:* my friends and colleagues all seem to be attaining significant birthdays more or less simultaneously. My first contribution to such a symposium, entitled 'Latin Participles as Slave Names' (not, it may be supposed, the most gripping of subjects), was written in honour of Paul

275

Kretschmer's seventieth birthday in May 1936; the *Festschrift* appeared as a special issue of the periodical *Glotta*, with which he was closely associated.

Sometimes, unhappily, the person to be honoured has died between the inception of the work and the intended date of publication, and what was designed as a *Festschrift* has to be produced as a *Denkschrift,* a memorial volume. This happened with the volume of *New Testament Essays* (1959) which was to have been presented to my predecessor T. W. Manson on his sixty-fifth birthday; it happened also with the volume entitled *Man and his Salvation* (1973) which was being prepared for the same landmark in the career of my colleague S. G. F. Brandon a few years ago.

Back in my Cambridge days Peter Giles, Master of Emmanuel College, used to tell us that any scholar who wrote an article for a *Festschrift* might as well dig a hole in his back garden and bury it, for in a year or two it would be forgotten and there would be no convenient means of recording its existence. The situation is a little better now with modern means of indexing: I have found very useful, for example, an *Index of Articles on the New Testament and the Early Church published in Festschriften,* compiled in 1951 by Bruce M. Metzger (with a supplement published in 1955). It also helps when such a symposium is devoted to one particular theme or field of study.

Two symposia of another kind to which I contributed many years ago were published by Pickering & Inglis: *The Church: A Symposium,* edited by J. B. Watson (1949), for which I wrote on 'Church History and its Lessons', and *The Faith: A Symposium,* edited by F. A. Tatford (1952), for which I wrote on 'The Scriptures'. More recently I wrote a chapter on 'Lessons from the Early Church' for the symposium *In God's Community* (1978), a work presented as a *Festschrift* to Cecil Howley, edited by David Ellis and Ward Gasque. My participation in the first two of these volumes (all three of which were published by Pickering & Inglis) perhaps helped to secure my reputation for orthodoxy in the minds of some right-thinking people, as did also my participation in various composite IVF publications, like the *New Bible Handbook* (1947) and the *New Bible Commentary* (1953). My contributions to the latter volume are clearly specified; to the former I contributed the chapter on the Four Gospels and Acts, but for anyone who did not possess direct information about this it could be discerned only by the application of higher criticism. The editor (G. T. Manley) treated the contributions with such sovereign freedom that some contributors would have had cause for complaint if they had been credited with the edited versions of what they submitted: hence the contributors were listed in alphabetical order at the beginning of the volume and no indication was given as to who was responsible for what. This led one distinguished reviewer to declare that we all shared responsibility for what he regarded as the serious defects of the work, but he was not taken seriously: it was generally recognized that the personality of the editor had been impressed on the whole volume.

This leads me to comment on an illegitimate exercise of editorial privilege, commoner in other parts of the English-speaking world than in this country, by which not only stylistic improvements but changes in subject-matter are introduced into a writer's work without his being given the opportunity to approve or disapprove of them. In a list of my writings published in 1970, for example, Ward Gasque points out that in an article on 'Plymouth Brethren' which I wrote for the 1967 edition of the *Encyclopaedia Britannica* (produced in USA), I 'should not be held responsible for the inaccuracies concerning the Plymouth Brethren in North America', since 'these statistics were added by the editor'. So they were, but they were not added as editorial addenda; they appeared as integral parts of the article over my initials. A further instance that comes to mind relates to another work of reference to which I made several contributions, in one of which I mentioned the 'Chronicler' (with a capital C) — meaning, as every biblical student might be expected to know, the author of the books of Chronicles. One member of the editorial staff replaced the capital by a lower-case initial, and then one of his colleagues, for reasons best known to himself, replaced the common noun 'chronicler' by its synonym 'annalist', so that between them they completely obscured the point I was making, without asking if I agreed to the changes.

Other orthodox symposia to which I contributed included a series edited by Carl Henry while he was editor of *Christianity Today*: these symposia were conceived as extensions of the ministry of *Christianity Today*. I think of such contributions as 'Archaeological Confirmation of the New Testament' in *Revelation and the Bible* (1958), 'The Person of Christ: Incarnation and Virgin Birth' in *Basic Christian Doctrines* (1962) and 'History and the Gospel' in *Jesus of Nazareth: Saviour and Lord* (1966). (This last essay was a revision of the C. J. Cadoux Memorial Lecture, delivered in Bradford in 1962.) What effect these had on my reputation in North America I cannot say: distinctions over there tend to be more finely drawn, and these symposia might be labelled 'neo-evangelical' — a good or a bad label according to one's point of view. In this country evangelicals generally (and wisely) prefer to be unhyphenated evangelicals.

So far as symposia or works of reference are concerned, it has never occurred to me that I should contribute only to those promoting a particular point of view (even if it be a point of view that I share). I should not, of course, participate in enterprises which I thought likely to be harmful in their purpose or effect, but where the cause of advancing Christian knowledge is concerned, I have gladly availed myself of opportunities to collaborate in this. I have already acknowledged the encouragement which H. H. Rowley gave me to contribute to composite works for which he had editorial responsibility. Although he was Old Testament editor for the new edition of *Peake's Commentary on the Bible* (1962) and (until his death) for the *New Century Bible,* it was not he but his New Testament colleague Matthew Black who enlisted my co-operation in these.

The 1962 edition of *Peake's Commentary* was an entirely new work, retaining nothing from the original edition of 1919. The publishers, however, thought it would be a pity to lose the good will of the old title, so they took it over from the old work, not realizing that in some quarters it was not *good* will that was attached to the title. The editor of a well-known evangelical weekly found this out when one of its issues carried a publisher's advertisment announcing the forthcoming publication of the new *Peake*; some of his readers sent indignant letters of protest on which he commented that he understood that the forthcoming edition would be 'practically' a new work. I think he was relieved when I wrote to say that it would be a 'completely' new work, adding that it would therefore 'be judged on its own merits, and not on the merits or demerits of the old commentary whose name it perpetuates'.

My reference a couple of paragraphs back to Professor Rowley reminds me that when I was invited to meet the committee dealing with the Manchester vacancy to which, in the event, I was appointed, he said across the table that he hoped I had not been embarrassed by contributing to works which he had edited. I assured him that I had not, and expressed the hope that he had not been embarrassed by having me as a contributor. He responded with an assurance to match my own, so we were both happy.

Since my field of study and teaching is text and exegesis, not dogmatic theology, I have always found it possible to maintain an objectivity of treatment which has made my productions equally acceptable for *Peake's Commentary* and the IVF *New Bible Commentary*, the IVF *New Bible Handbook* and T. and T. Clark's *Companion to the Bible*, the *Interpreter's Dictionary of the Bible* and the *New Bible Dictionary*, the *New Century Bible* and the *Tyndale New Testament* series, and indeed, the *Encyclopaedia Judaica* and the *Catholic Layman's Library*. If I am asked to say what the biblical text means, my answer will be the same no matter who asks me. This is not a question of following the apostolic example of being all things to all men; it is a matter simply of being myself to all men.

Anyone whose writings are published must expect to be criticized: why not? In a free country hostile reviewers are as much entitled to publish their criticisms as the writers whom they criticize are to publish their unacceptable opinions. I have already said what I think of those who make critical reviews an occasion for impugning a writer's integrity or imperilling his livelihood. But straightforward criticism is something that no one should be slow to welcome. Careful students of my writings might discover how greatly second editions have sometimes benefited from criticisms directed against the first editions.

Some people, however, find criticism difficult to take. An American colleague of mine, several years ago, published a work which received a predictably hostile review in a theological journal. (I say 'predictably' because the reviewer's outlook was notoriously opposed to his own.) When he was complaining to me about this review, I said, 'Well, at least you can't complain that your book was ignored.' 'I think', he said, 'I'd have preferred it to be ignored.' Evidently he did not agree with the remark in *Dorian Gray* that there is only one thing worse than being talked about, and that is *not* being talked about.

There is no reason at all why criticism and courtesy should not go hand in hand. When my *Expanded Paraphrase of the Epistles of Paul* appeared in 1965, my late friend Isaac Ewan of Abernethy, Scotland, wrote to me to say that he proposed to criticize some of my observations in one of his *Present Testimony Pamphlets* and that he would use great plainness of speech. I wrote to him at once urging him to do just that, and assuring him that I should not take his criticisms amiss. (I knew well enough that his thoughts on what was involved in biblical inspiration were so different from mine that some of my suggestions must have been quite unacceptable to him.) What I appreciated especially was the thoughtful courtesy which made him write and tell me what he was about to say: where criticism is practised in this spirit, good personal relations remain unimpaired. And in general, if reviewers think that I am compromising the truth as they see it, it is not only their right but their duty to say so.

As for those others who are abusive simply for the sake of being abusive, or in the hope of getting under one's skin, no harm need be taken from them; they quickly acquire a reputation for this sort of practice, and the result is that their criticism is discounted even when there is some substance to it. But for the most part the *odium theologicum* that used to be part of the stock-in-trade of religious disputants has now been left to political ideologues, who have taken it over and perfected its vocabulary for their own purposes.

After these comments on the art of reviewing, it is to be hoped that I practise what I preach. If a work is so bad that nothing good at all can be said about it, I prefer not to review it; if it is as bad as all that, it does not deserve even hostile publicity. Nothing ensures a wide circulation for a book so speedily as an attempt to ban it, or to discourage its reading with the warning: 'Avoid this book as you would the plague!' In the less enlightened days when the Vatican issued a periodical *Index of Prohibited Books*, intelligent Catholics, it is said, used it as their library list.

For the rest, the golden rule is as applicable to reviewers as it is to others: 'Review as you would be reviewed.'

35
On staying with the Brethren

In an earlier chapter it was suggested that I might take up later the question why in our successive changes of abode we have always thrown in our lot with a local church of the same order.[1] Let me take it up now.

The question often takes the form 'Why have you stayed with the Brethren?' Thus phrased, the question involves a certain presupposition at which I shall look in a moment, but it is quite plain what people mean when they ask it, and I will try to answer it in the sense which they mean. Strangely enough, my questioners are often a little dissatisfied with the true answer, which is that I have remained with the Brethren because it has never occurred to me to leave them. I say 'strangely enough', because the same reason holds good for most people who remain in the type of church order and fellowship within which they were born and brought up. It takes a greater effort to leave than to stay, and unless they have some positive reason for changing, they stay. I once heard Professor Rendle Short say, in the course of an address on guidance, 'No guidance to move is good guidance to stay where you are' — and although he was not speaking particularly of church association, the principle is as applicable there as in other areas of life.

My friends who find the true answer to their question inadequate try to probe further, and as I listen to them I sometimes get the impression that they envisage a stage in my career at which I reviewed impartially all the options of church order — Catholic, Episcopal, Presbyterian, Independent, Baptist and so forth — and reached a dispassionate conclusion. Had I come to the Christian faith for the first time after reaching years of discretion and found it necessary to decide which church I should join, I might have made my mind up that way (but I doubt it).

I have never found it a disadvantage to belong to the Brethren, and even if I did, that would be the worst possible reason for leaving them. I owe them an incalculable debt. It was among them that I learned my early lessons in the Christian way, and I hope I have been able in measure to repay that debt by passing on to others the lessons I have learned.

There are a few basic requirements for which I look in a church, and two of the most important are fidelity to the truth of the gospel and the maintenance of Christian freedom. It will be acknowledged by most evangelical Christians that the former has been characteristic of the people called Brethren, and many who, like myself, have spent a lifetime in their fellowship will acknowledge that the latter has also been characteristic of them. In the early 1960s the late Melville Capper of Bristol, writing as chairman a letter of welcome to members of what was then the Young Men's Bible Teaching Conference, said, 'One of the things that attracts many of us to the Christian Brethren is its breadth, not its narrowness.' In saying that, he spoke for all the members of the conference committee (of whom I was then one). By 'breadth' is not simply meant the principle and practice of giving an equal welcome for Christ's sake to all fellow-believers — that is what the Brethren movement was all about from its inception. The word also embraces the atmosphere of spiritual freedom, flexibility and spontaneity which marks the movement. I know very well that this is not universally so: one hears from time to time horror stories of dictatorship and legalism, such as that of the place where a visiting lady was admitted to communion because she produced a duly signed letter of commendation, whereas an elder of her church, who was actually one of the signatories of her letter, was not admitted because he did not come similarly equipped.[2] This story comes to me only by hearsay; I cannot vouch for its truth. I could match it with horror stories from my own experience — not, happily, in churches for which I had any responsibility. But the whole point of such horror stories is their exceptional character; they are so out of keeping with normal practice. What has been said about freedom, flexibility and spontaneity may not be universally true, but it is generally true.

We have our traditions, of course, and it is well that we should recognize them for what they are, whether they are helpful or the reverse. But we are not likely to codify them into canon law; for one thing, they tend to vary from region to region, so that with the social mobility of the present day they have little chance of being generally imposed. Towards the end of the 1960s a television conversation was broadcast in this country in which Malcolm Muggeridge discussed the Brethren situation with the late Thomas Elwood of Belfast. In this conversation Mr Elwood made a good deal of the fact that, since the Brethren have no conventional creeds to bind them, they enjoy more freedom than those communities which have such creeds. It might be interjected that subscription to creeds does not invariably ensure theological orthodoxy, but it cannot be denied that, despite the absence of such creeds among them, the Brethren have preserved a fairly high reputation for orthodoxy. It would be a good subject of enquiry how this has come about in such a loosely-knit, 'non-subscribing' community. A writer in *The Christian*, commenting on the telecast, remarked with regard to Mr Elwood's emphasis on the absence of creeds, 'I wonder if the "traditions of the elders" are not even more shackling.'[3] The answer to that is, 'No, they are not.' Any individual or group wishing to dissent from the 'tradition of the elders' can do so with impunity — and perhaps gain a wider hearing for that very reason.

Sometimes I can discern, behind the question why I have stayed with the Brethren, a curious misapprehension that they are an anti-intellectual lot, particularly antipathetic to academic theology, and that the likes of me might be supposed to find them uncongenial company. I have, indeed, come across evangelical Christians who talk as though academic qualifications in biblical or theological studies positively disqualified one from a right to be heard on these subjects, but outside rather than within the Brethren movement. Throughout my entire career, as I have indicated before, I have been conscious of no tension between my academic interests on the one hand and my fellowship and teaching ministry among the Brethren on the other. I have been encouraged to share the fruits of my studies with them in the fullest degree, and have enjoyed the utmost freedom in doing so. It could be asked whether or not this would have been equally true had I been born a woman instead of a man and pursued the same academic career. That would be a hypothetical question, but I suspect that the cause of freedom would have triumphed.

My staying with the Brethren has no doubt been helped by the fact that I am, by calling and preference, a persistent layman. Had I been called to the ordained ministry, it might not have been so easy to find an appropriate niche among them, since they are a completely (or almost completely) lay community. (When I say 'almost completely', I think of some men among them who have been ordained to the ministry of other bodies and resume their ordained status when they visit churches in which that status is relevant.) But in my experience the Brethren provide an ideal setting in which a lay theologian can put his gifts at the disposal of the church.

Some people employ a vocabulary which does not commend itself to me, and make a distinction between 'tight' and 'loose' brethren. In the sense in which these terms are used, I should be classified (I imagine) in the latter category, but I have found my ministry equally acceptable among those to whom the former epithet would be applied. I have tried to be a bridge-builder within the Brethren movement as well as elsewhere.

But now it is time to deal with the presupposition to which reference was made above — namely, that there is a distinctive ecclesiastical group designated the Brethren. If one uses language precisely, this is not so. As I have indicated before, I am, ecclesiastically speaking, a member (a) of the Church Universal and (b) of Brinnington Evangelical Church, Stockport — and of nothing else. (Am I a member of the church of God in Buxton, the town in which I reside? Not in any formal sense. If a letter were addressed to the church of God in Buxton, I can think of two or three places at which it might be delivered, but at none of them would it reach me.) As regards the designation 'Brethren', the reason this is given to us is that we prefer to call one another by this or other designations broad enough to comprehend all Christians, rather than choose one which would distinguish us from other Christians. When our brethren the Friends came to be known by *that* designation it was not because they limited their friendship to their own Society but because they liked to call one another 'friends', as their Master had called them (John 15:15). So with our friends the Brethren. From time to time protests are published against a sectarian use of the designation, like W. E. Vine's *The Mistaken Term 'The Brethren'* and Rowland C. Edwards' *The Use and Abuse of the Name 'Brethren'* — but to protest against a linguistic usage that has taken firm root is an unrewarding activity. For myself, when I am choosing my language carefully, I sometimes take a leaf out of John Wesley's book and refer to 'the people called Brethren'; but this could be a trifle pedantic. Instead of calling my pamphlet on this subject *Who are the Brethren?*[4] I could have called it *Who are the People Called Brethren?* but this would have been less appropriate in something intended for the general public. Another pamphlet, written by Jim Taylor of Mendoza, Argentina, bears on the front the still more forthright wording: *'Who are the Plymouth Brethren? By One of Them'.*

If the sum total of the people called Brethren do not constitute an ecclesiastical community, at least we share a historical identity (the Brethren movement is an important phase of nineteenth century church history) and (whether we realize it or not) we constitute a sociological entity. Invite any sociologist to have a look at us, and he will have no doubt on this score. Our local churches have (mercifully) no ecclesiastical superstructure but they are securely underpinned by a sociological infrastructure. I have no statistical information about the degree of intermarriage within our ranks, but I suspect it is significantly considerable. (On the other hand, we do not think that only marriage within our ranks is marriage 'in the Lord' in the sense of 1 Corinthians 7:39, as do members of some enclosed groups which apply to themselves in particular language which the New Testament applies to all the people of God.)

Consider the obituary column which is printed month by month in *The Witness*. The great majority of those whose names appear there have belonged to the people called Brethren, and since these people form the majority of *Witness* readers a helpful service is performed by this column, as readers by its means get to know reasonably promptly of the death of their friends in other places. If the names of other Christians occasionally figure in this column, that is because they were known over a wider area. (In recent years it has included obituary notices of S. H. Hooke, R. V. G. Tasker, C. H. Dodd, Rudolf Bultmann, G. R. Driver and William Barclay.)

Consider again many of our conferences, convened either at local or at national level. In addition to the provision they make for biblical ministry or missionary reports, they perform an equally valuable service on the social plane by affording those who attend them an opportunity for meeting old friends. And while 'all Christians are cordially invited', as the invitation cards say, the great majority of those who accept the invitation come from Brethren churches. There are many people, for instance, who enjoy the Westminster Missionary Meetings[5] not only for their primary purpose of hearing reports of missionary work all over the world but also for the annual opportunity of renewing acquaintance with friends whom they would not otherwise see. This is as it should be, and it serves as a further illustration of what is meant by a sociological infrastructure.

One might go on and think of a distinctive vocabulary and idiom current within the group but scarcely intelligible outside it. I have heard this vocabulary and idiom often enough, especially from public speakers, to understand it readily, although I do not use it — and I think that if I did use it, I should be accused of trying to parody it! A few years ago a friend in Ireland — R. J. Wright, formerly a missionary in Japan — compiled a glossary of this form of speech, which could enable preachers to turn simple expressions into circumlocutions and enable their hearers to turn circumlocutions into simple expressions. All this, again, is a symptom of a well-defined sociological group.

The useful directory of *Assemblies in Britain and Other Parts*, issued by our publishers, has no official status, but every one who uses it knows what kind of churches are mentioned in it — those referred to by R. W. Orr in his immortal couplet:

> Our churches are enrolled on high,
> And listed here by P. and I.

This is no haphazard catalogue of local congregations: it is carefully compiled with a sense of responsibility to its users. There will be a general family resemblance between most of the churches listed, together with marked individual differences. They may call themselves by different names, but their inclusion in the directory suggests that they have some distinctive features in common.

One Sunday afternoon several years ago a friend rang me up and told me that serious debates were going on in his home church as to whether it was a 'Brethren assembly' or not. But I was unable to tell him what the distinguishing features of a Brethren assembly might be. If a church wants to be a Brethren assembly, let it call itself that; I can think of some churches (my own included) in which that would be a question of the utmost unimportance.

Nowadays, with so many of our local companies adopting the designation 'Evangelical Church', there is an increasing tendency to associate them with other companies, not in the Brethren tradition, which bear the same designation. More and more, at the present day, the really urgent questions which arise in Brethren churches are those which arise in all evangelical churches. If this speeds up the breaking down of denominational or quasi-denominational barriers, so much the better.

The administrative autonomy of the local church is something which can coexist with all the sociological infrastructure whose existence is so patent. This autonomy need not become a sacred cow, nor should it hinder a church from doing anything that it may see fit to do. It relieves us of the burden of a top-heavy inter-church (not to say super-church) bureaucracy, but it does not inhibit the fullest fellowship and co-operation with other churches and Christian groups. If a local church wishes to join a Council of Churches in its area, or to be affiliated to such a body as the Evangelical Alliance, it can, just because it is autonomous, exercise its freedom to do so. If it wishes to collaborate with other churches in promoting an evangelistic campaign or a periodical convention, let it collaborate. A local church united under the guidance of a responsible body of elders in whom it has confidence can be a very effective instrument for the Christian good of its neighbourhood by such joint efforts as well as by its own activities.

I count myself happy in belonging to a church of this kind — one which is not federated with other churches but gladly practises fellowship with them. To such a church, whose constitutive principle is the confession of Jesus as Lord, all who call Jesus 'Lord' may come and be assured of a welcome for his sake. From such a church one may go and have fellowship with all who call Jesus 'Lord', with no compromise of 'denominational distinctives' — because (whatever may be said of family resemblances) we have no 'denominational distinctives' to compromise. In such a church I feel so completely at home that this, I think, is sufficient answer to the question: 'Why have you stayed with the Brethren?'.

Notes to Chapter 35

1. See p. 222.

2. Our practice in this regard at Brinnington Evangelical Church has been summed up thus: 'If you come with a letter, you are welcome. If you come without a letter, you are doubly welcome.' This is because the visitor with a letter of commendation feels secure in the possession of 'credentials'; the visitor without one may feel a little uneasy, wondering what kind of reception to expect, and will have to be made to feel more thoroughly at ease by a specially friendly and wholehearted welcome.

3. This remark provided the text for a series of papers on Tradition which I contributed some years ago to the now defunct Canadian journal *Calling*.

4. See Appendix (p. 313).

5. Large gatherings held year by year in the third week of October in Central Hall, Westminster.

36
Tools for the job

There is one question, regularly put to celebrities interviewed on the radio programme 'Desert Island Discs', which I find more relevant to myself than most of the questions they are asked. 'Which book, apart from the Bible, Shakespeare and the big encyclopaedias, would you like to have with you on a desert island?' The Bible and Shakespeare, for some unlikely reason, are said to be there already; big encyclopaedias are banned.

Once, at least, I was asked on a brains trust which books (apart from the Bible) I would wish to have with me on a desert island: I said Calvin's *Institutes* and Charles Wesley's *Hymns*. That was about thirty years ago; I am not sure if I would give the same answer today. The study of the *Institutes* would certainly keep the mind from going to seed, and Charles Wesley would keep the soul from drying up. I have, in fact, a set of *The Poetical Works of John and Charles Wesley* in 13 volumes, but these would be too bulky to take to a desert island: probably I should settle for *A Collection of Hymns for the Use of the People Called Methodists* (music edition, for on a desert island I could sing, when in the mood for it, without disturbing anyone).

My chances of having to spend any length of time on a desert island are negligible. I have, however, sometimes idly wondered which books I should take with me if circumstances beyond my control compelled me to seek refuge in an eventide home. Book-space in such a place would, I expect, be limited. However, I need not cross that bridge until I come to it. On the other hand, I have no wish to emulate the late Professor Charles Sarolea of Edinburgh, who bought a large house every room of which was occupied by his books, and when they outstripped the resources of that house, bought the house next door to accommodate the overflow.

Some books are more basic than others: those which serve as tools of the trade, books which one uses rather than reads. Which books do I use most often? At the back of the desk at which I am typing this, within arm's reach, stands a row of books which I regularly consult. They include a Hebrew Bible, three editions of the Greek New Testament, a one-volume edition of the Septuagint, several editions of the English Bible (RV, ASV, RSV, NEB), a small Hebrew dictionary, C. F. Hudson's *Critical Greek and English Concordance of the New Testament* (a useful Bagster reference work, long since out of print), the Book of Common Prayer, a five-year diary and a book containing people's addresses and telephone numbers. Probably I regard these as particularly basic since I can consult them without leaving my chair. But only a pace or two away are larger and more voluminous works — concordances and dictionaries — which are constantly used.

Moulton and Geden's *Concordance to the Greek Testament* had served me so well for over thirty years that my copy was beginning to fall apart when the editor of *The Expository Times* sent me a review copy of the new (fifth) edition of 1978; it will probably last my time. Hatch and Redpath's *Concordance to the Septuagint* is in better shape, but then I have not had it so long; my edition is the Vienna photographic reprint of 1954. Wigram's *Englishman's Hebrew and Chaldee Concordance*, in two volumes, I find more convenient than the unwieldy volume by Mandelkern (once the property of W. E. Vine), which stands on a bottom shelf.

As for lexicons, those by Brown-Driver-Briggs, Buhl and Baumgartner serve me well in the Hebrew field, supplemented by M. Jastrow's *Dictionary* for post-biblical Hebrew. Liddell and Scott's *Greek-English Lexicon* deals primarily with classical Greek, but no student of the New Testament can afford to ignore classical usage. I have met students who claimed to 'know Greek' on the basis of their acquaintance with the Greek New Testament; even if that latter acquaintance were exhaustive, it would no more amount to a knowledge of Greek than acquaintance with the English New Testament would amount to a knowledge of English. There is a story told of A. S. Peake writing a Greek word on the blackboard of his Manchester classroom, and one of his students saying, 'You needn't write it down, Doctor; we know Greek.' To which he replied, 'I wish *I* did.' To know a language, even an ancient language, involves having such a feeling for its usage that one can tell, almost as by instinct, whether a construction is permissible or not, or whether a translation is possible or not. Translation is not simply a matter of looking up a word in a dictionary and selecting the equivalent which one would like to find in a particular passage. It is this manifest mastery of Greek usage which makes William Kelly's New Testament commentaries, especially those on Paul's epistles, so valuable. 'And you know what is restraining him now,' says the RSV of 2 Thessalonians 2: 6, following some earlier interpreters. This construing of 'now' with 'what is restraining' Kelly describes as a solecism, pointing out that the 'now' is 'simply resumptive'. Kelly is right. But how did he discover that the construction of the adverb with 'what is restraining' is a solecism? No grammar-book or dictionary would tell him that; it was his wide and accurate acquaintance with Greek usage that made it plain to him, an acquaintance which is the fruit of long and patient study.

Where the New Testament is concerned, the best lexicon of our time is Bauer-Arndt-Gingrich's *Greek-English Lexicon of the New Testament and Early Christian Literature* (1957). But Moulton and Milligan's *Vocabulary of the Greek New Testament* (1930) remains worthy of consultation for the usage of the papyri and other non-literary sources. Those who have Bauer-Arndt-Ginrich, however, will find less need for the venerable Grimm-Thayer, not to mention Cremer — although Cremer's work, which was described in its title as 'biblico-theological', was really the parent of the ten-volume *Theological Dictionary of the New Testament*, edited by G. Kittel and G. Friedrich and translated (1964-76) by G. W. Bromiley. For the post-apostolic period Geoffrey Lampe's *Lexicon of Patristic Greek* (1968) is a storehouse of valuable information.

Then there are dictionaries of another kind: Bible dictionaries and other reference works of the same *genre*. Among older works · I still consult with profit the *Encyclopaedia Biblica* (making allowance for Cheyne's Jerahmeelite aberration in the later volumes[1]), Hastings' *Dictionary of the Bible* (both five-volume and one-volume editions, the latter revised in 1963), with his *Dictionary of Christ and the Gospels* and *Dictionary of the Apostolic Church*. Among more recent works the *Interpreter's Dictionary of the Bible* (four volumes) and the *New Bible Dictionary* (one volume) deserve special mention. I particularly appreciate works of this kind which provide bibliographies with articles on various subjects, as both these works do. Bibliographies, on the other hand, can be a matter for criticism: one review of the *New Bible Dictionary* complained: 'We have yet to find a Puritan classic recommended anywhere in this volume; indeed little published before 1900 is ever mentioned.' The reviewers, it appears, had not worked their way through to the entry on 'Sanctification', where they would have found the bibliography headed by Walter Marshall's *Gospel Mystery of Sanctification* (1692), a Puritan classic if ever there was one, followed by one eighteenth-century work and two from the nineteenth century.

On the score of bibliographical information special praise

is due to the *New International Dictionary of New Testament Theology*, published in three volumes by The Paternoster Press. The comprehensiveness and usefulness of the bibliographies in this work are quite exceptional, far exceeding what is provided in this respect by the German *Begriffslexikon* of which this is the English edition. Indeed, from every point of view the English edition is an improvement on its German original, and this is mainly due to the expertise and industry of Dr Colin Brown, editor of the English edition. Unlike the Kittel-Friedrich-Bromiley *Theological Dictionary of the New Testament*, the *New International Dictionary* is organized according to the alphabetical order of the English words. That, of course, is the way in which W. E. Vine's *Expository Dictionary of New Testament Words* was organized. The *New International Dictionary* is more detailed and comprehensive than the *Expository Dictionary*, but then, the latter was Mr Vine's single-handed production, while the former is the work of a large team of collaborators. A comparison of the two makes one admire Mr Vine's achievement all the more.[2]

However, if I had to choose between biblical and theological dictionaries on the one hand and linguistic lexicons on the other, I should hold on to the linguistic lexicons. With them I should couple one or two reference works on grammar, such as the *Hebrew Grammar* of Gesenius-Kautzsch (translated by Collins and Cowley) and the Blass-Debrunner-Funk *Greek Grammar of the New Testament and Other Early Christian Literature*.

These all belong to the category described by Charles Lamb as *biblia a-biblia*, books that are no books, 'things in books' clothing', among which he included not only directories, almanacks, scientific treatises and draught-boards disguised as books but also 'the works of Hume, Gibbon, Robertson, Beattie, Soame Jenkyns, and, generally, all those volumes which "no gentleman's library should be without": the Histories of Flavius Josephus (that learned Jew), and Paley's Moral Philosophy. With these exceptions', he added, 'I can read almost anything.'[3]

There are indeed some people who claim that they read lexicons as others read novels, but although I am not one of them, I find great use for many of those 'things in books' clothing', not excluding the works of Josephus. The edition which Lamb had in mind was probably Whiston's, which (as I remarked in an earlier chapter in this work) was judged suitable for Sunday reading in my childhood. But now I prefer the nine-volume Loeb edition, with Greek and English texts on facing pages. For New Testament background Josephus is indispensable. (I have not, however, invested in K. H. Rengstorf's Concordance to Josephus, now appearing in four volumes; at something like £100 a volume it is a work that I can live without.) Alongside the Josephus volumes stand the twelve Loeb volumes of Philo, the Jewish philosopher of Alexandria, whose life overlapped our Lord's by 15 to 20 years at either end. His writings are as useful for the cultural background of the New Testament as those of Josephus are for the historical background. With the two Loeb volumes of the Apostolic Fathers and the two of Eusebius's *Ecclesiastical History*, all these together make up a frequently consulted shelf.

Anything, in short, that illuminates the history and religion of the Near East between 300 B.C. and A.D. 300 is grist to the New Testament student's mill. R. H. Charles's two volumes of collected *Apocrypha and Pseudepigrapha* come into the picture here; so do the texts from Qumran, the earlier New Testament apocrypha (conveniently accessible in the two volumes edited by Hennecke-Schneemelcher-Wilson), the writings of the apologists and the ante-Nicene Fathers (pre-eminently Justin Martyr among the former and Irenaeus among the latter), and the writings of their gnostic opponents—many of them known to this generation, after the lapse of 1500 years, from the Nag Hammadi papyri discovered in 1945 (a volume entitled *The Nag Hammadi Library in English,* published in 1977, has now made their contents conveniently accessible).

I have already mentioned the new and completely revised edition of E. Schürer's *History of the Jewish People in the*

Age of Jesus Christ, the first volume of which appeared in 1973 and the second in 1979 (one final volume will complete the work). Another work of similar value is Martin Hengel's *Judaism and Hellenism*, studies in the encounter of these two cultures in Palestine in the early Hellenistic period, the English translation of which was published in two volumes in 1973. More recently still we have greeted the first two volumes in a new series of Jewish studies relating to the New Testament — *The Jewish People in the First Century*, edited by S. Safrai and M. Stern (1974 and 1976). But with all his gratitude for such aids to study as these, the New Testament student will bear in mind the necessity of going back to the sources — the first- and second-century authors themselves. Even the most erudite and judicious of modern scholars may at times misinterpret those authors: the student will want to consult them for himself and reach his own decision on their significance. So Tacitus and Suetonius and Cassius Dio on the pagan side will take their place with Philo and Josephus on the Jewish side. And not far away stands a row of *biblia a-biblia*, as Lamb would have called them: *Documents illustrating the Reigns of Augustus and Tiberius* (V. Ehrenberg and A. H. M. Jones), *Documents illustrating the Principates of Gaius, Claudius and Nero* (E. M. Smallwood), *Select Documents of the Principates of the Flavian Emperors* (M. McCrum and A. G. Woodhead) and *Documents illustrating the Principates of Nerva, Trajan and Hadrian* (E. M. Smallwood). These compendia of inscriptions and other contemporary non-literary documents from 31 B.C. to A.D. 138 are not the least important of 'tools for the job' of the New Testament student. The Christian story is anchored in world-history, concentrated pre-eminently in events which took place when Pontius Pilate was Roman governor of Judaea, and the story, with all the divine revelation which it embodies, is better understood in relation to the historical setting in which the events took place. A history of New Testament times provides an illuminating commentary on the opening clause of Galatians 4: 4: 'when the fulness of the time was come . . .'

But for a desert island? Provided a Bible, or at least a Greek New Testament, were available, I might choose a symposium entitled *Apostolic History and the Gospel*, edited in 1970 by Ward Gasque and Ralph Martin, which I value both for its scholarly contents and for a more personal reason, and with its aid produce a commentary on one or two New Testament books, beginning with Galatians. If a commentary on Romans could come a few years ago from a Belfast prison, why not one on Galatians from a desert island?

Notes to Chapter 36
1. See p. 137, n.6.
2. At the time of his death in 1949, Mr Vine left an incomplete work on Old Testament words along similar lines: this has now been published as *An Expository Dictionary of Old Testament Words* (London 1978).
3. 'Detached Thoughts on Books and Reading', *Last Essays of Elia*.

37

Three personal questions

I

'And as regards your own writings,' say my questioners, 'how do you maintain your regular output?'

I have indicated already that in this respect I have often contrived to kill two birds with one stone: to deliver material in the form of a course of lectures and then to publish it in book form. When so much of the substance of my writings is part and parcel of the regular business of study and teaching, it is not so necessary to take time off to write a book. At the moment I am engaged on writing commentaries on some of the shorter Pauline epistles. It will be evident that for one who has done so much lecturing and writing on Paul much of the material for these commentaries lies ready to hand: the work involved consists mainly in organizing and supplementing the material for the form required by these commentaries.

For the rest, it is a matter of making a disciplined use of time. When I accept an invitation to write something, be it a book or an article, I fix a realistic deadline and try to meet it. Unforeseen circumstances may make the meeting of a deadline impossible, but if they are circumstances of that kind, publishers and editors will understand. It may well be that in my way of life it has been easier to decide in advance what in the normal course of events would be a reasonable deadline; even so, I like to carry around in my pocketbook a sheet of paper with a list of the literary projects which I have undertaken and a note of their respective deadlines, ticking off each as I finish it. From time to time I take it out to refresh my memory on the situation: at the moment I see that I have come about half way down the current sheet. I recommend this simple device to friends who find deadlines difficult things to meet. But I suspect that even this would be of much assistance to the kind of writer who exceeds his deadlines by fifteen years and is unable even then to deliver the goods. But we are all cast in different moulds: some find it easy to switch their attention at short notice from one subject to another and are able to fill the odd half-hour with a paragraph or two on a subject quite different from those to which they have to devote their attention immediately before and after; for others this is quite impossible, since it would take them at least half an hour to adjust their minds to a fresh subject.

II

'Then', say some, 'would you care to comment on your reputation as a person who is always mild and restrained in criticizing others?' I am not sure what is the proper answer to this: perhaps it is largely a matter of doing as one would be done by, remembering the dominical admonition: 'with the judgment you pronounce you will be judged, and the measure you give will be the measure you get' (Matthew 7: 2). I think, too, that it may be very much a matter of temperament. I remember many years ago a complaint being voiced about Dr D. M. McIntyre, Principal of the Bible Training Institute, Glasgow, a scholar and saint of high repute in his day: 'We could never get him to denounce any one,' said the complainant. Probably Dr McIntyre was not the denouncing kind.

But much depends on what is meant by denouncing. Where someone deliberately sets himself to subvert the morals of those who are young or easily influenced, or to undermine their faith in God, no language is too severe to condemn such wickedness; it was with regard to such a person that our Lord said that 'it would be better for him to have a great millstone fastened round his neck and to be drowned in the depth of the sea' (Matthew 18: 6). But even our Lord named no names, and we should have to be very sure about the motives of any specific person before applying such language to him. As it is, we are so easily deceived about our own motives that it is wellnigh impossible to be sure about the motives of anyone else. Where, however, a man openly avows (as one or two have done in our day) that the demolition of people's faith or morals is his settled intention, he cannot complain if he is denounced by those who have a concern for faith and morals (although with their denunciation they may well endeavour to bring him to a better frame of mind).

But it was not denouncing of this kind that was intended when complaint was voiced about Dr McIntyre's unwillingness to denounce anyone, and similarly this is not the situation in view when I am said to have a reputation for mildness or restraint in criticism. In both instances it is criticism of fellow Christians that is in view. Where I consider that someone is wrong, I have no hesitation in saying so, and I try to show why I consider him to be wrong (remembering that it is I who may be mistaken). Whether my disagreement springs from a difference in basic presuppositions or from a difference of judgment about the significance of the evidence at some point along the way, no one can reasonably object to being disagreed with. But the way in which the disagreement is expressed could certainly be objectionable. One of my friends, expressing himself generously in a review (as my friends tend to do), said of me: 'You will search his work in vain for anything like contempt for some liberal or radical thinkers with whom he finds himself in disagreement.' One might have hoped (having regard to the canons of ordinary human courtesy, not to speak of Christian grace) that this sort of thing hardly needed

301

to be said, except that there are some Christian writers or speakers who find it difficult not to mix some measure of contempt or sarcasm with their expressions of disagreement.

I may be wrong, but I often detect a note of unnecessary censoriousness on the part of some who, like myself, stand in the tradition of 'Reformed' theology — not in their treatment of 'liberal' publications (where it might be expected) but in their treatment of evangelical works. One takes it for granted that the publications of the Inter-Varsity Press will not be greatly appreciated by those who reject the basis on which the IVF/UCCF stands. But sometimes the sharpest criticism has come from Christians who accept that basis. I have referred in earlier chapters to criticisms voiced against the *New Bible Commentary* and *New Bible Dictionary*. Similarly, when Pickering & Inglis' *New Testament Commentary* appeared some years ago, claiming to be in its entirety produced by writers 'associated with the churches of the Christian Brethren', the severest strictures which it attracted came from some who could be described in those same terms. More recently, the *New International Dictionary of New Testament Theology* — written, edited and published by evangelicals in Germany, Britain and the United States — has received its most relentless censure in a British Reformed periodical, which indeed did not scruple to level a charge of dishonesty against it.

In all these instances the common ground between the work reviewed and the reviewers was far greater than the area of disagreement; yet it was the limited area of disagreement that provided a basis for the unfavourable estimate of the work as a whole. The situation is not unlike what we sometimes find in religious denominations or political parties, where two similar groups, differing from each other on points which to the outsider are almost imperceptible, are more wholeheartedly hostile in their public assessment the one of the other than in their relation with groups much farther removed from their common position. If my reputation for restraint in criticism simply means that I give due weight to areas of agreement as well to those of disagreement, well, that is how I like to be reviewed myself, and that is how I like to review others.

Another recollection occurs to me here. In 1964 I reviewed for an evangelical weekly C. H. Dodd's *Historic Tradition in the Fourth Gospel*. I thought it was a very valuable aid to the appreciation of the Gospel of John, and I said so. A correspondent wrote to the editor quoting a number of less valuable things from a book issued by the same author thirty-five years earlier (before he had broken loose from the influence of the liberal theology in which he had been brought up) and complaining by implication that I had not dealt in my review with other writings of Professor Dodd in addition to that which I had been specifically asked to review. A book reviewer who thinks it his duty to review the writer as well as his book may land in difficulties; for example, any one reviewing John Robinson's critically conservative book *Redating the New Testament* (1976) will do his work better if he does not drag in the theologically radical work which Dr Robinson produced in 1963 (although even in *Honest to God* the discerning reader could see that the biblical criticism at least was conservative, with regard, for example, to the apostolic authorship of the Fourth Gospel).

I have said that contempt is an attitude which should play no part in criticism. Equally, no part should be played by imputations of dishonesty or by the raising of doubts about the personal integrity of those with whom we disagree. Indeed, from time to time I have heard or read public attacks which I am sure would be actionable if those attacked cared to invoke the law relating to slander or libel. The fact that they did not invoke the law might suggest that they were better Christians than their accusers. And, quite apart from that, the imputation of dishonesty rules out further communication. If I disagree with someone, I can enter into correspondence or conversation with him over the points at issue, and both of us may find further enlightenment. But if I impugn his integrity, this possibility is excluded.

When all this has been said, however, perhaps we should

be thankful that our mutual criticism is not so exuberant as the sort of thing in which our forebears were wont to indulge, in the days when A. M. Toplady could head his attack on John Wesley *An Old Fox Tarr'd and Feather'd* or when, a century later, the seventh Earl of Shaftesbury could condemn that inoffensive work *Ecce Homo* as 'the most pestilential volume ever vomited forth from the jaws of hell'!

III

There is another question which I am asked from time to time, more personal than any mentioned thus far. 'Why do you say so little about your wife and family?' There are several answers to that question, and all of them have a measure of truth. One is that, if I began on that subject, I shouldn't know where to stop. Another is that (in my experience) listeners are not so interested in a speaker's family life or the achievements of his children as the speaker himself is. Over twenty years ago I was entertained to lunch in a London hotel by a well-known American preacher. I could see from the direction in which he was guiding the conversation that he wanted to probe my orthodoxy, so I diverted it along another track by asking about his children and their careers. From that point on I could relax: he became expansive. I was not nearly so interested in the subject as he was, but I gladly let him go on: quite soon the lunch was finished and he had another appointment. If any blame was involved in his enlarging on his family, it was mine for encouraging him, not his for responding. But, if I did not know it before, that experience was sufficient to teach me that others are not likely to be at all so interested in my family as I myself am.

But the main inhibition lies in the fact that my wife and family are so much part of my life, as I am of theirs, that I cannot speak of them objectively. I can see my parents and grandparents in better perspective now than when they were around in mortal body, so I can speak of them more freely than was possible then; but I am very much involved in the lives of my wife and children and grandchildren. Moreover, they are all very much persons in their own right, with their own 'remembrance of things past', enjoyment of things present, or expectation of things future (according to their generations), and are not to be treated merely as incidental to my own reminiscences. But it always gives me special joy when my wife's contribution to our life's work is recognized. In 1971 a number of my friends very generously collaborated in producing a special issue of the *CBRF Journal* to mark a recent milestone in my career. The next *CBRF Broadsheet* (No. 7) contained a letter to the editor from one of our extra-special friends, Raymond Payne of Sheffield, pointing out that the tribute in the *Journal* was incomplete because it took no account of the part my wife had played in 'creating the atmosphere' in which I had been able to do my life's work — a part which he truly described as 'difficult to overestimate'. But this was something of which he and his dear wife Florence had private knowledge denied to many contributors to that issue of the *Journal*. My professional life has been most satisfying throughout, but more satisfying still, at a deeper level, has been our domestic life. For the rest, let me apply to my wife (changing the initial 'he' to 'she') the tribute paid to her husband by Pamela Hansford Johnson (Lady Snow),[1] 'She has been all I could wish. More might be said, but it isn't going to be.'

Note to Chapter 37
1. *Important to Me* (London 1974), p. 81.

38

In conclusion — for the time being

By now 'remembrance of things past' has turned into 'reflection on things present', and it is well to call a halt before it develops into 'prediction of things future'. As I look back over my reminiscences, I find that it is the first quarter-century that comes most vividly to life: the record of my earlier years is the product of wellnigh total recall, and could have been expanded disproportionately. This superior clarity of early recollection is a familiar feature of advancing senility, and I must draw the appropriate conclusion.

While some readers have observed that in these chapters I have said little about my domestic life, others have wondered why I have been so reticent about my religious experience. The reason is probably the same in both instances: I do not care to speak much — especially in public — about the things that mean most to me. Others do not share this inhibition, and have enriched their fellows by relating the inner story of the Lord's dealings with them — one thinks of Augustine's *Confessions* and Bunyan's *Grace Abounding*. But it calls for quite exceptional qualities to be able to do this kind of thing without self-consciousness or self-deception. It is helpful at times to be able to draw on one's own spiritual experience in the privacy of personal counselling, or in a small 'sharing' group, but to expose it to indiscriminate publicity makes no appeal to me.

From one point of view, life may give the appearance of a series of progressively diminishing options. Many people, I realize, have very little option in matters of career, residence and so forth; but to one who has taken a university degree in the humanities the range of choice, to begin with, is fairly wide. One career must be chosen in preference to others, and if that career is an academic one, one area of specialization must be chosen in preference to others. The particular part of the world in which to live and work may itself be a matter of choice. The same may be said of church fellowship: one may choose to join a church because of its order, or because of its location, or because of its provision for the interests of young people, or because one has friends among its members — but once the choice is made, it carries certain commitments with it. With regard to marriage and family life, one may choose whether to marry and whom to marry (if the choice is reciprocal, so much the better), but once the positive choice is made and carried into action, it imposes a limitation: 'forsaking all other, keep thee only unto her/him'.

I have had all these choices to make, and theoretically they have been accompanied by their corresponding limitations; but since the choices were free choices, the limitations have never been felt as real limitations. 'It is ordained of Almighty God', said E. G. Robinson (obviously a wise man), 'that he who dips into everything will never get to the bottom of anything'; and it is much more rewarding to take decisions and abide by them than to live in a state of perpetual indecision.

For the Christian, this business of repeated choices and diminishing options is bound up with the experience of divine guidance. Some of my friends can relate quite exceptional experiences of divine guidance. For myself, I have found it easier to trace divine guidance in retrospect than to recognize it at the time, but I must add that the consciousness of free choice has often been accompanied by a

307

not incompatible sense of following a predetermined course. To commit one's way in advance to God, especially (but not only) when a momentous choice has to be made, is to have the assurance that one's way will be ordered or overruled by him for good. In none of the departments of life which I have mentioned could I wish that I had chosen differently, or that the overruling guidance of God had been otherwise. In this I realize how much cause I have to be thankful. I know that many Christians have to cope with uncongenial jobs or unhappy marriages, or to endure severe trials of faith in other ways. To be spared such experiences is perhaps something that carries its own test of faith with it, but it is certainly a much more comfortable test. Some have sacrificed professional prospects for the sake of the kingdom of God; to me, on the other hand, it came home rather forcibly some years ago that every professional ambition that I could reasonably have cherished had been attained. Happily, the Christian has ambitions of a higher order; there is always something left to live for. Like Paul, he does not count himself to have 'arrived'; he continues to press on toward the goal.

Questions are frequently addressed to me about the more intellectual side of my faith over and above the more inward and personal side. When such questions are asked by people who are themselves in need of help, or by people who have been giving personal thought to certain articles of doctrine and want to compare notes with me, I am very ready to give an answer. But when the questioner is concerned simply to know if I am as 'sound' as he is (and suspects that I am not), then I feel under no obligation to play into his hands. Some people remind me of the inhabitants of Assynt, in the north-west of Scotland, of whom it used to be said that, while others went to church to hear the gospel preached, they went to hear if the gospel was preached or not. But there are right and wrong ways of declining to answer questions, and the wrong way may lead to an awkward situation. A generation ago, at the end of a public lecture in Edinburgh, the lecturer was asked from the floor: 'Are you prepared to answer a question?

Did Christ rise from the dead?' The lecturer, a naturally shy man, answered the first question with 'No', but because of his hesitant utterance the second question had been asked before he got the 'No' out. Hence he was loudly accused of denying our Lord's resurrection — an embarrassing accusation for a Church of Scotland minister to put up with.

In 1975, about the time of his retirement, my late friend William Barclay published his *Testament of Faith*. In it he combined some account of his personal experience of God with a statement of certain things which he did and did not believe. So far as personal experience is concerned, his faith had been tested by fire as mine has not, and one could listen to his 'testament' with the more respect on that account. The time has not yet come for me to publish a 'testament of faith', but a perusal of some of the reviews which his book received might well deter me from ever publishing any such thing. Another of my friends once produced a book entitled *But That I Can't Believe!* I could, if I were so minded, write quite a sizeable book with that title, but the things which I can't believe would not include any essential article of the Christian faith.

When I try to review as objectively as possible the movement of my mind over the years, one thing that impresses me is the increasing clarity with which I see as fundamental to my thought and life the justifying grace of God, brought near to mankind in the vicarious sacrifice of Christ and offered for acceptance by faith. I cannot remember a time when I did not hold this to be the essence of the gospel, but questions which attached themselves to it in earlier days have apparently resolved themselves out of existence. It is for this reason that I am always happy to be called an evangelical, although I insist on being an unqualified evangelical. I do not willingly answer, for example, to such a designation as 'conservative evangelical'. (Many of my positions are indeed conservative; but I hold them not because they are conservative — still less because I myself am conservative — but because I believe they are the positions to which the evidence leads.) To believe in the God who justifies the ungodly is to be evangelical. On many points of New Testament criticism I find myself differing from such post-Bultmannians as Ernst Käsemann and Günther Bornkamm, but critical differences become insignificant in the light of their firm understanding and eloquent exposition of the Pauline gospel of justification by faith, which is the very heart of evangelical Christianity. I deplore the misuse of the noble word 'evangelical' in a party sense.

I emphasize this account of what it means to be evangelical because from time to time speakers or writers try to limit the scope of the word by imposing further conditions, as who should say: Unless you subscribe to *b, c* and *d* in addition to *a*, you cannot be recognized as evangelical. All that this amounts to is that they are imposing their own 'pickwickian' sense on the word.

To the same general category belong those people who want me to confess my faith in language of their choosing, not of my own. I do not object to confessing my faith in well-established statements drawn up by others, whether it be the Apostles' Creed or the doctrinal basis of the IVF/UCCF. I have been signing the latter basis annually as a Vice-President of the IVF/UCCF for a long time now, but no one imposes its terms on me as a test of orthodoxy, and I have never found it to inhibit the freest-ranging enquiry in biblical or theological studies. If I did not of my own free will agree with the doctrinal basis of the IVF/UCCF, I should not wish to be a Vice-President of that body; my consent to serve it in that capacity carries with it an acknowledgment that its understanding of the Christian faith is consistent with mine. But it occurs to some people that the vocabulary of time-honoured creeds and confessional statements has become so worn with repeated recitation or subscription that it no longer retains the incisiveness which it once had; accordingly they introduce fresh terminology and use it as a criterion of orthodoxy: unwillingness on the part of others to use this terminology is a sign of unsoundness. If, however, it is advisable at times to abandon the familiar vocabulary of creeds and confessions and to express the faith in untechnical language, I prefer to make my own choice of untechnical language. Best of all, I prefer to say 'I know whom I have believed' — and leave it at that.

For many years now the greater part of my time has been devoted to the study and interpretation of the Bible, in academic and non-academic settings alike. I regard this as a most worth-while and rewarding occupation. There is only one form of ministry which I should rate more highly; that is the work of an evangelist, to which I have not been called. (About a hundred years ago, J. N. Darby remarked, in the course of a Bible reading in Edinburgh, that he considered the gift of an evangelist to be the highest gift in the church today. He was heard with keen delight by W. T. P. Wolston, who thought that some of his brethren should take this to heart and accordingly interposed: 'Would you please say that again, Mr. Darby?' 'No, my dear young brother,' said the great man; 'I won't flatter your vanity.')

I should not find the career of a Bible teacher so satisfying as I do if I were not persuaded that the Bible is God's word written. The fact that I am so persuaded means that I must not come to the Bible with my own preconceptions of what the Bible, as God's word written, can or cannot say. It is important to determine, by the canons of grammatical, textual, historical and literary study, what it actually does say. Occasionally, when I have expounded the meaning of some biblical passage in a particular way, I have been asked, 'But how does that square with inspiration?' But inspiration is not a concept of which I have a clear understanding before I come to the study of the text, so that I know in advance what limits are placed on the meaning of the text by the requirements of inspiration. On the contrary, it is by the patient study of the text that I come to understand better not only what the text itself means but also what is involved in biblical inspiration. My doctrine of Scripture is based on my study of Scripture, not *vice versa*.

The question 'how does that square with inspiration?' is

perhaps asked most insistently when one part of Scripture seems to conflict in sense with another. I suppose much depends on the cast of one's mind, but I have never been bothered by 'apparent discrepancies', nor have I been greatly concerned to harmonize them. My faith can accommodate such 'discrepancies' much more easily than it could swallow harmonizations that place an unnatural sense on the text or give an impression of special pleading. If the 'discrepancies' are left unharmonized, they may help to a better appreciation of the progress of revelation or of the distinctive outlooks of individual writers.

Where inspiration is supremely important is here: the voice of God in Scripture is best heard in dependence on the Spirit who spoke by the prophets and taught by the apostles. The primary work of the Spirit in the lives of believers is to bear witness to Christ. It is by no mere coincidence that Scripture itself is said to bear witness to Christ: the witness of the Spirit, borne through prophet and apostle, has been recorded in written form in the biblical documents, and by their means the Spirit continues to take what relates to Christ and to make it plain to us. The Spirit of Christ who was in those early spokesmen of God is the Spirit of Christ who indwells believers today: we may distinguish his work in them and his work in us as inspiration and illumination respectively, but the work is his, whatever we call it, and Scripture is the sovereign instrument by which he performs it. There we can hear, aided by his grace, what he is saying to the churches of the twentieth century as clearly as what he said to those of the first. When this is grasped, the precise terminology in which our doctrine of Scripture is formulated is seen to be of minor importance and will not be treated as a test of sound or unsound thinking. To hear the voice of God in Holy Scripture oneself, and to help others to hear it, is a worthy cause to which to devote one's resources; to be commissioned to devote them to this cause is a sacred trust, not to be undertaken lightly, not to be refused irresponsibly, but to be fulfilled thankfully.

Appendix 1
Who are the Brethren?

The Brethren, or 'Christian Brethren', are given this name because they prefer to be known by a designation comprehensive enough to embrace all their fellow Christians. There are two main groupings among them, commonly described as 'Open Brethren' and 'Exclusive Brethren'. The terms 'Open' and 'Exclusive' are intended to denote their respective principles of communion. These pages are concerned only with the people called 'Open Brethren'; the writer has no authority to write about his 'Exclusive' friends.

It may be useful to make one point in this connexion, however. In the early 1960s considerable publicity was given in the press to the withdrawal of a number of people called Brethren from various business and professional associations, and from universities. These people belonged to one section only of Exclusive Brethren, and their policy in such matters was not shared by other Exclusive Brethren, and still less by Open Brethren. This distinction has not always been clearly observed, and the result has been considerable confusion in the public mind.

The Open Brethren have no central organization. They belong to a large number of local churches or assemblies, spread throughout the British Commonwealth, the United

States, the European continent and many other regions. Each of their local churches is independent so far as administration goes; there is no federation or union linking them together. Yet there is a recognizable family likeness between them, and their sense of a spiritual bond is strong.

Origins

The Brethren movement originated around the year 1825, although the Brethren commonly insist that their roots are really in the apostolic age, for they aim as far as possible at maintaining the simple and flexible church order of New Testament times. In the earlier part of the nineteenth century the barriers separating the various Christian denominations were less easily surmounted or penetrated than they are today. The founders of the Brethren movement were a group of young men (many of them associated with Trinity College, Dublin) who tried to find a way in which they could come together for worship and communion simply as fellow Christians, disregarding denominational barriers. They had no idea that they were starting a movement; still less had they any thought of founding a new denomination, for that would have defeated the very purpose for which they came together. For a time some of them continued to be members of their original churches, in which indeed a few of them were ordained ministers; but in general this situation did not remain practicable for long.

One of their early leaders was a Church of Ireland clergyman named John Nelson Darby (1800-1882), a man of unusual strength of intellect and personality, who envisaged the establishment of a corporate worldwide witness to the unity of the Church of Christ in an age of ecclesiastical fragmentation. His views were perpetuated by the Exclusive Brethren rather than by the Open group; when the cleavage between the two took place in 1848 it was to those who sided with Darby that the name Exclusive Brethren was given.

From Dublin the movement spread to England. In England the first Brethren assembly was established at Plymouth in 1831; hence arose the popular term 'Plymouth

Brethren'. Two leaders of the Brethren's meeting at Plymouth, Samuel Prideaux Tregelles (1813-1875) and, in a lesser degree, his relative, Benjamin Wills Newton (1807-1899), were responsible for one of the best critical editions of the Greek New Testament to be produced in England in the nineteenth century.

Another important meeting of Brethren was Bethesda Chapel, Bristol, which had as its joint-pastors the Scottish Hebraist Henry Craik (1805-1866) and the German-born George Müller (1805-1898), best known for the orphanage which he established in that city in 1836 and which survives to the present day. (Dr T. J. Barnardo was also a member of the Brethren when he founded his equally famous orphanage in London in 1870.)

Overseas Missions

George Müller's brother-in-law, Anthony Norris Groves (1795-1853), has claims to be regarded as the first of the 'Open' Brethren. He gave up a dental practice in Exeter to become a pioneer missionary, first in Baghdad and then in India. He was a man of large-hearted sympathies, who never forgot that the things which unite Christians are immeasurably more important than the things which divide them. 'I would infinitely rather bear with all their evil', he said of some people with whom he seriously disagreed, 'than separate from their good.' Whether those features which he thought to be evil were so in fact or not, his words express the attitude which Open Brethren acknowledge as their ideal.

The Brethren missionary movement launched by Groves continues to the present time in every continent, and over a thousand missionaries are engaged in it. Some Brethren missionaries have been pioneers in more senses than one. Among these were two Scots, Frederick Stanley Arnot (1858-1914) and Dan Crawford (1870-1926), who explored uncharted areas of Central Africa; it was Arnot who first opened up Katanga to the knowledge of the outside world in the 1880s. Brethren missionaries are located principally in Central Africa, India and Latin America; they co-operate with other missionary bodies in the practice of mission comity. Their work is registered under the designation 'Christian Missions in Many Lands'.

Doctrines

So far as their doctrines are concerned, Open Brethren have no peculiarities. They hold the historic Christian faith, because they find it plainly taught in the Bible, which is to them, as to all children of the Reformation, 'the only infallible rule of faith and practice'. They are wholeheartedly evangelical in their understanding and presentation of Christianity, proclaiming Jesus Christ, the Son of God, as the all-sufficient Saviour of those who put their trust in him and as the only hope for mankind. For this reason many of them find it specially easy to co-operate in Christian witness with others who share this evangelical emphasis, and in many interdenominational evangelical causes their influence is greater than their numbers might lead one to expect.

The beginnings of the Brethren movement were attended by a keen interest in the fulfilment of Biblical prophecy, and many of them are still characterized by this eschatological awareness. Their hymnody gives quite a prominent place to the Second Advent of Christ. But no single line of prophetic interpretation is held or imposed by them. Indeed, one of the features which many people find attractive about their fellowship is the spiritual and intellectual liberty which is enjoyed there in an atmosphere of brotherly love.

Practices

It is practice rather than doctrine that marks them out. Among Open Brethren baptism is administered only to people who make a personal confession of faith in Christ, whether they are adults or children; and the mode of baptism is immersion. They observe the Lord's Supper every Sunday morning (and occasionally at other times), and hold that the Lord's Table is for all the Lord's people. This, in fact, is their most distinctive gathering. When they meet for communion, together with any Christians who care to join them for this occasion, their devotions are conducted by no presiding minister and follow no prearranged sequence, but are marked nevertheless by a reverent spontaneity and orderliness. Various members contribute to the worship by suggesting hymns to be sung, by leading the congregation in prayer and thanksgiving, or by reading and expounding a passage from the Bible.

The Brethren have no ordained ministry, set apart for functions which others cannot discharge. A considerable number do give their whole time to evangelism and Bible teaching, but are not regarded as being in clerical orders. The various local churches are administered by responsible brethren called elders or overseers, but these have no jurisdiction outside their own local churches, and inside them they try to guide by example rather than rule by decree.

Numbers

The Brethren have always manifested a supreme lack of interest in their numerical strength. Their numbers are difficult to assess, partly because no precise statistics are available and partly because there is no hard-and-fast line of demarcation between Brethren assemblies and other independent evangelical churches. A common estimate of their strength in Great Britain and Ireland is 100,000; but this is at best approximate. They are to be found in all grades of society and in all walks of life.[1]

Note to Appendix 1

1. This appendix first appeared as an article in *The Witness*, November 1961; it was then issued as a pamphlet. It has now been slightly revised and brought up to date.

Appendix 2

An Anonymous Poem

In 1906 three sisters, the Misses Haig (relatives of the distinguished soldier who later became Field-Marshal Earl Haig of Bemersyde), bought the estate of Maviston, near Ballater, Deeside, and took up residence there. They had Brethren associations and were concerned about Christian witness in their new environment. Not long after their arrival a gospel tent mission was conducted in the district by two well-known northern evangelists, Francis and Matthew Logg; and to provide for follow-up work after the mission the Misses Haig converted stables, and later also the coach-house and laundry, at the back of their house into a meeting-hall. One of the forms of 'outreach' carried on there in the winter months was a gospel service at which attendance was encouraged by the provision of a meal before the preaching. The preaching was entrusted to brethren from Aberdeen and other parts of the north-east.

A local versifier, a shrewd but unsympathetic observer of this activity, described it in a poem which I know only from a single manuscript copy. It is reproduced here simply in order to prevent its becoming completely lost and forgotten. It has some local historical interest; the brethren alluded to were conspicuous figures in their day among our north-eastern assemblies. I suspect that the unknown author, for all his cynicism, represents the main thrust of the ministry fairly accurately. But the good ladies' enterprise was by no means spiritually fruitless.

318

In Ballater a plan's been launched
    Tae wean folks frae the pub —
A hybrid, double-barrelled scheme,
    Half kirk, half Dorcas club.

The founders o't hae set themsel's
    An ideal high indeed,
Tae save the soul, as weel's relieve
    The sinner's temporal need.

When stormy weather pits a stop
    Tae dellin yairds an' ditchin',
The needy sinner gets his dinner
    At Maviston soup kitchen.

The preachers come frae far an' near
    Wi' voices lang an' lood;
There's Brithers Logg, an' ither stars
    O' lesser magnitude.

There's Brimstane Robbie frae Schoolhill,
    Pits shivers doon yer spine;
The wrath tae come's a favourite theme
    Wi' the grocer frae Aboyne.

Salter aboot the burnin' lake
    Lays aff a gruesome tale;
Ye'd almost think ye saw the lowe
    An' fan' the sulph'ry smell.

'Beware!' the Speyside joiner cries,
    'Ye're on the brink o' woe;
Unless like us ye're saved by grace,
    Doon the backstairs ye go.'

The brethren sit wi' reverent air,
    Each face as lang's a fiddle;
They've heard the story telt sae aft
    They dinna care a diddle.

My text's in Matthew twenty-four,
    An' there, I think, ye'll see
That wheresoe'er the carcase is,
    There will the eagles be.

DATE DUE